FEROCIOUS MINDS

POLYMATHY AND THE NEW ENLIGHTENMENT

BOOKS BY DAMIEN BRODERICK

FEROCIOUS MINDS

POLYMATHY AND THE NEW ENLIGHTENMENT

Great Issues of the Day
ISSN 0270-7497
Number Eight

Borgo Press, an imprint of **Wildside Press**
www.wildsidepress.com

Great Issues of the Day: Number 8
(ISSN 0270-7497)

HARDCOVER: 0-8095-4473-3
PAPERBACK: 0-8095-4474-1

To Anders Sandberg
and the memory of John Maxwell Foyster
enlightened polymaths

TABLE OF CONTENTS

Acknowledgments

Much of the material in this volume, as with my previous Borgo/Wildside book *x, y, z, t* (2004), has appeared previously in rather different form. I thank the editors concerned, especially the *Weekend Australian*'s Barry Oakley and Jim Hall, Professor Malcolm Walter for a chapter from *To Mars and Beyond,* Alasdair Foster for a piece in *PhotoMedia*, Brian Edwards of Deakin University's *Mattoid*, the editors of *Vogue Australia* for seeking my thoughts on the return of Halley's comet, Janeen Webb and Andrew Entice for material from *The Fantastic Self,* and Alex Imich for encouraging me to write about spirituality from an unusual angle. I am grateful beyond measure to the innumerable writers I have cited, and who have helped stock my overloaded and often confused mind, especially such friends and e-friends as Rory Barnes, Russell and Jenny Blackford, Greg Burch, Dale Carrico, Serafino Cerulli-Irelli, Paul Davies, Hal Finney, Spike Jones, Barbara Lamar, Eugen Leitl, Fotini Pallikari, Yvonne Rousseau, Anders Sandberg. Thanks to Andrew Hartman for permission to adapt his striking photograph of a Chinese temple lion (http://andrew.hartman.tripod.com/info/afe18a.htm) to the book's cover. I am also happy to thank, for their continuing support, the Department of English and Cultural Studies at the University of Melbourne in Australia, where I have the good fortune to be a Senior Fellow, a post with no pay but no teaching duties. And of course I thank above all my delightful wife Barbara Lamar, for her love and encouragement, and for her generosity in creating (before we met) and maintaining (even afterwards) a website about my work at www.thespike.us.

Aleph and Omicron

> A very great deal of good, undoubtedly, was done, suffering mitigated, injustice avoided or prevented, ignorance exposed, by the conscientious attempt to apply scientific methods to the regulation of human affairs. Dogmas were refuted, prejudices and superstitions were pilloried successfully. The growing conviction that appeals to mystery and darkness and authority to justify arbitrary behavior were, all too often, so many unworthy *alibis* concealing self-interest or intellectual indolence or stupidity, was often triumphantly vindicated. But the central dream, the demonstration that everything in the world moved by mechanical means, that all evils could be cured by appropriate technological steps, that there could exist engineers both of human souls and human bodies, proved delusive.
>
> Sir Isaiah Berlin,
> *The Age of Enlightenment* (1960: 28-9)

i

Two hundred years ago, that intoxicatingly hopeful but doomed European age of critical, encyclopedic reason perished. It was slain, arguably, by its own hand, or the fists of its rebellious offspring in the French Revolution and the rise of Romanticism. The most recent century of science, bent to unequalled good and ill, may be regarded as an ambiguous re-run up to a new Age of Enlightenment. Admittedly, much of the twentieth century seemed diabolical rather than enlightened, a kind of appalling *parody* of reason, so the Enlightenment is not in good odor among critics who see humanism as a comfortable middle class PR device, a *bien pensant* sentimental apparatus blocking any authentic challenge to widespread human misery.

Typical in their broad-brush detestation of Enlightenment tradition are Jake and Dinos Chapman, postmodern artists most famous for 'Insult to Injury', their vandalized or 'rectified' appropriation of Goya's *Disasters of War* prints, in which they pasted fiendish clown and puppy heads over every victim's grimace: 'The Enlightenment project still virulently infects the earth. In comparison to the atrocities of reason, violence itself is laughably innocent of the crimes with which it stands perennially accused.'[1] But I will argue that today's reviving

---

[1] Cited by Sebastian Smee, 'Clowning with humanity', 12 March, 2004: http://www.theaustralian.news.com.au/common/story_page/0,5744,8938325%255E16947,00.html The Chapman brothers were favored to win the 2003 Turner Award at Tate

9

Enlightenment, despite such fashionable rumors to the contrary, is no recuperative sham, let alone a path to doom and ruin.[2] To the contrary: it is our single, best highway to deliverance from a future of accidental or malign oppression.

ii

We are seeing a recovery of the Faustian hunger to know everything that can be known. It is precisely this Enlightenment appetite, of course, which alarms some people. And the pace only quickens. There is a term for that hunger's goal: polymathy.[3] You do not have to be a universal genius or a Renaissance Man or Woman to be a polymath (although obviously it would help). All that's required is an informed enthusiasm for more than one narrow field of knowledge or expertise, framed by a capacity to gain a certain measure of competence in several realms that might seem distant from one another.

The *philosophes* of the eighteenth century Enlightenment—erudite, urbane, witty, combative, committed practical intellectuals—made up perhaps three generations of true polymaths in various European nations and America for the astounding century between the English Glorious Revolution which threw out King James II in 1688-89 and, following the American revolution and War for Independence of 1775-83, the much bloodier French Revolution of 1789-99. They were not necessarily very comfortable people to be around. As the Enlightenment was about to be crushed out, English Gothic writer Horace Walpole denounced the *philosophes* in 1779 as 'solemn, arrogant, dictatorial coxcombs—I need not say superlatively disagreeable' (cited Gay, 1977: 16).

Uncomfortable or not, is such polymathy *possible* any longer, even assuming it is desirable? Clearly, the flowering of knowledge in the last two centuries, and the ever-more specialized means of obtaining it, suggest powerfully that nobody can hope any longer to attain such breadth and depth of available insight. This need not deter us from

---

Britain gallery but were beaten by potter Grayson Perry. In an interview, with Simon Baker (*Papers of Surrealism*, 1, winter 2003), Jake Chapman offered this item of throw-away bad boy provocation in response to his work regarded as an act of transgressive force: 'Yes—a good social service like the children who killed Jamie Bulger.' http://www.surrealismcentre.ac.uk/publications/papers/text_only/issue_1/issue1_contents.h tm
Interestingly, the British Museum would open an exhibition entitled 'Enlightenment' in December, 2004.

[2] The originating German name for the Enlightenment, *Aufklärung*, implies 'clearing away fogs of ignorance', as does *L'Éclaircissment*, its French name.

[3] Voracious readers often recognize many words we never have heard anyone say aloud, and pick up the meaning from the context, without ever checking their strict dictionary definition. Polymathy, in case you're wondering, is pronounced Puh-*lim*-uthy.

aspiring to the condition of polymathy, as long as it is sought with suitable (if inevitably ironized) modesty and an unblinking awareness that the best any of us can do these days is sip cautiously from the torrent of knowledge.

A third of a century ago, the French philosopher Michel Foucault reprised a key meditation by his great German predecessor Immanuel Kant on this vexed topic of *Was Ist Aufklärung*, published by Kant in November 1784 in the German periodical *Berlinische Monatschrift*. Here is what Kant had told the burghers, not mincing his words (which I here render in a somewhat less constipated translation that we are accustomed to with Kant):

> Enlightenment is our emergence from self-imposed intellectual submission. I mean the refusal to trust your own grasp of reality. I mean bowing to the dictates of authority. What's lacking in submissive people isn't any raw capacity for understanding, but rather the resolution and courage to use it without kowtowing to imposed direction. So here's the motto of enlightenment: Have the guts to use your own intelligence, to follow your own reasoning!
>
> Why do so many people happily submit lifelong to authority? Laziness and cowardice! And that allows a few among us to set themselves up, all too easily, as guardians over the rest. It's so convenient to drift along! If I can depend on a manual of instructions, a spiritual adviser to serve as my conscience, a doctor to choose my prescriptions, all the rest of it, I needn't make any effort. Don't think, just pay up and toe the line; let others take over the tedious job of thinking for me.
>
> Those do-gooders who generously accepted the task of running our lives quickly made sure that the majority assume that to take any step in the direction of self-command must be frightfully dangerous and difficult. First they dumb us down, then they lead us by the nose. In reality, the danger isn't so very great. Despite a few early topples, everyone learns to walk eventually. But falling on your face intellectually is intimidating, and usually frightens us off from further attempts.

If a new enlightenment calls for polymathy, or the best approximation we can manage, that is perhaps no more than a demand for Kantian intellectual and emotional maturity in a world of daunting overload. Foucault's response to Kant's project sustained a certain pitch of uncertainty, as befits a postmodernist radical profoundly in tension with traditionalist ideologies of rationality and scientific aspirations to global knowledge, but in the end, perhaps surprisingly, he endorsed the often-ridiculed Enlightenment project:

> I don't know whether society at large will ever reach adult maturity. Experience persuades us that the 18th century Enlightenment failed to produce many mature adults, and we're still waiting. However, in reflecting on the Enlightenment, Kant formulated a critical questioning of the present and of ourselves that remains meaningful. Through the last two centuries, it seems to me, Kant's meditation has importantly and effectively championed a particular approach to the activity of philosophy. It's this: no critical ontology of humankind can establish a definitive theory or doctrine, not even as a permanent, accumulating body of knowledge. A philosophical life has to be conceived as an attitude, an ethos, in which our critique of what we *are* is at once an analysis of the limits that are imposed on us by our historical locality and contingency, and an experiment in the possibility of going beyond those limits.... I do not know whether it must be said today that the critical task still entails faith in Enlightenment; I do still think that this task requires patient work on our limits, manifesting our impatience for liberty. ('What is Enlightenment,' 1969)

Still, this is not the usual assessment, and certainly not Foucault's own. In the astringent summary by contentious scholar Frederick Crews, for Foucault (like the Chapman sibling artists), 'The whole Enlightenment was a continuing nightmare of ever-harsher social control—a movement to draw "reasonable" distinctions (rational-irrational, sane-insane, innocent-criminal, normal-abnormal) so as to stigmatize and punish behavior that threatens bourgeois self-regard' (1986: 171). There's some truth in that, although rather more of bourgeois self-loathing. In my own view, the finest impulse of the first as well as the second Enlightenment is captured by the admirable philosopher and historian of science, Stephen Toulmin: 'From the Judgment of Solomon on, literature and scripture have preserved stories showing how hard it is to treat situations "rationally" (without distortion) and also "reasonably" (without injustice)' (2002: 94).

Eighteenth century Enlightenment polymaths such as Thomas Jefferson helped design their own homes and ran a complex farm or business—on the backs, dreadfully and ironically, of slaves. They read widely in both the classics and contemporary literature and philosophy, investigated the available sciences, involved themselves in politics, studied the workings of the human mind, and all of this in a spirit of open-minded, exploratory enthusiasm and optimism tempered by a realistic appraisal of human weakness and temptations. It's no accident (despite slavery's tormenting irony) that an insistence upon personal liberty marked these Enlightenment polymaths. The liberty to ferret out what is true in the midst of contesting opinions and dogmas was seen, rightly, as the necessary footing for freedom to act.

In the same year Foucault cautiously affirmed these values, a historian of the Enlightenment, Peter Gay, concluded his notable two volume interpretation with an endorsement that I believe still stands, more than three and a half decades on:

> We have known horrors, and may know horrors, that the men of the Enlightenment did not see in their nightmares. Yet, though few are today inclined to believe it, none of this impairs the permanent value of the Enlightenment's humane and libertarian vision, or the permanent validity of its critical method... It remains as true today as it was in the eighteenth century: the world needs more light than it has, not less; the cure for the shortcomings of enlightened thought lies not in obscurantism but in further enlightenment. Our recognition of human irrationality, self-centeredness, stupidity beyond the philosophes' most pessimistic appraisals demands not surrender to such forces, but battle against them. (1969: 567-8)

iii

In the frankly personal exploration that follows, I hope to show how urgently we need an embracing return to the best of those values, and for the ferociously curious minds that advanced them with such passion. As a bonus, there is the very considerable pleasure that knowledge offers intelligent citizens of the twenty-first century—an age when, with luck, the lofty yet quite practical hopes of those eighteenth century visionaries will be translated finally into simple fact.

Here are just a few of the wildly various yet cross-linked topics we will touch upon, in what I hope you can regard as a sort of darting after-dinner conversation:

How many universes can dance on the point of a pin?

What happens to a genetic boy's inner life when she is raised as a girl?

Are the strings from which the world is woven near to being unraveled by science? Or is there no limit to the flowering complexity of the universe, fated always to evade our grasping theories?

Should we care that Sigmund Freud was a cocaine addict during the time he concocted his most influential ideas?

Is science itself sexy? No, really?

Or might science do away with natural sex entirely? Once human cloning is perfected, should we expect to see a dystopian world of cloned backups, waiting for their organs to be rifled by the rich? Or is that prospect, in turn, no better than catchpenny hysteria? Do literature and art possess the resources to render, with nuance and emotional relevance, today's disturbing outlook on a barely imaginable tomorrow?

Can you create a red triangle in your mind, turn it upside down, and make it change to a deep luminous blue? If you cannot, what happens when you try to write poetry or fiction?

Will humans rocket to Mars some year soon, begin rebuilding that dry ancient planet in the image of our own blue home? That was the ambitious pronouncement of President George W. Bush in 2004, after the successful landings and deployment of the rovers Spirit and Opportunity, but his successors might not feel bound by his commitment. Indeed, a mere six days later Bush himself omitted this expensive bid from his State of the Union message. But even if we can go, should we? If we do, need it be by rocket, whether chemically propelled or driven by nuclear engines? Will technicians instead dangle a diamond string from the sky to the Earth, an elevator shaft we'll climb up as fairytale Jack climbed his Beanstalk, into the giants' world of the greater cosmos beyond our planet?

How did 'Darwin's Bulldog', agnostic evolutionist T. H. Huxley, cope with the death of his own child?

What will happen to us when medicine learns how to repair and rejuvenate every cell in our bodies, putting an end to automatic death by aging? Or is that promised prospect just misplaced religious hope?

Are we moving inexorably toward a future where most people abandon real reality for the powerful attractions of authentically *virtual* reality?

What will happen to us when artificial intelligences, those ultimate polymaths, finally arrive from the labs, perhaps by 2025 or even sooner, and swiftly soar past our own attainments?

Are there realms of knowledge beyond art and science? Can human beings touch each other's souls, and the world, by a kind of direct, intimate psychic access? Or is that recurrent wishful dream just the final backlash by superstition against a renewed Enlightenment?

We tend to look askance at medieval thinkers with their time-wasting obsessions. Thomas Aquinas and his thirteenth century scholastic colleagues, tonsured and celibate, racked their formidable brains over questions so silly we cannot even utter them today except as mocking metaphor: *How many angels can dance on the head of a pin?* Unless you live in Hollywood and feel sure you have a personal guardian angel to go with your personal trainer, you probably find this the very model of an ancient foolish question.

Well, perhaps not. Years ago, I had a salutary shock, learning that this is *not* what the Scholastics argued about, not really. Angels were a kind of code or stand-in. The Schoolmen were plumbing the same mysteries that centuries later would baffle mathematicians: infinity, endlessness, the limits and boundaries, if any, of pure number.

Angels, Aquinas supposed, were undivided beings of absolute intellect, spirit untouched by matter. 'Each angel,' Frederick Copleston, S. J. informs us, 'is pure form,' each a species unto itself. 'There are as many species as there are angels' (1962: 49). Here is the mathematical equivalent: it would be centuries before Gregor Cantor understood that between the number 1 and the number 2 there is not merely a huge bunch of fractional and irrational numbers such as 1.00087 and 1.8553. Jammed in between those are *infinitely* many numbers, and between each of those a further infinity, all the way down.

From one edge of a pin's head to the other, then, it is a mathematical continuum, infinity within infinity. Like choirs of angels, these numbers array themselves in hierarchies of appalling, impossible multiplicity. How many angels? How many numbers?

Looked at this way, the question is not nearly as foolish, as arbitrarily extravagant as we took it to be. Indeed, it is impressively deep, or so mathematicians assure us. Followed through, it draws us into hierarchies of infinites, each infinitely larger than the one before. These transfinite numbers have a general name: they are Alephs.

The kind of countable infinity we are all comfortable with, the one you get by starting with 1 and going on to 2, 3, 4, and the rest of them, never stopping, is Aleph-null or Aleph-nought: the zeroth Aleph number. Above Aleph-null, the universe of number swirls dizzyingly into ever more infinite, transfinite compressions, numbers ever more tightly packed.

Consider that tale a metaphor in turn.

Then again, perhaps the metaphor has rather a different meaning. The story itself turns out to be wrong. I'd read that engaging mathematical gloss years ago, but when I went searching through my library for its source I could not find it mentioned anywhere. Naturally, this being the twenty-first century and not the thirteenth, I turned at once to the Google search engine on the World Wide Web, a monstrously vast Internet repository of instantaneous links to facts, arguments, fantasies, advanced scientific preprints, mad misconceptions, pernicious scams, urban legends and ancient truths. The trouble with Google is, notoriously, this: how can you trust anything you read on the Web? That is the latest version of a very old question: how can you trust *anything*? Your own senses and thought processes can lead you astray, as anyone who has wandered home singing off key from a late party can tell you.

No medieval theologian debated how many angels might dance on a pin, or at least none is recorded as having done so.

The charming absurdity's source was Isaac D'Israeli's *Curiosities of Literature*, 1791, which attributed it to a 1741 satire by Tory scapegraces Alexander Pope, John Arbuthnot and Jonathan Swift. That satire, by the way, 'The Memoirs of Martinus Scriblerus', made no such mention, according to Stephen Clark, who does note that 'the image of Angels on the point of a needle appears in Joseph Glanville (1661), and in Nicholas Cudworth's *True Intellectual System* (1678)'.[4]

So much for polymaths. Well, at least we can be trusted upon to try to clean up our own messes, and with a grudging good grace.

vi

It does not really matter, though, not here and now, not for our purposes. Many matters of fact turn out not to matter too much, when all is said and done. It pleases me to imagine a leap through imagination from angels to Aleph-null. As we now know (or think we do), the world is a hierarchy of Aleph infinities. But is the very universe infinite, entire and blazing about us in the brilliance of the night sky? Born in the ferocious furnace of the Big Bang, bursting outward in its own simultaneous creation of space and time, the universe seems all there is, all there can ever be. Perhaps that is not the case.

Increasingly, specialists in cosmology find themselves tempted by a vision transfinitely larger than the simple cosmos we see, spread out to a mere 13 billion light years on every side. If the old universe of faith and myth ran from Alpha to Omega, start to finish, first to final letter of the Greek alphabet, this new great world extends, we might say, from Aleph to omicron. That 'little o', unlike the single austere Omega we once thought comprised the final fall of the curtain, stands in my figure for a creative ferment of new little universes, budded off at right angles to our own, cast outward into unimaginable new spacetimes in a frothing foam

---

[4] http://www.liv.ac.uk/Philosophy/angels.html

of universes born from quantum vacuum nothingness and flinging themselves endlessly into actuality.

How many universes can dance upon the head of a pin? As many, perhaps, as there are—and perhaps that is transfinitely many little omicrons.

This is strange knowledge indeed; perhaps, in a strict worldly sense, useless knowledge. But it can make the blood sing. It is knowledge born not of mystical visions or ancient lore but from the most careful observations ever made by human senses, amplified by brilliantly inventive devices, analyzed by other superb machines, and built into a ceaselessly expanding fabric of comprehension. It is knowledge that gives us new capacities to act, and to act with subtlety and power.

No deity revealed these truths—these provisional guesses, rather, based on evidence that might be overturned at any moment by fresh, more complete observations—and no authority vouches for them, beyond the earned authority of skilled, imaginative human minds. Plenty of people do not wish to know, admittedly. Plenty of people yawn and flip channels, searching for sports stars running back and forth, or soap characters with winsome smiles and reassuringly formulaic pseudo-lives and loves.

The sort of people who wish to know this strange knowledge are... well, let's admit it: they are the belated and perhaps embattled children of the Enlightenment, marooned here on a planet where, in the twenty-first century, educated Californians voted down plans to erect a new police and fire building because the new structure would violate the town's *feng shui*—the alleged flow of magic luck—blocking the movement of benign spirits and encouraging the ruinous entrance of bad demons.[5] In 2004, Democrat State Assemblyman Leland Yee, representing San Francisco, introduced a resolution urging that public building officials accommodate feng shui (while not making it obligatory).[6] Feng shui masters reportedly guide media billionaire Rupert Murdoch's News Corporation in choosing office spaces. 'A birth date,' the *Los Angeles Times* added blandly, 'can determine how a person's energy will coincide with the Earth's magnetic pull, as well as a building's energy force.'[7] In the wealthiest nation in history, most insurers now unblinkingly pay a benefit to Christian Science practitioners who simply *pray* for the recovery of policy holders.[8] In 2004, even as the Mars rovers beamed back

[5] http://www.usatoday.com/news/nation/2002/03/07/building-feng.htm

[6] http://www.cnn.com/2004/US/West/01/31/offbeat.feng.shui.ap/

[7] Sallie Hofmeister, 'Want a Corner Office? First Check the Chi', *Los Angeles Times*, 21 March 2004.

[8] *The Skeptic*, Autumn 2002, Vol. 22, No. 1, 9-10. But is it possible that such intercessory prayer *works?* A number of medically linked studies argue that it can; see, for example, Sicher and Targ, 1998. Tragically, Elisabeth Targ herself died of glioblastoma multiforme,

news of water seas in that planet's past, and perhaps of a separate evolution of life outside our own world, the townsfolk of Darby, Montana, were locked in fierce dispute over the teaching of 'intelligent design' as part of the school science curriculum, a revision that received the preliminary vote of the school board. [9]

Perhaps some measure of ferocity is called for, in response to such grimly comic absurdities.

vii

Or is this too menacing a prospect? Why *ferocious* minds? Shouldn't those aspiring to enlightened polymathy seek calm, balance, evenhandedness, a suspended caution in reaching judgment, sweet kindliness: the very contrary of ferocity? Well, yes, these are desirable traits, to be sought in one's heart and cultivated in one's dealings with other people—and not always or easily attained by the intellectually wideranging. A certain ferocity of mind is, indeed, not readily peeled apart from the concentrated energy and demands upon self and others that goes with the territory. Recall Walpole's waspish assessment of the Enlightenment *philosophes*. Perhaps, to bring matters down a notch or two, a personal recollection can help explain why many people are bound to find polymaths rather daunting.

For four decades I had the unnerving fortune to know a brilliantly intelligent, witty, articulate and diverse man whose death eight days short of his 62nd birthday was due, by a gruesome irony, to a glioblastoma multiforme tumor swelling in his left parietal lobe, where language lives, so that as he died, his quick words were taken away from his mental grasp. I had met John Maxwell Foyster briefly when I was 17 and he was 20, airily clever, confident, a budding know-all who in adolescence had been immobilized for a year by polio, a now-defeated plague whose ill effects returned in later years to trouble him. (Post-polio syndrome affects many former sufferers, such as Sir Arthur C. Clarke.) Somehow he botched his first attempt at a science degree, became a high school teacher for a time, published world-renowned science fiction fanzines in profusion (often with self-derisive titles like *The Journal of Omphalistic Epistemology, or JOE)*, returned as a young husband and father to the mathematical physics of cosmology ('The classification of the Ricci and Plebanski tensors in general relativity using Newman–Penrose formalism', with C. B. G. McIntosh and A. W. C. Lun), only to

the same brain cancer that felled my dedicatee John Foyster (Bronson, 2002). Attempts to heal Targ by prayer had not proved effective.

[9] http:// www.jpl.nasa.gov/releases/2004/90.cfm; 'Montana Creationism Bid Evolves Into Unusual Fight', *New York Times*, Feb 29, 2004, 19. On 'intelligent design', see the discussion below of Michael Behe's ideas.

abandon his doctorate in disgust at the machinations and dishonesties of the academy, read everything with terrifying speed, a couple of books a day—Basho's poetry, Proust, anarchist theory, Kaluza-Klein physics—developed statistical methods in educational testing and evaluation, guiding policies in several nations, died too soon. When we both were in our twenties, he and I and other science fiction enthusiasts met the prize-winning Australian novelist George Turner. Foyster the scientist became his close friend, and one of his most acute and useful literary critics. In his memoir *In the Heart or in the Head* Turner recorded his initial impressions of the Australian science fiction world, in which Foyster played a major role, in terms that remain, all these years later, cause enough for some chagrin:

> Some of the more consciously intellectual were hard to take. I met John Foyster and Damien Broderick, a pair of fairly ferocious mentalities, and found their conversation so allusively remote as to constitute a shutting out of the intruder. I gathered that they found me uninteresting, but times change and we with them, and we all know each other much better now—sufficiently to disagree profoundly while yet finding each other's brains worth the picking. (1984: 129)

At a public tribute to John Foyster, a bright meteorologist friend who had known him for four decades explained: 'I found John both incredibly stimulating and very, very frustrating... because he was highly intelligent, because he knew what criticism was about, he knew what literature was about... I found John extremely irritating for exactly the same reasons.... He knew more about literature, he knew more about music...' Another friend admitted: 'I found him intimidating,' but added: 'He was never unkind.' This last brought a buzz of skeptical comment from the audience, perhaps from some stung by Foyster's swift ferocity. 'He was devastating when he found he had to be. He took people as he found them and, if he found he could communicate with them at close to his level, he did.' Another old friend found him 'often charming and funny, sometimes acerbic and upbraiding.' Devastating, irritating, blunt, not suffering fools gladly—yet not unkind, not really. One of his oldest friends was the lively film critic and biographer John Baxter, who never attended college but has taught in one, and is now a millionaire bibliophile in Paris. At a time when C. P. Snow's shibboleth for breaking down the Two Cultures barrier between the science and the arts was a grasp of the principle of entropy, Foyster, he noted wryly, 'really understood the Second Law of Thermodynamics—and, we suspected, the First and Third as well.' Baxter recounted a youthful, heated conversation. 'The subject of cinema came up, and I cited the French magazine *Cahiers du Cinema*. "What magazine?" John enquired. I told him. Reprovingly, he corrected my pronunciation. Not "Ka-heers" but "Ki-ay". He knew French too! It just wasn't fair.'

A new Enlightenment polymath, in short: a ferocious mind, hoisted high on the shoulders of giants. By contrast, I am confessedly a dabbler, usually trying desperately to peer past the giants' kneecaps. Still, to mutilate Isaac Newton's dictum even more: If I have occasionally seen further than others, it is because I have trodden, now and then, on the toes of dwarves.

Beginnings

> The one-man monograph is vanishing. That is the result, in part, of the growing ocean of known facts and the consequent narrowing of focus of the human mind. The 'universal genius' is gone forever. Nowadays, it is almost impossible to find a man who considers himself qualified to write all about some small subdivision of biochemistry, which is itself a subdivision of biology and chemistry, which are themselves subdivisions of the field of the physical sciences which are themselves subdivisions—
>   ...the literature relating to efforts to handle the literature is too great to be handled easily.
>
> Isaac Asimov,
> 'The Sound of Panting' (1955: 106, 113)

i

In his memoir *Wisdom, Madness, and Folly* (a title drawn from King Solomon's famous investigation, in Ecclesiastes), the controversial psychiatrist R. D. Laing told how he learned to read rather early, and of the hauntingly Platonic consequence of this skill:

> A lot of my time was spent absorbing two sets, several volumes each, of an illustrated history of the world, and of an illustrated history of world literature. By the time I went to school I was beginning to read the texts of these encyclopedias. Parts of literature and history are two subjects I've always felt I've always known but largely forgotten. Finding out about these things always felt as though I was simply refreshing my memory. (1985: 42)

Few of us are as smart as Ronald Laing, but many (that modest constituency who actually enjoy reading) do seem to treasure the image of some fat, battered volume, usually at least a generation out of date, choked with the stuff of wonder and expectation: gigantic gleaming locomotives, strange animals nothing at all like pussy cats or puppy dogs; atoms and bacteria too small for the naked eye; or mysteries so distant only the telescope's lens might reveal their shape—the rings of Saturn, say, or a spiral galaxy like flour strewn on Mother's kitchen counter top.

I relish such memories, though I cannot put a name to the multi-volume set, owned by an elderly neighbor of my grandparents, which I was permitted to borrow, just one book at a time, during visits. Later, I read Isaac Asimov instead.

Of course, twenty years earlier, Isaac Asimov hadn't had that option.

> For years I had wanted an *Encyclopedia Britannica* and finally my father managed to scrape together the money to buy a copy, and on March 11 [1942] it arrived. I began a project of reading it from cover to cover—not every word, to be sure, but lots of them, and at least I looked at every entry. (1979: 356).

Asimov was 22 at this time, America had entered the War, and the recent graduate was about to take up war-related work as a civilian chemist in the Navy Yard. He left home on May 13, 1942. 'I was in the third volume when I left, and my last words as I left were, pointing to the encyclopedia, "Gee, now I'll never know how it came out"' (356).

A smart aleck as well as a damned know-all. But notice: when the call of duty snatched him away, he was already into Volume Three... a little more than two months after the set had arrived! A volume a month! Perhaps this is the clue any budding polymath needs for a life of success.

ii

I was born, as it happens, a couple of years later.

When I was 11 or so, a workmate friend of my toolmaker father made the lucrative move to selling, approaching all his friends with the Newnes encyclopedia. Ten volumes for 39 pounds, and an 8-guinea dictionary, the thickest book I had ever seen not excluding *The American Woman's Cook Book*, thrown in at a bargain 6 pounds. There was no high pressure; my parents were happy to buy the lot, and today one of my brothers has it still on his own shelves.

When the row of red leatherette-bound books duly arrived, it was immediately (and justifiably) stockaded behind a fence of prohibitions and warnings. The glamor quickly wore off anyway, and though I delved into the things for homework, I never developed any real love for the Newnes.

I must have seen the *Encyclopedia Britannica* in the free municipal library. Great heavy volumes in embossed leather, imposing and terrible. But as a kid I was not much interested in anything I could not borrow. What would it have been like, living in a household which owned a set? Surely one's parents would have felt impelled to place it out of reach, which is exactly what you must not do with knowledge, jammy fingers and torn pages or not. Knowledge has to open its arms to you. Ideally it should slouch against the wall with a roguish gleam in its eye, whistling slightly out of tune.

By the time I got to university in the early sixties I had picked up a vague distrust of encyclopedias. They were vulgar (thought this kid from the rough, working-class suburb of Reservoir, then near Melbourne's outer boundaries). Certainly their reputation was not advanced by the night I arrived home at two a.m. to find my exhausted parents trying to evict a Britannica salesman who had started his spiel five hours before. A fellow St. Gabriel's parishioner, this worthy labored through an entire memorized routine, replete with punishing and unanswerable thrusts: Your children would be hard pressed to matriculate without a set of the *Britannica* in the home, and certainly they'd never make it through University. I listened to this claim with some astonishment. When at last he could no longer deny the galling fact that he had wasted his time and theirs, that he was not going to unload his 200 pounds' worth of truths, he caved in and got them to sign a chit to prove to head office that he had gone through the motions. No commission, but a few shillings for trying.

The Enlightenment idea of an alphabetized gathering and compression of all human knowledge has gone into deeper decline since those days. A recent academic conference noted that the turn of the new millennium

> marked the 250th anniversary of perhaps the most famous encyclopedia in the West, the *Encyclopédie ou Dictionnaire raisonné des Sciences, des Arts, et des Métiers* (1751-1765), edited by Diderot and D'Alembert. The Encyclopédie contained contributions from many eminent scholars and scientists of the day, and was built around the idea of a complete classification of knowledge. Its basic assumption was the sense that the cultural and natural world formed a cosmopolis, a bounded and finite system which was orderly, knowable, and recordable; something which would produce benefits for humanity, with social and human engineering following scientific description and classification. In the twenty-first century, that basic assumption is no longer secure: the boundaries and limits of our world have shifted, our methods of classification are less stable, and the optimistic vision of the Enlightenment seems no longer achievable.[10]

Plainly, this is so, just as we no longer dream of flying by attaching teams of swans to our chariots but use noisy jets instead, just as we no

---

[10] Report on the conference *The Idea of an Encyclopedia*, held at Lucy Cavendish College, Cambridge http://www.crassh.cam.ac.uk/events/events2001/reportencyclopaedideaof.html

longer expect to speak Leibniz's perfect language free of all ambiguity but make do with English and web browsers. This need not require us to abandon a reasoned, polymathic project which, as Peter Gay acknowledged, 'may appear to be a truly utopian prescription' (1969: 568). For, as he noted at the outset of his second volume on the Enlightenment: 'in the eighteenth century, for the first time in history, confidence was the companion of realism rather than a symptom of the Utopian imagination' (3). In the twenty-first, as we are starting to realize, confidence grounded in new knowledge, and the new means of attaining and applying it, is—wonderfully enough—a companion of both realism and utopian hope.

iii

Half a century and more ago, I was raised within an Australian working class family so fervently Roman Catholic, as vectored through a clergy steeped in Irish tradition, that its beliefs and chosen way of life seem to me now to have verged on derangement. The often vicious moralizing constraints of Catholicism—the kind I was exposed to from pulpit and primary school nuns, and later from Jesuit and Christian Brothers, and later again in the French-influenced seminary where I spent my last two years of school, aged 15 to 17—had the usual double impact. While I managed to avoid being sexually molested, still my relationships with my own body and with other people were at least somewhat harmed by wretched men and women terrified of the flesh yet apparently obsessed by it, a sorry saga that is now so boring and ubiquitous in the laments of Catholic and ex-Catholic writers world-wide that I will not tire you with it.

At the same time, this ancient tradition of purportedly rational belief—Aristotle! Aquinas! Duns Scotus!—provided a durable framework for viewing the world as a place that made sense, that had moral depth and called out a certain strength of mind, if not always of heart, in those persuaded (or more often, in the first instance, brainwashed) by its principles.

The odd thing about such an upbringing is that after you break free you retain a background metaphysics (think of James Joyce) that prevails even when you come to understand that in fact the universe is *not* intentional, was not designed by a higher intelligence. That it is, in fact, neither benign nor malign but just *there*, evolving in the darkness, cooling into eternity.

Absurdly, you tend to respond to the world with an optimism that is strictly unfounded. (Of course, some luckless souls, like nauseated Jean-Paul Sartre or the Australian novelist Gerald Murnane, respond instead with a deeply irrational and lifelong terror. Curiously, theological fright can be a source of considerable art as well as personal heartache, or so I have observed without, I'm relieved to say, experiencing it.) Luckily, we live at a time when science and technology are yielding solutions to many of the miseries of human life. Perhaps, indeed, that will eventually include an answer to our otherwise inevitable mortality. Confidence in the human prospect is not now as fatuous or gratuitous as it was a thousand years ago, and is more firmly grounded than the famous optimism of the encyclopedic Enlightenment in the second half of the eighteenth century, crushed prematurely by Romanticism and the Terror in France, and then more dreadfully by murderous totalitarian ideologies in the twentieth century.

Plainly, for an evolved consciousness in an uncaring universe, no 'technical fix' for the drawbacks of life can solve these deep metaphysical conundrums. Still, the incessant biological decay that now causes us to age and die might be remedied within the next half century, granting us, or more plausibly our children or grandchildren, the space, time and basic comfort and security to work our way toward some answers that are not wholly contrived out of self-delusion. We find ourselves in an epoch I believe might become a full reawakening of the Enlightenment's best hopes.

iv

Such polymathic scholars as Richard Dawkins (1998), Edward O. Wilson (1998), Steven Pinker (2002) and Daniel C. Dennett (2003) now toil to prevent its second fall, arguing with a certain desperation that we still might get it right this time around.

Wilson is the magisterial authority on insects, and more controversially the founder of sociobiology, the Darwinian doctrine that genes, bodies, minds and cultures co-evolve. Dawkins is the superb explainer of science who coined that celebrated and much misunderstood term, 'the selfish gene'—and another important concept, the 'meme'. That is his conjectured unit of culture that propagates from brain to brain like a virus or indeed a useful computer program. Already it has replicated itself neatly inside Wilson's immense and growing synthesis, driving out its clunkier competitor, the 'culturgen', a concept and failed term formulated by Wilson and his colleague Lumsden. Pinker is the Chomskyan linguist who is attempting to convey to the intelligent public the nature of the evolved powers and limitations of the mind and its brain/body, of the inherited bent that allows us to speak and act one to another as social beings. Dennett's contentious philosophical enquiries into the naturalistic sources of self and freedom are declaredly polymathic; closing his book *Freedom Evolves,* he notes:

> perhaps the most radical feature of this book by a
> philosopher is the preeminence given in it to the work of

non-philosophers. My point has been that philosophers, *as philosophers,* cannot claim to be doing their professional duty to their very own topics unless they pay careful attention to the thinking of psychologists... economists... biologists... (2003: 306-07)

The allure and embattled significance of this renewed Enlightenment seems pitched against two foes, themselves enemies: a redemptive environmental holism verging on Luddism, with roots in sublime mystery, and the ruinous cupidity which gladly rapes the planet's future in the name of no creed beyond the short-term bottom line.

Wilson, an ardent reductionist who deplores the woolly and ill-informed thinking of New Agers, is (no doubt to their astonishment) a prophet of *biophilia:* reverence for global biological diversity. And Dawkins, for all his steely atheism and even more devoted reductionism, urges union between science's relentless curiosity and the expressive, searing power of the arts. This hoped-for synthesis is aptly caught in Wilson's term *consilience:* a conjectured deep coherence and consistency of realms of knowledge apparently sundered during the nineteenth and twentieth centuries into testable sciences versus artistic and religious domains of feeling.

The first Enlightenment failed two centuries ago because its dream of clarified reason ran into the willful passions of obdurate humans. It is even arguable, as Wilson admits, that it had a 'dark-angelic flaw' (1998: 21), its noble idealism leading directly to the twentieth century's totalitarian nightmares. The neoDarwinian variant is more open-eyed. Enlightenment *philosophes* were nurturists, supposing a baby's mind to be an unmarked slate written afresh with each generation. Had that been so, humankind might be perfected by purified thought. It was a redemptive vision of endless mutability that led to a range of atrocities, from the behaviorist excesses of American education and psychology to the far more monstrous crimes of Stalin, Mao and Pol Pot.

Wilson and colleagues know better. We are shaped by 'epigenetic rules', which are 'the neural pathways and regularities in cognitive development by which the individual mind assembles itself' (139). But the linkage between genes and culture is flexible. We weave our own patterns, but on a loom built by evolution: in a word, human nature.

That loom endures because its cloth is suited to the world we live in. Wilson's deepest assumption, unprovable and perhaps absurdly ambitious, is that our brains and bodies echo to fundamental regularities in the cosmos. The world is always-already unified, even if we are not smart or sensitive enough to learn its grammar. So Wilson is an admitted reductionist. 'I plead guilty, guilty, guilty. Now let us move on...' (9). While his grasp of theory in the humanities is insecure, out of date, even naive and embarrassing (a lapse found also in Pinker), I find that ambition admirable.

Dawkins, too, is besotted by the continuing promise of diverse yet unifiable knowledge. Our time's tragedy is the shattering of that Enlightenment link between science, law and poetry. The Romantic poet John Keats, Dawkins reminds us, deplored Newton's unweaving of white light into a prismatic spectrum, reducing the glories of the rainbow to nothing more than a lab experiment. Yet that assessment, in turn, was a vulgar and unimaginative error. In his customary clear and, yes, poetic voice, Dawkins draws us into a world hugely grander than anything known to the Romantics—much of it opened to us in science's splendid unweaving.

The Enlightenment impulse does not break down and unweave in drunken revelry, for the sake of harm. It reweaves, builds up secular cathedrals—the entire vast, ancient cosmos itself—for the admiration of our hearts and minds. Its goal is, indeed, consilience. Its enemy is not appropriate scrutiny, but gullible or arrogant mystification. Dawkins is routinely scathing about the usual suspects—astrology, the New Age, superstition—but like Pinker and Dennett, Dawkins and Wilson share a humane search for communal cooperation in a world built from the blind scurrying of selfish genes.

v

I was long ago persuaded by Jacob Bronowski's claim (1964, 1967) that the practice of science, far from being malign or even ethically neutral, requires and calls forth at least some of the basic virtues, civic and personal. To function well, scientists must be honest in their work and public reports, to be diligent, to work with others, and perhaps to care what other people want (since, at the very least, its practice is now often so expensive, and its funding dependent on the good will of taxpayers and private benefactors).

Bronowski acknowledged, though, that perhaps the softer virtues of the heart are not required for the exercise of science, let alone mercantile technology, and might even to some extent be excluded. Blazing ambition that catalyzes success in science can be so savage and all-consuming that its practitioners can ignore the needs of those close to them. Granted, that imbalance applies equally to artists, who are often praised and admired for the intimidating purity of their obsessions—all too often just a cover story for self-importance and lazy refusal of empathy. The particular peril implicit in scientific attainment is its awful power. Beyond the costs levied upon the ambitious scientist's family (no greater, perhaps, than those charged to the artist's) are immense consequences to the world at large: to all the other humans on the planet, to the creatures with which we share the earth, perhaps to the very endurance of that world.

Beyond these standard minatory considerations, though, new disciplines such as evolutionary psychology have begun to lay bare the deep roots of ethical conduct, and of those drives and urges that impel us to act in ways usually regarded as wicked or at least shamefully self-centered (by contrast with those many ways that are quite properly self-regarding in an individualist). The classic Humean argument seemed to deny this possibility, showing that 'ought', strictly speaking, can never be implied by 'is'—that morality is always absolutely distinct from the facts of the world, including facts about human actors. Yet that argument might break down somewhat as this elaborate evolutionary narrative unfolds.

Arguably, as the Enlightenment *philosophes* were perhaps the first to understand, science at last *introduces* moral accountability by bringing forth knowledge that strips away rote faith. Previously, in the absence of systematic knowledge based on experimental investigation and theoretical elaboration working hand in hand, moral accountability often took the form of kow-towing to dicta handed down 'from above' (as Kant himself noted). The gods spoke, but they mouthed the proclamations of human authorities possessed of the mandate of force or eager to obtain it. Freed of base and baseless faith in supernatural warrant, we are able to investigate the genuine, non-superstitious sources of moral decision-making.

These might often turn out to be prudential and situational—I will not kill you if you agree not to kill me unless you are extremely irked, we shall both act in a trustworthy fashion most of the time, etc—but while prudence lacks the metaphysical zing of divine ordinance, to the unbrainwashed it is both less craven and a more plausible basis for right conduct. But is it true that morality—ethics, if you wish—is prudential? Let us assume that it is not. Then you are driven into absurd self-subverting loops like: 'Tell me *why* I should be moral?' which unpacks, uselessly, into 'Give me a moral account of why I *should* be moral; repeat'.

To be able to act prudently implies and requires several subsidiary factors. We must be able to know with some accuracy—to model effectively—how the brute or unintentional world works. We need an adequate model of our own current and long-term needs, desires, aversions. More, we have to model effectively and fairly the complex interplay of other intentional conscious beings like ourselves with that brute world. Failure in any of these subordinate competencies compromises the effectiveness of how well we understand the likely impact of our actions. If we cannot foresee the consequences of our actions, it is meaningless to suppose that we are obliged to act rightly.

Yet failure is unavoidable. Complex dynamical systems veer away from their starting points in unpredictable jinks and swerves. These limitations on understanding and prediction, imposed by what it became fashionable in the 1980s to call 'chaos', mean that even the best stocked mind and heart is going to make errors in modeling. That is not necessarily a counsel of despair; we adjust a tad and start again. Actually we often learn from our mistakes. Chaos does not govern everything in the world; it can be self-limiting. The billiard balls of Newton's and Hume's universe wander blindly across the green baize after only a few consecutive strokes with the cue, but they do not change color and tunnel through the edge of the table and into the next room, not even in a quantum universe.

Nothing about the complexity of world and self denies us the opportunity to reassess our goals in the light of new information. In fact, it almost ensures that we must do so, from time to time, as more accurate information about the world and ourselves is gathered, and as our theoretical models are improved. In that sense, I see no real gulf between Is and Ought, only that we need to keep ourselves informed on the best available picture of what actually *Is*, so as to optimize our chosen *Oughts*.

Today, more than ever, the largest new ingredient of that knowledge will come from scientific research.

A Child's Garden of Change

> My thesis... is not doubt-for-doubt's-sake, but doubt as
> a necessary barrier which the valid can overcome and
> the nonvalid cannot. The more a finding seems to
> destroy the basis of the scientific structure, the higher
> the barrier of doubt. Of course one must remember that
> 'doubt' is not synonymous with 'refusal to listen'.
>
> Isaac Asimov (2002: 263)

i

Four hundred years ago, you sat in your study with René Descartes and
said with him, 'I think. Therefore, at the very least, and doubt whatever
else I will, I know that a thought exists. I may reasonably put in doubt
any perception, any deduction from my observations of the external
world, except for that: *a thought exists*. Hence, since it is the last to go
down under the blowtorch of skeptical inquiry, thinking—
consciousness—appears to have some priority in the scheme of things.'

Nowadays, instead, you sit in a lab and watch a functional magnetic
resonance display, while small distinct parts of the brain flicker on and
off as someone thinks of the color red, or recalls her first birthday, or
moves a toe, or recalls a musical tune, or thinks 'I think, therefore I am.'

How could that not make everything abruptly different? If, instead,
the machines had shown the whole brain switched on in a holistic blaze
of activation *whatever* you did, you might develop a more traditional
kind of story about consciousness, the kind that overwhelmed the
original Enlightenment thinkers with their often-derided 'mechanical'
model of the mind. Now you can literally *see* that the activation of a
salient portion of the brain always occurs some distinct part of a second
before the person reports making a choice. The 'you' that regards itself
as executive, sacrosanct and unitary is clearly some kind of non-stop
juggling act, an illusion that fools itself. It is a theme that shall recur in
this book.

My own sympathies are with philosopher Daniel Dennett and
evolutionary linguist Steven Pinker, rather than, say, philosopher David
Chalmers, who still insists that consciousness is the 'hard problem'
whose solution will require a fundamental revision of science. On the
other hand (balky as usual), I retain a scandalous interest in some of the
more carefully researched findings of parapsychology, which suggest that
maybe intention and perception sometimes exceed the boundaries of
current physics and psychophysics. Orthodox science, in all its
comprehensive and attested glory, seems to own no easy place for these
observations to rest—except, unexamined, into the waste bin. That
might be far too easy a solution to the disgraceful data.

Do I therefore wonder if the mind might be extra-dimensional, or utterly other (a 'spirit', say, whatever that might be)? Certainly not. But I have to say it is odd that the inner feeling of awareness, of qualia, of rich smells and hues, still evades adequate reductive explanation, as do the shocking anomalies of parapsychology. Maybe, after all, there is some link between the two unknowns, beyond the simple fact that they both *are* unexplained. With any luck, if the nanomedicine machines arrive from the labs to repair me before I am dead or brain-dead of old age, I might still be alive when scientists uncover the answers. Perhaps the hyperintelligent Artificial Intelligences that I expect we will see before the middle of the century will explain it all to us. That would be a very nice joke on human pretension.

What *is* a human, in the age of science? Are we naked apes, protein computers, or something deeper and more wonderful? Can we retain human dignity without turning our backs on reason and its sciences that seem ready to shred us into meaningless fragments? These are questions posed at the intersection of gene and history.

When two international teams released the complete sequence of the human genome, the first big surprise was that it is only a third as long as experts had expected. That seemed genuinely shocking to some observers, demeaning to our self-estimate. The twisting, coiled DNA we inherit from our parents contains little more than 30,000 genes plus a tremendous amount of sheer hitchhiking rubbish sneaked in by viruses. Not much to build a brainy body from, starting with a single cell. Not enough, perhaps.

Or so some imagined. The news delighted commentators who regard classic evolutionary theory—Darwinian natural selection modified by genetics—as ridiculously oversimplified. Look, they say: here is a human, noble in reason, infinite in faculties, and yet this paragon of animals emerges from a genetic recipe just half again as long as the DNA recipe needed to build and operate a nematode worm. So much for the mighty gene! All the extra information must come from somewhere else. Where? Well, from the environment, of course. This looked like good news for those who doubt the ruling power of biology over choice.

Might it be the kiss of death to reductionists, recently returning to fashion with the doctrine that our lives are ordained by an evolved, persistent human nature? Actually, no. After all, everything in the cosmos—star, dust, worm, human—is made from just a few varieties of elementary particles plus four forces shunting them around. Take two kinds of quark, whimsically named the *up* and *down* varieties, build protons and neutrons from them, throw in electrons, neutrinos and some radiation, and you can build most of the universe. It is impossible to get much more reductive than that. Yet nobody doubts that this is how it works.

It is precisely the same with genes. Even if we have only 30,000 genes—protein patterns, and construction codes—those genes differ among themselves at 60,000 known locations. A single coding letter for a given gene often varies from one person to the next without actually spoiling the message (like spelling 'tyre' as 'tire' or 'center' as 'centre').

So what are the implications of these dazzling new discoveries? Are the skeptics right to mock genetic reductionists? No, because that scorn is nearly always misplaced and poorly founded. Of course, human genes are inevitably expressed within a specific environment that provides sustenance, training, the embrace and discipline of parents, the boisterous fun or cruelty of playmates, all the inexhaustible memory of culture that each growing child drinks down in gulping draughts. Our 30,000 genes are sliced and diced and recombined while weaving our bodies, programming them with temperament, abilities and social talents. The insistent impact of those genes is undeniable. Twins really *are* much more alike than random classmates from the same socioeconomic background. And yet people who share a similar culture and upbringing have a great deal more in common, obviously, than they do with other humans speaking a strange tongue on the other side of the globe, or in a drastically different period of history, even if all these people share most of their genes.

Soon enough, all of today's cultural and biological variants are going to seem tame and familiar, by comparison with the changes on their way.

iv

Although I have always lived in the future, I am always surprised when it actually happens. Nevertheless, it is difficult for me to grasp how *truly* strange the future seems to most other people, how little deep change is expected. Indeed, I find it almost impossible to understand the usual response to our technology-shaped future, which is typically a blend of dread, denial, scorn and boredom.

We are governed by men, and a few women, most of whom were young and impressionable back in the late '50s and early '60s—the horrible Baby Boomers and their predecessors. (I myself am too *old* to be a Baby Boomer.) They have lived through this accreting future, dragging it with them like a shell that fits less comfortably with each year. Here is the problem: the future is not just coming relentlessly to us, bringing changes for good and ill. It is doing so faster and faster—not uniformly, by any means... frequently with skids backwards and sideways... but *accelerating* is what change is doing, on the whole.

In my own nation, forty years ago Aboriginal Australians did not have the right to vote, and the contraceptive pill was unavailable, and pubs closed at 6 o'clock, and it cost an arm and a leg to phone overseas, nor could you fly there, however uncomfortably and ill-fed, in 24 hours by jet. Nobody had Xerox copiers or desktop computers or video recorders, and we all ate awful stodge, and the biggest public celebration of the year was the Melbourne Cup rather than, as today, the Gay and Lesbian Mardi Gras. So the 40-year gap between then and now brought its measure of future shock. It is likely that the next *twenty* years will be harder, faster, brighter, more shocking... *at least* equal, when people look backward from the 2020s, to that gap.

An on-line friend of mine in the United States is a terrifyingly brilliant computer prodigy named Eliezer Yudkowsky. In his 20s now, he works on artificial intelligence, but when he was just 17 he noted on his web site:

> *Future Shock* was written in 1970 and proposed that the rate of change had exceeded the human ability to deal with it. *1970! Ha!* Since then, of course, things have gotten so bad that we could speak of 'inflation-adjusted 1970 years' when making futurological predictions. A 1970 year now buys only three months. Fifty years from now, adjusted for inflation, is about 2010. If we try to account for future inflation, at around 5 per cent inflation per 1997 year, we find that *eternity* is only 2017 or so.

By and large, people of my parents' age who grew up in the 1920s are ill at ease with the Internet... the impact of cheap mobile phones and instant global news, of imminent human cloning and nervous system repair, cures for some cancers, the swift mapping of the human genome... There are people who were awe-struck children when humans flew aircraft for the very first time, who now watch crisp pictures of small machines rolling along in the ancient sea beds of Mars.

Squeeze all that change into two or three decades.

That is the scale of the thing. That is what will smash into us, if technology advances at the current rate of exponential change, by the first third of this century.

And what is causing this dislocation, this disruption, this fabulously difficult and fertile future? Well, computers. It has been observed that computers get more powerful each year in a remarkably predictable way, following what is known as Moore's law. Currently, this doubling of computational power for your dollar happens every 12 months. That might not seem so startling, but it is. If you keep doubling year after year, by compound interest you reach truly gigantic amounts surprisingly quickly. If you invest a dollar this year and earn another dollar at the end of the year, then reinvest at the same rate, by the end of ten years you'll own $1000. In 20 years you will not own $2000, which is the sort of linear expectation that is built into our naive expectations, and most of our political forecasts. You'll have a million dollars. In 30 years, you'd have a billion dollars. Just from one dollar and an annual doubling rate. It does not work with money, alas, but it *does* work with computer power, and has been doing so faithfully for more than half a century, with no obvious reason for it to plateau out any time soon.

A curve like that runs away up the page. It looks like a spike. But let us defer our discussion of that truly unnerving prospect, and return for the moment to the still contentious mysteries of the genes.

Darwin's Beige Box

> If Darwinian mechanisms can explain the existence of a skylark, in all its glory, they can surely explain the existence of an ode to a nightingale, too. A poem is a wonderful thing, but not clearly more wonderful than a living, singing skylark.
>
> Daniel C. Dennett (2000)[11]

i

Horse walks into a bar. Barkeep asks, 'Why the long face?' (Boom boom.)

That would not have been funny at all had it been an elephant and the question had been, 'Why the long nose?' or 'Why the big ears?' In fact, these are not such silly questions. Answering them calls for an unusual approach to life—looking at creatures not just from an evolutionary point of view, but from the angle of a quizzical engineer. Why do the big lovable beasts sway from side to side as they plod along? Because they are so massive. You cannot spring about as lightly and gracefully as a gazelle when your twin tusks each weighs more than a sturdy human. African bulls can reach 13 tonnes, rarely less than 4 tonnes. Plodding under the tropical sun, all that hot meat and fat is packed inside a bald, tough rind. It needs to radiate away the heat of the elephant's internal engines, or risk boiling the poor beast in its own juices. So, big ears. All the better to hear you with? No, they are radiators, dispersing metabolic waste heat from a huge array of blood vessels close to the cooling air.

And that long trunk? Well, if you had a head as big and high off the ground as an elephant's, mounted on a thick, sturdy neck, you could not readily get your mouth down to the grass and a long drink of water. An elongated, prehensile nose does the job of hands and straw in one—and, at a pinch, serves to spray water over the hot, radiating ears. Mammoths, those defunct hairy elephant lookalikes, had small, furry ears. They needed to retain all the warmth they could during the Ice Ages.

It is simple engineering. Well, not all that simple. Life forms are more complex than machines, and developed by strange and twisty paths. Not every feature of an animal can be 'reverse engineered' as readily as the elephant's ears and trunk.

Still, we share inner mechanisms with lions, lambs, koalas and dinosaurs: 'nature's engines' (Lavers, 2000). Do we really have that much in common with extinct species such as the mighty saurians,

---

[11] 'In Darwin's Wake, Where am I?', http://ase.tufts.edu/cogstud/papers/apapresadd.htm

doomed in the random smash of an asteroid into our planet 65 million years ago? Weren't they cold-blooded folk, lumbering stolidly through their marshy world? Motion pictures such as *Jurassic Park* have encouraged us to doubt this, and indeed for several decades there has been a vigorous heresy claiming that many dinosaurs were warm-blooded. If we are not extremely careful, we might end up exterminating ourselves in a vast new species dieback that has already begun.

But won't science have an answer to such impending doom, to that loss of biodiversity due to human rapacity and carelessness? After all, we now know the very sequence of human DNA, the recipe of our kind. With such knowledge in hand, perhaps we will be able to correct such temporary setbacks and rebuild the lost biota? Perhaps (I am inclined to think so), but Marxist geneticist Richard Lewontin, for one, scorns such confidence (2000). Equal scorn arises at the far end of the scientific spectrum: among those who wish to reinstate a religious perspective under the sobriquet Intelligent Design (as we shall see in a moment), and some who hope to see a kind of revival of Darwin's rival Lamarck. And then there are those many intelligent, happily ignorant people who cannot be bothered learning anything about evolution beyond the word and how to pronounce it with a suitably mocking sneer. Consider this utterance by the self-deconstructing artist/theorist Jake Chapman:

> Temporality implies a kind of Darwinian evolution, the idea that there's some ideal being pursued. I think the presumption that there is some kind of refinement going on towards an ideal perfection, an absolute success and idealization is inherent to all forms of the understanding of art. (Baker and Chapman, 2003)

Here Chapman, author of the drolly-titled assemblage *Meatphysics,* repudiates teleology while attributing it to the most acerbic anti-teleological science the world has ever known, Darwinist evolutionary theory. Darwin's model of descent with modification, winnowed by contest, is precisely *not* a narrative of 'some kind of refinement going on towards an ideal perfection'. At a time when varieties of Darwinism are themselves still in vigorous contest, this is a dismaying slip for a cultural artisan to inscribe in his pronunciamientos.

ii

I was walking with friends in their pleasant backyard when a flock of dear little birdies swooped and sang their hearts out above a tree. 'Ah, look how they sport and carol for the very joy of it!' a friend cried, clapping her hands to her breast.

You could see her point, and it was a gladdening thing to behold. 'Actually,' I suggested, 'what they're really saying is either "This turf will be defended with lethal force" or "Feel like a quickie? I'm sure you'll like it."' My friend stared at me in disgust. But this cynical estimate was not my fault. Darwin made me do it. Or perhaps it was Wallace, as we shall see in a moment.

Isn't this a dreadfully reductive way to look at the world? There are other dear little birdies, after all, that shout at the top of their voices when a dangerous intruder approaches, saving the flock at great risk to themselves. Rather than gorging alone when it stumbles on a carcass, a raven will call others to join the feast. Surely this is natural altruism in action, the very antithesis of those notorious 'selfish genes' that Richard Dawkins made famous—and which were disputed hotly by his territorial rival, the late paleontologist Stephen Jay Gould?

At least with ravens, we now know, reality is less than noble. If a juvenile bird without territory chances upon something dead and tasty, it will be seen off by the larger adult who holds the turf. By calling in other young ruffians, it can overwhelm the incumbent's defense. Everyone gets a share, but that is smart (if automatic, 'hard-wired') politics, not the golden rule. The recipes for such political strategies have been conserved as behavioral genes selected by brute survival. For Dawkins, evolution is finally about the preferential survival of clumps of adapted, co-operating genetic replicators—selfish only in the sense that unless they create effective bodies, they'll perish. Stephen Jay Gould, by contrast, wished to stress the role of the whole organism and indeed of species lineages, often interrupted by natural catastrophes that disrupt locally effective adaptations, making them suddenly irrelevant. No gene is rewarded— selected—on its own; it takes a village to put many genes into effect (at least among humans). Many of these apparent deadlocks are matters of emphasis rather than theological doctrine, as innocent onlookers might suppose from all the thunder and lightning. For the budding polymath, they can be an occasion of both insight and fun—like those charming birds swooping in flight.

In a charmingly clever book, Geoffrey Miller (2000) has argued that charm and cleverness are no mere froth on Darwin's cappuccino, but actually the motive power behind human distinctiveness. We have evolved song, art, sport, jokes and skiing as part of a non-stop courtship repertoire, an extreme extension of the dancing birds' gavotte. Women's sexual choices for a hundred thousand years and more have shaped men, including the much reviled penis, and their own choosy and reluctant clitoris. Both sexes built intelligence out of millennia of cries and whispers: 'The mind evolved by moonlight' (7). It sounds glib but Miller mounts a handsome and enticing argument.

At a far extreme from the subtle glances and sighs of sexual selection, molecular chemistry reveals a dizzying realm of genetic shenanigans. Are selfish genes engaged in endless contest and grudging co-operation, or is life more than molecules red in tooth and claw? If Leicester genetics professor Gabriel Dover (2000) is right, 'molecular drive' happens when small mutations literally jump around the chromosomes, spread swiftly by 'adoptation', and colonize an entire genome, even leaping between species. Dover argues passionately that we idiosyncratic individuals, not the swarms of genes whose unique interactions help build us, are the key to evolutionary selection. The late zoologist S. Anthony Barnett also resented the Dawkins-style selfish gene story and distrusted such neuroscience terms as 'hard-wired'. Everything in the brain, he insisted, is connected to everything else. Like Dover, Barnett saw genes and brain cells as a symphony orchestra, not a set of competing buskers. His prescription: 'The most momentous task for humanity is to arrest the destruction of the biosphere, to manage what remains and to guide its future growth' (2000: 179). It will be exceedingly difficult to manage this transition if we cling to the myths of difference and identity that have formed the unconscious bracing of nearly all human cultures to this date. In the next chapter, we shall return to that all-but-intractable problem, and see if the new Enlightenment understanding can help us understand its sources.

iii

Despite these demurrers, the Human Genome Project has now mapped effectively every item in our collective genetic recipe. (There is no *single* human genome, of course.) It is a suitable time to take stock of what is known, and of what changes we can expect as biology builds the 21st century, rather as electricity and the atom built the 20th. We humans lace our genetic instructions on twin pairs of 23 chromosomes of different sizes; now we have begun to interpret their messages. That is an engaging and demystifying way to approach those deep, ancient encryptions that construct our bodies and, to some extent, our minds. Huntington's disease, say, lethal, terrible and delayed, is caused by a kind of stutter in the genetic word or paragraph that ordains a certain protein. The more stutters, the more deformed the protein, and the earlier the disorder sets in. But our genome is not primarily about illness. Nature and nurture cannot easily be peeled apart; our lives, even so, are going to be remade entirely by this extraordinary new knowledge.

Science is about compression. It is the informed art of squeezing what is knowable about a topic into the neatest possible package. Intensity is a virtue for science just as for art (or religion). But you can go badly wrong with a goal like that, squeezing the juice out, leaving only a husk. Science and technology can reach too eagerly for absolute explanations and power over nature can miss or crush complexity.

Understandably, one response is a kind of born-again mysticism, painting us not as masters of nature but as her custodians or even worshipful children. The name increasingly given to this portrait of the world as vulnerable mother, under assault by her rash offspring, is Gaia.[12] According to Gaia's devotees, our planet is no mere jumble of animals, vegetables and minerals. It is a profound but fragile harmony, a system of living systems that our wildly growing technologies place at risk. Earth is no mere ball of rock and air infested with evolving life forms—she is a single great organism, the largest of all endangered species. The mutual partnership of diverse living creatures, from bacteria and fungi to the finned, furred and feathered, is called symbiosis. The mother of the Gaia theory, professor of geosciences Lynn Margulis, argues (1998) that life is better understood symbiotically, co-operatively, rather than as a red-in-tooth-and-claw Darwinian contest.

In her view, we are all symbionts, creatures linked in vast recycling circuits of matter and energy. In turn, we contain multitudes of symbionts, from the tiny bacteria that live in our guts and help us digest food to the even smaller remnant organisms that power our cells. These mitochondria were once free-living microbes that long ago entered a pact with larger cells and now dwell inside the enormous multi-cellular animals that roam the world and sometimes dream up science and art. Does this mean Margulis is a kind of New Age sage, a mother figure for Gaia-worshippers? Far from it. She is justifiably irascible at the way her deep idea has been pilfered and misused. 'The co-optation of Gaia-theory by science-haters and media-mongers is striking,' she writes. 'Gaia is neither vicious nor nurturing in relation to humanity; it is a convenient name for an earth-wide phenomenon: temperature, acidity/alkalinity and gas composition regulation' (120).

But that is not as dull as it sounds. For billions of years, the changing ecologies of life have nudged our world into a global ecosystem—Gaia—that subtly stabilizes the amount of oxygen, methane and other gases in the air and regulates the greenhouse effect. Without the feedback flows summarized in the name, Earth would be cold and inhospitable. This immense process is brainless as a thermostat, but persists through catastrophes that wipe out most of its constituent species.

So are we Gaia's chosen children? No. 'We cannot put an end to nature; we can only pose a threat to ourselves' (128). The mindless systems of balance we call Gaia will expunge us, she says, if we try to grow without limit. Her argument is elegant and audacious and the telling wonderfully personal. We hear about the passionate, abrasive time she had as Carl Sagan's young wife and the scorn from narrow pedants that greeted her startling grand theory. Nowadays, when it is

---

[12] Pronounced 'Guy-uh', after the Greek earth goddess.

taught in high schools, 'I find, to my dismay if not to my surprise, that the exposition is dogmatic, misleading, not logically argued and often frankly incorrect' (30-1). That is the lament of more than one evolutionist trying to tussle with the boundaries between opinion and knowledge, art and science and faith, as we shall now see.

iv

In 2002, the world's most popular evolutionist since Darwin and T. H. Huxley died, aged only 60, leaving a trove of richly flavored essays and books centered on natural history. Death did not still his fluent, polymathic voice. In a posthumous volume, Gould carried forward his intrepid attempt to solve bitter demarcation disputes that have tormented Western culture for centuries. The still smoldering war between religion and science is the most famous, hotly followed by a prickly stand-off between natural sciences and humane arts (C. P. Snow's 'Two Cultures', seen more recently in action as the 'science wars'). Gould hoped to dissolve these conflicts by showing that it had all been a terrible blunder, rather like the fake headline: *Duke Ferdinand Found Alive, Great War a Mistake*.

Is it possible? Suppose each of these realms of human experience and knowledge (or doctrine) is an independent 'Magisterium', an authoritative stand-alone body of teaching. They could not conflict, as none of them should covet the other's ground. This purported principle of NOMA or Non-Overlapping Magisteria (NOM was perhaps insufficiently mellifluous) was deployed in Gould's 1999 book, *Rocks of Ages*. Soothingly, he explained that religion actually never made claims disputable by observation, theory and experiment—or, if it did, it shouldn't. This does have the merit of seeing off 'creation science', long the target of Gould's ridicule, while accepting the Pope's belated recent apology to Galileo. Oddly, it also means physical miracles must be dismissed as rank superstition, a solution which will scandalize many believers.

Gould daintily declared himself an agnostic. Admitting that he was 'not a believer', that an immaterial realm had no strong claim on 'factual existence', he allowed both faith and reason at the heart of 'the fullness of life' in a spirit of consilience—unity amid diversity. Since ethics cannot be derived directly from scientific facts, he was happy to place moral judgment and religion within the same catch-all Magisterium. This, though, is absurd, making ethical atheism a clandestine religion.

In 1998, his great foe and fellow Harvard professor Edward O. Wilson, founder of the reductionist evolutionary program once known as sociobiology, borrowed the 19th century term 'consilience' to epitomize an ambitious intellectual goal. Wilson hopes to see all the world's plenty captured in a single powerful hierarchy, from the tiniest quantum particles to geology and astronomy, to life and mind and society, with science and the arts themselves finally enfolded into a unified edifice. Gould discerned an error at the very core of this project. Complex things, especially people and societies, crystallize around historical accidents and choices: in a word, contingency. Such events are lawful enough, understandable in hindsight, but can not be predicted, unlike the repeatable phenomena of traditional science. Evolution itself takes this form, since it is not only physics and chemistry but history. You can explain how an animal came to have its special shape and habits, as we just saw, but *not in advance*.

As with his florid, ornamented collections of essays, Gould argued his case in no desiccated, passive voice but with all the enthusiasm of an art lover. His final book, *The Hedgehog, the Fox, and the Magister's Pox*, took a delicious, wandering course through his private collection of beloved antiquarian texts, leading us through the compressed Latin and beautiful engravings of animals real and imaginary. Here we swiftly find the thread that threatens to unravel his separate but equal Magisteria. A great 16th century zoological treatise by Protestant Konrad Gesner was systematically and comically defaced by an ecclesiastical censor, one Magister Lelio Medice. These laborious blottings and obscurations are 'the Magister's pox'. They leave the scientific content unmarred while obliterating the names of scientists from the wrong side of the faith tracks.

One of those was the brilliant but unorthodox Catholic scholar, Erasmus of Rotterdam, whose quip about foxes and hedgehogs forms the rest of Gould's title. Borrowing an even older military adage from seventh century B.C. poet Archilochus, Erasmus (and much later Isaiah Berlin) told us that some thinkers use many diverse strategies, like wily foxes, but others, the hedgehogs, single-mindedly pursue one great way of knowing. Gould advised a blend of the two approaches. As a polymath, he was naturally attracted to the fox's multiple paths, yet as an evolutionist he saw a single bright thread running through the world's history. Similarly with the distinct Magisteria, which are not identifiable with those two contrasting strategies. Passionately, he argued that 'a fruitful union of these seemingly polar opposites can, with goodwill and significant self-restraint on both sides, be conjoined into a diverse but common enterprise of unity and power'.

Such wholeness cannot be gained, he warned, by 'shearing off the legitimate differences... that make our lives so varied, so irreducibly, and so fascinatingly, complex'. E. O. Wilson's reductionist version of consilience, according to Gould, tempts us to that awful constricted cropping, to an imperialist ambit-claim by science that would swallow up the complexity and hazard of life. It is difficult, though, to find this in Wilson, who clearly respects art and philosophy and is, ironically, himself a religious believer.

Gould's accumulating assault on a one-eyed consilience—another small irony, as Wilson lost an eye in a childhood accident—serves to warn us against a too-easy fall back into the spiritual aridity of mid-20th century positivism. What it risks is its own magisterial pox, infecting foxes and hedgehogs alike with reluctance to go where angels, and their barmy but fashionable New Age magisterium, fear to tread.

v

Natural selection, evolution by heritable variation and environmental sieving ('darwinnowing' is a nice term for the process), has come a long way, then, since Charles Darwin stepped off the *Beagle* and started his long voyage toward a shocking Victorian truth. A century and a half ago, his ideas were on the borders of accepted science. Today they stand at its very heart. Some argue, though, that the well-off and finally agnostic Darwin filched his notions from a struggling working class Anglican, Alfred Russel Wallace, who had had only seven years schooling. Traveling the world with no less valor than Darwin, he suffered abominably. At 25, racked with illness, he carried back from the Amazon 400 butterflies, 450 beetles, 1300 insects, notes and journals. The ship caught fire and nearly all was lost.

In the Malay Archipelago six years later, delirious with malaria, Wallace realized that in nature the stronger, healthier animals would die less readily than their kin. Varieties would emerge, and eventually diverge into species. He wrote up this brilliant theory in two nights and sent it to the already famous Darwin, who had dithered with his own equivalent treatise for two decades. In a 'delicate arrangement', papers by both naturalists were read to the Linnean Society in 1858. Fifty years later a joint medal was struck in commemoration. Incredibly, Wallace was still alive, and would not to die for a further five years.

In *Skeptic* magazine editor Michael Shermer's view (2001), this amiable accord is a fine instance of a 'plus-sum' method, perhaps found more often in science than elsewhere, for dealing with disputes. He is less charitable toward other borderland topics such as the postmodern embrace of hideously cruel cultures not built by dead white males, racist claims, and purported paranormal powers. It is intriguing, though, that Wallace himself was a cautious believer in telepathy (179-98), although he saw through the worst spiritualist warblings of his day. Do the swoopings and cries of scientists and cranks alike have any greater content than birds' territorial defense? Certainly, and Shermer makes clear the very great merits of science as a path to truth. Can we expect a joint medal to be struck some day, with a head of Gould on one side and of Dawkins on the obverse? I rather doubt it. But 2008 should be a time for some vigorous celebrations among evolutionists of all species. Let us trust Wallace's memory survives.

A polymath entirely unlike Gould, and from the far side of the science tracks, was Nobel physicist Richard Feynman. Charming and feisty, he was one of the deepest minds of their century yet with a gift for limpid explanation. He looked unblinkingly at the impact of science upon politics and religion. Science, he concluded, is a special method of finding things out, a knowledge archive, and a set of derived technologies (1998: 5). The method 'involves a most terrible test of human reasoning ability... tightropes of logic' (15), and the practical trial of observation. You make a guess at how things work, then go and see if you can knock down your guess by looking hard at the relevant bits of the world. A guess that survives makes it into science.

So science is based on imagination, but not the sort familiar to an artist. You try to 'imagine something that you have never seen, that is consistent in every detail with what has already been seen, and... different from what has been thought of' (22). But your guess must be definite, not vague or slippery or metaphorical. Where does that leave religious and other non-scientific intuitions? Feynman is generous: just because a claim 'cannot be subjected to the test of observation, this does not mean that it is dead, or wrong, or stupid' (16). Some such claims, he agrees, 'are, in fact, in many ways the most important' (17): ethical dictums, say. Actually, during the last three or four decades, evolutionary psychology—arguably at the heart of the emerging Enlightenment project—has probed deep into the biological sources of ethics, but Feynman's modesty was refreshing.

The controversialist Michael Behe has something of the same gift as Feynman. He can discuss molecular biochemistry's blood-clot cascade proteins and keep you smiling. Behe is a Roman Catholic professor of biochemistry who became a US media celebrity several years ago when his ingenious assault on Darwinism first appeared (1998). In the age of the Internet, we can instantly compare his curious claims with rejoinders from defenders of orthodoxy. He was lambasted by witty experts such as H. Allen Orr, Russell F. Doolittle and Jerry A. Coyne, finding support in others such as James Shapiro.[13]

Behe is a deft, entertaining writer. His relentless attack on Darwinism stems from his claim that certain systems at the sub-cellular level are 'irreducibly complex', so that their development cannot be explained by evolution. The way blood clots to close an injury requires a vast cascade of enzymes. None can be left out of the feedback loops but each is worthless by itself. Reaction paths where you need chemicals A, B, C and D can lead, in the Darwinist story, to an organism evolving a

---

[13] All of whom may be sampled on the web-site
http://www-polisci.mit.edu/bostonreview/evolution.html

way of making spare D from C if the supply of D runs out. Simple, Behe notes scathingly: 'after all, they're right next to each other in the alphabet'. Real chemistry is not so convenient: it is harder to credit that 'carboxyaminoimidazole ribotide was sitting around waiting to be converted to 5-aminoimidazole-4-(N-succinylocarboxamide) ribotide' (152).

Behe asserts that intelligent design from beyond the system is the sole plausible account for such living structures. My own mind closes down with a palpable bang as I reach these assertions, but that is no rebuttal to his strongly-presented case. In some places his argument is flawed, as Orr and Coyne show, in others it is surely premature—but it does deserve a critical hearing (though probably not in routine high school classes). After all, leaving deity aside, Earth life might have been designed by aliens, as Nobelist Francis Crick once suggested (1981).

Ted Steele's heresy is not quite on Behe's scale, but it got him drummed out of the UK several decades ago, and almost out of science. For a time he was associate professor of biology in Wollongong, in regional Australia, where he and colleagues tried to prove that while Darwin was right, his ideological rival Lamarck was also right. Lamarck argued for the direct transmission to offspring of physical changes acquired during a parent's life (as did Darwin's own early theory of 'gemmules'). Mendelian and DNA genetics show that life (mostly) does not work that way. Germ cells mutate, grow into slightly variant offspring, and natural selection sieves the contenders. Somatic or body cells from the parents do not get a look-in.

Steele and others have argued that probably this is not true of some immune system cells. His important but infuriating book *Lamarck's Signature* made shockingly heavy work of explaining this, loading the hapless non-specialist reader with heaps of detail shuffled out of logical order. Oddly, arch-Darwinist Richard Dawkins gave a fine précis of the same idea back in 1982, in *The Extended Phenotype,* but is treated with outraged indignation by Steele. Crammed to the cruppers with real science, Steele and his collaborators abandon their general audience at the outset. They extrude acronyms, illustrate their stodge with unreadable diagrams in tiny print, then jumble the mutated result into something evolution would never select. If you wish to learn about somatic hypermutation, the few paragraphs on the topic in Behe or Dawkins make far more sense. Steele's trek has been arduous, made painful by conservative enemies, but his stronger claims still elude replication. It is hard to see how the limited immune retrogenes and 'mutatorsomes' he describes could have genuinely Lamarckian effects in the large—imprinting the gains of a short giraffe's straining neck, to draw once more upon that chestnut of mistaken inheritance, on the genome of its offspring.

Not all radical evolutionary theories need be fundamentally heterodox, let alone based in religion. If zoologist Andrew Parker is correct in his ambitious theory (2003), the beginning of complex life on our planet can be captured in an almost-familiar but not quite Biblical phrase: 'Let there be sight!'

It is slightly shocking that for nearly four billion years our planet's most complicated creatures were bacteria, algae, single-celled primitive creatures: bland, living on sunlight like plants but unable to see by its illumination. For most of the tenure of life on earth, long before insects and dinosaurs and rats and us, the light was on—but nobody interesting was at home. Life changed and diversified, but at an excruciatingly slow pace. A little more than half a billion years ago, everything accelerated, in an extraordinary burst of evolutionary inventiveness. That surge in novelty, when complicated life galloped into existence, is known as the Cambrian explosion.

We don't have much instinct for these sorts of numbers. Yes, half a billion years is a tremendous span, equivalent to ten million pre-industrial human lifetimes strung out one after the other, and for all our antiquity humans have only been here for a thousand generations. If an average lifespan today represents the history of life on the planet, a human would be a very strange monster indeed. For the first 68 years or so, you would remain a single celled embryo, patient and mindless in your mother's womb. Abruptly, in a single month, you would start developing in earnest. Clumsy speech and dexterity would be delayed until the closing days of your 80th year, and true intelligence would not blossom until the final few hours.

Self-preening, we stress that final burst into brilliant intellect, and disregard a tormenting question: why the extreme delay at the starting line? How is it that almost nothing happened for the first seven-eighths of life's history? What kept the brakes locked down on evolution, and what released them at long last, permitting an explosive flowering from just four basic kinds of very ancient inner and outer body design into 10 times as many, giving rise to everything we see and much that is already extinct, like the dinosaurs?

The Cambrian explosion took place between about 543 and 538 million years ago. Into those five million years were crammed all this rococo fabrication of complex life's ground rules. Why so fast, and why so long to get started? It would be neat and satisfying to resolve both questions with one answer. Parker, a Royal Society research fellow at Oxford University, deemed by the *Times* one of the three most important young scientists in the world, took an interesting shot at the task seven years ago. His popular account is readily accessible to non-scientists. Possibly too accessible, since he leaves out any pointers to other research, except for some names mentioned in passing, which makes it hard to follow up claims hotly contested by other experts. Still, his book is richly crowded with altogether fascinating details, the very stuff of polymathy: how our planet was frozen for hundreds of millions of years under kilometers of ice, stopping life in its tracks; why the working insides of animals vary more than their defensive shells; exactly what causes the shimmering opalescence and iridescence of a pearl or a beetle's wing.

For Parker, the key to the Cambrian event was the long delay before vision evolved. For vast stretches of time, creatures navigated and sought prey (or evaded the hungry) using touch, smell, taste, magnetic sensing: intimate and blurred. The world lay in fog. Then light-sensitive patches on the skin evolved with striking swiftness into true eyes, conscripting from other purposes the nerve wiring needed to turn images into a map of the world. Parker calls the epoch when sight came into useful focus the 'Light Switch'. Once its switch was thrown, you could see others across a crowded room (or pool, or paddock) and they could see you. Under that spur, that naked transparency, natural selection was ruthless and quick, testing and conserving a vast number of sighted creatures such as trilobites, Parker's favorite candidate for the first eyed animal. It seems he is wrong, though, since trilobites (as Cambridge zoologist Simon Conway Morris argues) appeared as the Cambrian explosion was subsiding, not igniting. Well, details, details. Parker's key idea is fresh and fertile and fun.

In the luminous shallows of Australia's Great Barrier Reef, he ran into a dark brown cloud of cuttlefish ink. As it cleared, he faced thirty of the animals, forming 'an exact arc around me, tentacles to face, eye to eye. Their brown bodies instantaneously bleached as I moved toward them... [then] displayed a wave of color changes. Brown and white synchronized undulations... suddenly a 'loud' red...a calming green as I retreated... their eyes remained silver, like mirrors' (4). This is deliciously vivid, exactly capturing how crucial the sense of sight has become since the first clear-lensed eye opened half a billion years ago.[14]

Even if eyes were the crucial breakthrough to explosive diversity, why did they take so long to arrive? My guess, reading toward the end of this detective story, was that air or water had perhaps long been murky, and cleared with a change in the environment. Either that, or the great slow orbit of the solar system into the dusty arms of the galaxy and out again might have modified the intensity of the Sun's light. Parker tries all these notions, and more, but fails to find a totally satisfying culprit. Still, his theory insists that there must be one, and so provokes a new and exciting scientific quest.

---

[14] In his efforts to be lucid as well as engaging, Parker does sometimes slip into unintended comedy. 'Chemical detectors,' he explains carefully, 'detect chemicals' (282).

> Now the true and lawful goal of the sciences is none other than this: that human life be endowed with new discoveries and powers.... But by far the greatest obstacle to the progress of science and to the undertaking of new tasks and provinces therein is found in this—that men despair and think things impossible. For wise and serious men are wont in these matters to be altogether distrustful, considering with themselves the obscurity of nature, the shortness of life, the deceitfulness of the senses, the weakness of the judgment, the difficulty of experiment, and the like; and so supposing that in the revolution of time and of the ages of the world the sciences have their ebbs and flows; that at one season they grow and flourish, at another wither and decay, yet in such sort that when they have reached a certain point and condition they can advance no further.
>
> Francis Bacon,
> *The New Organon,* LXXXI, XCII (1620)[15]

i

Bigots and racists lump people into pre-judged groups using some blindingly apparent but absurdly skin-deep discriminator: sex, or age, height, melanin tone, eye shape, hair type, verbal accent. However did this get started? We do seem to have a penchant for carving the world into kin (loosely and modifiably defined) against the rest. Some people we proudly gather inside the 'us' boundary. The others we lock out behind the 'them' boundary. All too often, these groups get confused with 'friend' versus 'foe', 'sexually unappealing' versus 'wickedly attractive', and many other opposed categories. As it happens, many people do look and act differently from us, and these days, in many parts of the planet, large numbers of them live just down the street. Racism is one of history's stupidest reactions to that fact. Will today's treasury of genetic discoveries help expunge such stupidities (the promise of the new Enlightenment)—or reinforce them? Genes hold intriguing clues to our past. The stories they tell can be confronting, especially to those who preen themselves as ethnically spotless and superior.

---

[15] From the translation from Bacon's Latin text, posted at http://www.constitution.org/bacon/nov_org.htm , which notes: 'This rendition is based on the standard translation of James Spedding, Robert Leslie Ellis, and Douglas Denon Heath in *The Works* (Vol. VIII), published in Boston by Taggard and Thompson in 1863.'

Bigotry, after all, quickly feels all too natural. Even those of us who pride ourselves on being 'color-blind' can slip into old habits. White against black is only the crudest of these arbitrary divisions, apparently sanctioned by common descent from sacred or secular heroes steeped in some blood-drenched landscape. Soccer teams make a fetish of it. Identifying ancestry-based groups of humans as 'races', then ranking them, is not just arbitrary, grounded in ancient wrongs and self-interest, but systematically misleading. Unpacking the genome means uncovering the immensely complex endowment of various alleles (that is, the gene variants underlying physical features—for eye color, say, or blood type).

Humanity's genes map out a vast, tangled history of virtually identical tributaries in the great river flowing out of Africa 100,000 years ago. All the world's human plenty funnels back to one common maternal ancestor 200,000 years ago, dubbed Mitochondrial Eve, and one common father 50,000 years later, whose Y genes form the basis of every male alive. Obviously these are not the Biblical first parents, just those individuals whose lineage has never once faltered along the road to us. The variant haplotypes, or slightly different versions of mitochondrial and Y chains, are a sort of chemical map of the peoples they have passed down through; we shall return to this topic shortly in greater detail.

Obviously we are not all identical, so the enterprise has its risks. An expert in Hawaii, with its remarkably mixed population, warns against using genetic markers to prove ethnicity: 'I don't believe that biology is destiny. Allowing yourself to be defined personally by whatever your DNA sequence is, that is insane. But that is exactly what some people are going to be tempted to do' (Olson, 2002: 236).

But are not some groups of humans—some 'races'—known from IQ tests to be smarter or dumber than others, even though nobody is allowed to mention this any more? The claim is fallible. The Buraku of Japan are 'a minority that is severely discriminated against in housing, education, and employment. Their children typically score 10 to 15 points below other Japanese children on IQ tests. Yet when the Buraku immigrate to other countries, the IQ gap between them and other Japanese gradually vanishes' (62). Conservative black American scholar Dr. Thomas Sowell observed recently that over five times as many black girls as boys score above 140 (highly gifted). Social not inherited factors are at work.

Chinese specialists still favor the idea that different peoples evolved separately from proto-human stocks spread about the globe. Molecular probes quash this possibility. Everyone on earth is African, although most of us have less genetic variability than those who, like the Bushmen, remained in the original continent. That is because some gene variants were lost during the migrations. But one charming discovery cited by Olson is that much of Southeast Asia was seeded from Australia and New Guinea, 20,000 or more years after their first ancestors arrived there (130). Arguably, the boat people refugees into Australia from Southeast Asia are just going home.

ii

How would we have lived in 20,000 BC? Life then was more than a little uncertain, made easier by some early technology: fire, woven fabrics, chipped stone tools, wooden weapons. Yet there were just a few tens of thousands of people on the whole planet. You did not get sick very often, because your clan was too small to support the raging epidemics that eventually would fell whole nations. In fact, those organisms probably had not infested humans yet. So you'd have lived reasonably well, thin and muscular, with good teeth (but eyesight fading with age), singing your history, dancing your skills and places, rejoicing in your children, the old dying in a sacred haze.

We humans evolved to thrive in that way of life, give or take the odd climatic cataclysm, the occasional megafauna torched or hunted to extinction. That is also what life was like in 19,000 BC, and 10,000 BC, and for many it had not changed much by 5000 BC. Yet now, with immense speed, we are about to rewrite the deep codings of evolution and ecology. As we prepare in earnest, it pays to know just what those rules are. Geneticist Steve Jones' revision of Charles Darwin's ground-breaking classic is a fine place to start (1999).

Here is the scary aspect of this story: almost everything we now know is news, and not just by the standards of 20,000 BC. Jones carefully retains the structure of Darwin's own elaborate evolutionary solution to species diversity: limited inherited variations in bodies and behavior, many more offspring born than can survive amid limited resources, resulting in 'natural selection' of individuals best suited to their circumstances, who pass down those same winning traits with further random modifications. But brilliant Darwin, writing in the mid-19th century, missed some key elements in the emerging explanation. He did not know about genetics, for a start. He made some clever but mistaken guesses. Luckily, his key insight remains valid, once mathematical and molecular genetics fill in the blank spots.

The most extraordinary thing is how shockingly new all this knowledge is. The peoples of 20,000 BC and 10,000 BC, whatever part of the world they lived in, shared essentially the same reality. Yet I can vividly remember the stunned elation I felt, mere decades ago, when a friend showed me an article in the glossy US magazine *Life Illustrated* with simplified diagrams of the DNA molecule, its helix curling open as its code was explored for the first time. DNA's secret mechanism had been unlocked to specialists just nine years earlier. Half a century after James Watson and Francis Crick broke the code, the first sequencing of a complete human genome was achieved years ahead of schedule. Free on

49

the World Wide Web, it is available to anyone with a cheap computer and a phone line.

Jones is a mordant foe of Richard Dawkins-style 'ultra-Darwinism', which puts the selfish gene at the heart of evolution and seeks Darwinian explanations for mind and culture. Jones likes to offend fashion: 'Karl Marx got it (as usual) more or less right' (166). Even so, he is uncompromising about evolution's pain. To Darwin, he notes, 'evolution had no commonwealth: self-interest is what matters. He was right. There is no charity in nature' (160). These views are not inconsistent. They oblige us to act as humans, with foresight and conscience, not just as gene composites thrashing wildly for reproductive superiority.

Just as well, perhaps. Hermaphrodite slugs, say, have a tough time, since neither wants to be lumbered with the children, leading to each courting partner 'trying to bite off the other's penis' (86). There is kinkiness rampant in Darwin's garden. Sexual opportunists among male bluegill sunfish 'begin to resemble females, until they can saunter unafraid on to a territory, the sole risk one of courtship by its besotted holder. When a real female appears a transvestite's deception pays off. He fertilizes her eggs and makes a hurried exit' (91-2).

The sensitive, cross-dressing fish has an eerily contemporary ring to it.

With the new genomics we might find it easy literally to change sex. If so, being a human really will be extravagantly different in the 21st century, as we finally leap free of Darwin's fishing net.

iii

A century ago, in the middle of his life, the great Irish poet William Butler Yeats ached with love of poetry and women both. In a poem called 'Adam's Curse', he wrote of a beautiful mild woman who told him:

> 'To be born woman is to know...
> That we must labor to be beautiful.'
> I said, 'It's certain there is no fine thing
> Since Adam's fall but needs much laboring...'

That is the classic Biblical curse upon the human race: that man must earn bread by the sweat of his brow. But there is more sweat and effort in graceful, simple verse, Yeats insisted, than in scrubbing a kitchen pavement or breaking stones. He was trying to impress the lady, but it is true that work's a curse. Neither poetry nor scrubbing, though, is what genetics professor Bryan Sykes has in mind in naming his study of the Y chromosome *Adam's curse* (2003). Men are literally doomed to extinction, he claims. Give the human species another 150,000 years and we will be gone—those of our kind, at least, who bear in each cell the tiny, shriveled remnant of a chromosome, the Y, that turns a fertilized egg into a boy instead of its default condition as a girl. Females might persist via cloning or genetic engineering, so the species could continue even after the last male has died off, taking his garbled genome with him..

Sykes made his mark with a popular book on the genetics of human lineage, *The Seven Daughters of Eve* (2001). Using new methods for probing the gene code, he concluded that all Europeans were descended in an unbroken line from just seven ancient clan mothers. The earliest was perhaps 45,000 years ago, the most recent from 10,000. The heart of the new understanding was first revealed in the double adventure of mitochondria, those ancient assimilated bacteria which Margulis told us are handed down the maternal line, and Y-chromosomes, carrying the male sex genes. Mapping the four-unit sequences of DNA bases along these genetic threads, scientists find the places where mutation or random change added variety to the basic coded message. Sexual reproduction mixes and re-sorts our gene variants, and over time new mutations enter each lineage. In isolated regions, the variants narrow and persist, while in the melting pots they spread and multiply. Tracking these markers lets us estimate how long a particular group has been away from the African homeland, and more intriguingly which geographical routes its ancestors took to get where they are today.

Sykes's first study, then, looked at those tiny bacterial hitchhikers inside our cells that provide our energy and are handed down only through the female line. Might there be an equivalent tool for studying male lineage? Obviously, yes: the Y gene package, matched with one X chromosome from mother, is what makes a boy male. A pair of X's, one from each parent, is the recipe for a girl. Recent genomic methods allowed Sykes to look for the equivalent Sons of Adam. He did not mean this quest literally, since evolutionary theory holds no role for a single pair of original parents. But it is clear that paternal lineages can die out if every sub-branch of the family produces no sons. So we cannot track back to *all* the men who were alive 100,000 years ago—only to those few whose offspring sustained at least one son in each generation. Unlike the neat clumps of mitochondrial DNA that pinpointed the clan mothers, though, there were no plain ancestral signatures to be found. Male DNA tracked odd filiations and contortions through time. What is more, Sykes began to suspect something very strange, never noticed before by science: some families have an uncanny excess of boys, others of girls, generation after generation.

Genetic theory had already raised suspicions that sperm and egg are in some ways deadly rivals. Can't live with 'em, can't live without 'em. More exactly, while spermatozoon and ova go together like a horse and carriage, the Y chromosome (which specifies boys) and the mitochondrial genes (which need girls for their transmission) will be skewed by

natural selection to maximize their own kind. Even if that means nob-
bling the opposition. This unpleasant gene-scale version of the Sex War
does appear to be real.

Whether it accounts for an increase in gay tendencies in later-born boy
babies, as Sykes suggests, seems less likely, if not farcical. But that is not
why the Y might be doomed, if Sykes is right. His case was intriguing:
male cells appeared to have no way to repair their handful of sex genes
when they get corrupted by mutation, because they have no backup near-
twin copy (as the 22 non-sex chromosomes do). A female has those two
X chromosomes, each with a slightly different version of the human
female-building genome. A male has one X from mother, and the Y from
dad, so there's no spare copy of the code for the Y-carried sex genes if
they get mutilated or lost. The result is plain, even under a microscope:
today's Y is shrunken, a mere stump of the gene package on the X. Sykes
argues strenuously that without an archival copy for repair purposes, the
Y is doomed to unremitting degradation, and finally must perish 6000
generations hence.

It made an entertaining story, replete with a great deal of genealogi-
cal exploration and colorful landscape portraits as Sykes trawls Britain
for evidence. Alas, just as his book was about to appear, new findings
scuppered his central argument. He tried (manfully, one might say) to
salvage what he could in a last minute two-page postscript, but it looks
as if Adam's curse has been lifted. It turned out, remarkably, that the
shoddy, denuded Y has a trick up its sleeve. In various places along its
diminished length, it contains reversed versions of the key code. These
mirror images allow it to check the sex-building template for fidelity,
and to repair mutations. So Adam is safe, at least for a while.

Sykes downplayed the true threat to Adam's children, and Eve's. The
onrush of the very technology that allowed him to explore the genome's
nooks and crannies will soon allow science to remake our genetic constitution. Humans will gain the power to edit, repair, augment and redesign
our very recipe. Will we like the result? Many won't, but some surely
will. The children of those brave or reckless souls who do might well be
around in 150,000 years time to see who gets the last laugh. More likely,
as we shall see, humanity will have long-since been replaced by a swarming diversity of posthumanities.

Languages and cultures, like genes, mark out groups and peoples,
although they change faster than genes, and can be adopted without
marrying into new families. Still, historically, the two went hand in
hand. A celebrated geneticist, Luca Cavalli-Sforza, has traced genes and
tongues alike, mapping a controversial history of dispersion. His views
are becoming accepted as ever more nuanced genomic studies draw out
the ancient blends of migration, marriage (and rape), spoken and written
languages.

The details are dauntingly complex. In a poetic flourish, Steve Olson cites Hermann Hesse's Siddhartha: 'Each one was mortal, a passionate, playful example of all that is transitory... continually had a new face; only time stood between one face and another' (238). Olson foresees a future in which panmixia—the blending of all today's peoples—will reverse the dispersion of our genes. That is surely too tame a prediction. The same genetic technology that revealed Mitochondrial Eve will allow us to blossom forth in such a profusion of chosen variety that racism will be laughed to scorn and then forgotten. The mother of that new epoch might be, perhaps, Mitochondrial Dawn.

iv

'As far as science can tell us at present, our kind is all alone in this vast universe, and when we look to the long journey of evolutionary time there is nobody at the controls.' (Bolton, 251).[16] Once you accept the perspective of tested and accumulated wisdom built up during the past 150 years, that conclusion is not at all shocking, although for a lot of people the news still has not sunk in. Is that because new memes must fight their way through the thorns of prior memetic doctrines? Only one in 10 polled Americans believed in Darwinian evolution while, by contrast, only 7 per cent of senior scientists expressed belief in a personal God.[17] Australians are quicker off the mark, but their grasp is still tentative. A recent poll in France, nominally a Christian nation, does show some trends toward the opinions of the new Enlightenment.[18] In 1994, some 60 percent felt that astrology explained character; by 2003, that was reduced by more than a third, to 37 percent. The proportion of self-described rationalists rose from 22 percent to 52 percent. Among the young, the leap was from 22 percent to 67 percent. Belief in occult practices was halved from 41 percent, although that still left a fifth of the nation persuaded of the value of enchantments.

The press are not blameless in spreading confusion. Each day's news announces another genetic link to dire diseases, often presented as if each gene were coded for a single characteristic: *a* gene for criminality, or

---

[16] The delicious cover art (by Katharine Vanderwal) for Melvin Bolton's *The Road to Now* catches the eye and makes you reach for it, something every good meme should aspire to. In a droll parody of those classic museum tableaus showing early man emerging from the slime, a bent, ape-like beast evolves, rises, strides powerfully naked across the book's spine, then slowly sinks back under the burden of tools, until modern man crouches compliantly before a computer. It is funny, it speaks to our discontents.

[17] Public belief: http://blogs.salon.com/0001561/2002/12/13.html ; scientists' belief: *Nature*, Vol. 394, No. 6691, p. 313, cited http://www.stephenjaygould.org/ctrl/news/file002.html

[18] In a commentary published in *Le Monde* <http://www.lemonde.fr/article/0,5987,3232—317031-VT,00.html>

intelligence. This is ridiculously oversimplified. Genes work in suites, coding for a range of effects. When you plant seeds in hot, sandy scrub, the leaf, stem and flower you grow are different from what springs up in rich loam. Humans grow differently as culture changes, as we change it in turn, ranging from the basics of primitive life through the long epochs when people were, in a sense, wildlife, and on to the tumultuous cascade of urban humanity. The sheer speed of cultural change is dizzying. Our fairly recent ancestors were often ecological ravagers: 'In a pattern repeated in many parts of the world, fertile places near water were settled, fortified, fought over, farmed to exhaustion and abandoned' (Bolton, 131).

Some fear that we are on the verge of doing precisely that to the whole planet, with nowhere else to go, ruled by brittle computer rationality. Hope remains, though. In this long perspective, nothing remains unchanged, especially humankind. We respond brilliantly to challenge, or our memes do. The computer need not be our master: it is an emblem of advanced, cheap technologies that will carry us along the road to now and into a future where, with luck and effort, we can set right the errors of ignorance and start acting like mature humans rather than like grumbling or overawed slaves.

Environmentalist Bill McKibben, in *Enough: Staying Human in an Engineered Age* (2003), has advanced a nightmare prospect of genetic engineering that will tear the human species from our ancient roots and turn us into something terrible, robotic, without meaning. Such medical options, he has urged, ought to be made illegal (in more general terms that cover any germline enhancements): 'People shouldn't be allowed to choose things this deep for their children (and for every generation thereafter),' (192)

The slip of logic is customary in such Jeremiads, but no less bizarre for that. Watch McKibben's hands carefully: If we gain the power to make *any changes we wish* in the DNA of our offspring, this should be forbidden. Why so? Because these changes will thereafter be *permanently embedded* in the species. Note how the argument starts by assuming what it then denies: that science will provide us with the power to alter, enhance, add, or delete genes. The boogeyman of 'permanent embeddedness' is precisely a relic of previous, more restricted technologies.

McKibben goes on to draw out dire recommendations from his misunderstanding. Making such germinal-choice changes illegal, he admits,

> will involve limiting freedom, just as forbidding people to drive their cars the wrong way down one-way street limits freedom. The liberty of one generation, ours, would be in some small way constrained... in order to protect the far more basic liberties of those yet to come.

To demand this right is to make a mockery of liberty.
It's to choose, forever, against choice. (192)

What we are headed toward, McKibben asserts (in his wooly confusion), is a regime of 'programmed' lives, known totally in advance, which will be 'ineradicable' (because by then, even if the prowess remains, our will shall have been sapped; we will be contented Stepford Hive drones). Absurdly, given where he is avowedly coming from, he writes as a simple-minded genetic determinist. Once those devilish genes are locked in place, we will be obliged to march forever to their drumming, without passion or challenge or the poignancy of death and its rewarding, decent return to the embrace of Nature.

In reality, the danger is not primarily from gene technology. Genes, and the proteins they code for, do significantly ordain our bent, and some of our limitations and abilities, but they do not *program* us. The true danger arises from the conceptual mischief liable to be spread by pseudo-arguments like McKibben's. A more measured response to these risks and opportunities will serve us far better. Where broken genes are found, we should be permitted to correct their corrupted code if that is technically feasible and safe. Where extra genes might add immense benefits, we should permit their introduction into people who so chose, and arguably into their children. After all, we already allow parents to make consequential decisions on behalf of their offspring. In particular, we not merely *allow* but *insist upon* the right of parents to prepare and shape their children's minds through choice of companions, education, faith or avoidance of it: not through added genes, but in their exposure to *memes*. What is at stake is, indeed, freedom.

Or is that, too, just a fantasy, a mirage casts by the competing beliefs raging almost invisibly in our communities and our heads? Let us turn to that question.

Freedom and Folly

> ...it was European germs that brought Western Hemisphere populations to the brink of extinction, since those people had had no history in which to develop tolerance for them. In the next century it will be our memes, both tonic and toxic, that will wreak havoc on the unprepared world. *Our* capacity to tolerate the toxic excesses of freedom cannot be assumed in others, or simply exported as one more commodity.
>
> Daniel Dennett, *Freedom Evolves* (2003: 304)

i

People hold—and embody—extremely diverse ideas and beliefs; why is that? It cannot be explained by genes alone. Only a fool would claim that it can, and such fools are very hard to find, despite the denunciations of those opposed to any account that finds continuities between humans and the rest of the animals. Still, perhaps culture and genes have some key features in common; this is, in short, the meme postulate.

Both genes and cultural features are replicators, persisting through time only if they are so structured that they get themselves copied faithfully and eagerly. Yet the means of replication of these two species can be grossly at odds. Religions, for example, are perfectly capable of thriving by attracting able men and women into lives of dedicated celibacy, hardly the optimal methods for spreading the genetic features supporting belief. And of course some people prefer their own sex, reproducing only if pressured by society. If genes ruled the roost, how could any of this happen? How can lifestyles biased against reproduction persist in a world shaped by reproductive pressures?

Another notorious puzzle: people are generous, even to the point of self-sacrifice. We support others who do not share our familial genes or language or faith. What kind of inept replicators are we dealing with here? Psychologist Susan Blackmore (1999) has amplified zoologist Richard Dawkins's famous idea of the selfish gene. She develops a startling answer suggested by Dawkins himself. The world of humans is built from the jostling of two distinct kinds of replicators. Genes are one sort, providing the recipe for our brainy bodies. What she dubs the 'second replicators' infest and sculpt those brains, forming the cultures that make us truly human and not just smart pack animals.

In 1976, we recall, Dawkins named these replicators *memes*. They are any fragments of behavior that can be imitated with some fidelity. A science of 'memetics' has slowly emerged. Suppose Britney Spears or Leo DiCaprio shows up with purple ears. Millions of fashion slaves catch this meme and dye their ears. The craze lasts for a week or several generations (as blue jeans have done). In this way, a meme can travel sideways through a culture. A second way for memes to travel is down the family line, more or less as genes do. Parents teach their kids to pray or drive a car. In such cases it can be hard to untangle genetic from memetic influences. The really high-impact news, if Blackmore is correct, is that we are not just *influenced* by memes—our minds and selves are literally *built out of them*.

Think of an ant nest, which acts in ways that the mindless ant sub-units never could. Our brains are made of cells evolved from swarms of bacteria living together. Those cells are still as stupid as germs. Individual memes are also mindless, just fragments of human activity that can be observed and copied, remembered, spread to others. Words and phrases are an obvious example, recipes and computer programs are another. Sciences are packs of memes, as are religions.

You, too, might actually be an organized parliament of memes, condensed into a working unit. Blackmore calls these bunches of copied ideas 'memeplexes', a term that is itself a new meme in the making. A person would be a 'self-plex'. This resembles Buddhist teaching that the self is an illusion, a kind of story. It is also a claim quite similar to accounts offered these days by both brain sciences and the humanities, despite their traditional hostility.

Blackmore's approach helps explain why popular magazines print *feng shui* advice on how to attract 'good luck energies' into the house by arranging your mirrors and running water properly. Such preposterous mind-viruses are contagious. Our brains evolved to harbor and spread memes, whether or not they are true. Memetics claims to explain how the human brain evolved spectacularly fast, driven by memes, and why we like chattering so much: Memes 'R' Us.

The meme proposal has mostly met resistance from experts in fields it has tried to invade, like a virus faced down by a robust immune system. Blackmore's model—a genuinely provocative idea, even if it is rather too simple to be true—has already benefited from development and criticism, for example in Aunger (2000), a panel of expert anthropologists, psychologists and evolutionary biologists who tend to be skeptical if not scathing. 'Science on the frontier often has an anarchic, nervy flavor,' observe cultural evolutionists Robert Boyd and Peter Richerson, 'because it must deal with multiple uncertainties' (159). In fact, they remain uncertain that the object of their study even exists. Still, Dawkins and Blackmore have infected a lot of people with the meme meme.

ii

Even if memes are what comprise our minds as well as what fills them, they are not omnipotent—or, at any rate, some memes are able to oust others. We can face down silly ideas with either ridicule or careful analysis. For nearly half a century, one of the most likable warriors against zany self-delusion has been science journalist Martin Gardner. His 1957 classic *Fads and Fallacies in the Name of Science* remains in print, wonderfully unmasking the comic antics of pseudo-scientists, biblical literalists and devotees of newly minted cults. His subsequent books followed the same trail, examining such topics as 'reflexology, numerology, urine therapy, and other dubious subjects'. Urine therapy is drinking your own piss for its alleged life-enhancing properties, a suitable metaphor for most of these crackpot doctrines.

Gardner is astute, droll, tireless in tracking down fresh idiocies (renewed claims for deliberate design in biology, psychic UFO myths, much more) and exploring old oddities such as Thomas Edison's plans for a machine to record messages from the dead, the legend of the Wandering Jew, and a fundamentalist chestnut: did God create the first humans with navels? That would have been a lie, in effect, since navels imply earlier existence inside the womb. Or lacking them, leaving Adam and Eve 'imperfect'?

Physics professor Robert Park is Gardner's heir apparent, pursuing a similar ambit claim: 'The road from foolishness to fraud' (Park, 2000). The public information face of the American Physical Society, Park sees a thin barrier between foolishness and fraud. 'Because it is not always easy to tell when that line is crossed, I use the term voodoo science to cover them all: pathological science, junk science, pseudo-science, and fraudulent science' (10). Voodoo is a useful analogy, being false science, although it is impolite to say so. Even when voodoo witchcraft works, by placebo psychology, its magical explanations are simply untrue. Most of Park's voodoo science, however, does not work at all. Yet people fling away money to buy inane cures (homoeopathy, iridology), fanciful doctrines (quantum healing, UFO abduction), or bogus engineering that offers free magic energy. Critiques like Park's could help consumers of fringe ideas pick a little more carefully among the broken glass and slippery snake oil, but most would refuse to read his pungent analyses, dismissing him as a spoilsport scientist peddling nothing better than his own contrary opinions. (A typical ecumenical pronouncement, from the 'World Forum Statement on Life and Evolution' signed by Fritjof Capra, Ervin Lazlo and others, declares absurdly: 'We recognize the validity of the different ways of knowing that have been developed in different cultures *and the equivalent value of the knowledge* gained within these traditions' [my italics].)[19] A recent survey found that those who rely most strongly on faith rather than science have the most negative perceptions of genetic engineering. It was a better clue than age, educational level,

---

[19] In Heinberg, 1999: 234.

gender, even level of scientific knowledge (the second strongest indicator).

Is the widespread belief in a human-induced greenhouse effect science or faith? Although the Bible does not comment on the allegedly sickening effects of power lines and silicone implants, many embrace apocalyptic dread as a substitute faith system. Strong scientific refutations of those last two alarming claims exist, demonstrating that there is no good reason for fearing either power lines or breast implants. But neither are the scientific and engineering lobbies immune to snake-oil. The International Space Station, a favorite icon of many scientists, is a preposterously expensive boondoggle of little scientific value. Critics such as Gardner and Park do not just mock foolish beliefs; they pull such claims apart and show why they are wrong. Increasingly, though, the new faiths are pseudo-scientific rather than religious, or a weird blend of the two. Maybe informed laughter will embarrass the gullible—but it will not be surprising if silliness ends up winning. That is one risk of a society that prizes freedom.

iii

Four typical samples of life in the 21st century:

In Geneva, researchers announced that they might finally have seen a Higgs particle, the fundamental particle of mass sought for 30 years, capstone of physics' quest for deep explanation. In Oklahoma, a 15-year-old took legal action against the assistant principal who suspended her from school for witchcraft after she cast a spell, allegedly causing her teacher to get sick. The International Space Station has a reduced crew, and risks closure following the destruction during re-entry of the shuttle orbiter *Columbia*. And, as we saw earlier, a craze for *feng shui* prompts opinion leaders and businesses to redesign buildings at huge expense, thus warding off evil spirits and maximizing flows of luck and good magic.

Ironic, yes, but that is the postmodern world. Is this blend of superstition and the raw power of knowledge hilarious or scary, even dangerous? People do believe the craziest things, and not just *believe* loony ideas—cling to them in the face of overwhelming evidence. Fight and die for them, send our kids to die in our stead, unto the seventh generation. It is not always so lethal. Someone in Port Germein, South Australia, noticed that when a street light shone through a certain itchy powder tree, it cast an image of Jesus Christ, complete with crown of thorns, on the wall of a nearby caravan park. A miracle! People flocked to marvel and pray in the street. Cognitive scientists quietly pointed out that human brains are replete with specialized feature detectors. These useful nerve cells scan the world for other humans, clamoring for attention when they find anything that looks a bit like a familiar face.

Blotches of shadow, in other words, trick people's brains into seeing something that literally is not there. But, like Mulder in *The X-Files*, the devout wanted to believe.

Sometimes, irrational notions can be wildly dangerous. Jasmuheen (formerly known as Ellen Greve) is a Queensland guru who teaches that people can live without food. According to her alleged revelation, we can gain all the nourishment we require from the air, plus a little faith. One hapless 'breatharian' died after following this really very stupid plan. But she *had faith*, didn't she? At least she was *following her heart.* You have to wonder what is going on in people's heads. Or is it in their hearts? We are often urged to fear those who place too much trust in reason. Go with your feelings, we are told, go with faith. Reason, allegedly, is far too limited. Or maybe rationality is a plot by the brainy to crush the rest. Cold, heartless rationality might show us how to build a machine, but it cannot tell us how to live our lives. That is the role of faith. Stephen Jay Gould, as we saw, supported this view, declaring that faith and reason have dominion over two quite distinct and exclusive domains or 'magisteria'.

Still, if you were trapped inside a temple next to a ticking bomb, who would you rather have trying to defuse it: a well-trained rational bomb disposal expert or the local holy man with a direct line to divine intervention? By the way, who is more likely to have planted the bomb, a member of the Rationalist Society or one of your faith's doctrinal rivals?

iv

My municipal council recently banned genetically modified food. Reporting this, the local suburban newspaper opened with a mention of *Soylent Green*, the movie about an over-populated future dependent on synthetic food. Soylent Green, revoltingly, turns out to be people. 'No one,' the article went on blithely, 'is suggesting that the newly emerging genetically modified food industry is grinding up human corpses, but... there are still too many unknowns about the effects of biotechnology to be silent on the issue.'

No one is suggesting, says the reporter disingenuously, having done exactly that. It was a disgraceful leap, reminiscent of racist claims that some ethnic group or other eats the babies of their persecutors. Such is the odium that science can attract. Granted, it is prudent to pause before introducing proprietary crops gene-engineered for high resistance to pesticides. Widespread adoption could leave us eating food with more pesticide residues, and make farmers dependent on modified seed, a kind of agribiz monopoly. But to cite *Soylent Green* in that context is reckless escalation of the rhetorical stakes, instant overkill. It is what the writer Greg Egan has brilliantly dubbed 'Frankenscience'—demonization of science and technology out of fright, ignorance, malice or political opportunism.

That is not to say science is above reproach, off-limits to criticism. On the contrary, its palpable power and ubiquity demand that we keep the strictest eye on scientific research and its (often state-funded) practitioners. Instead, what we see is a slide from sensible caution to jokey but grotesque anxieties, borrowed literally without a moment's thought from the lucrative nightmares of Hollywood hacks.

Irrational behavior is not restricted to a few odd-balls. We all do it much of the time, but we use nicer words for it. We call it 'faith' or 'patriotism' or 'the right thing.' Or quite often: 'Shut up and do what I say, God love ya, or I'll give you such a thump.' The funny thing is that after you have been thumped a lot, you tend to come around. You find yourself clinging to those ridiculous claims you have been thumped for questioning. Maybe even embracing them with all your heart, dying for them. 'The heart has reasons,' as Blaise Pascal famously asserted, 'that reason knows not of.' But such debates start from phony contrasts. Reason is not some weird mental disorder used by cold-blooded creeps because they lack a heart. You could not get across a busy street unscathed if you did not use elementary reasoning ('Look right, look left...'). We all have emotions and values, feelings of love, fear, curiosity and revulsion, that provide the motor for our choices. Are those feelings irrational? Wrong question. They are appropriate or not, useful or a hindrance. As neuroscientist Antonio Damasio argues, feelings are not only important to the quality of life but crucial to the human exercise of reason. Feelings, he notes, are 'a window that opens directly onto a continuous updated image of the structure and state of our body' (1994: xiv).

René Descartes took the wrong path back in the 17th century by supposing that humans are cobbled together from a mechanical android body and a mysteriously invisible, untouchable soul, an immaterial essence designed to survive the corruption of the flesh. It seemed obvious that pure minds could not get angry or sexually excited or sentimental, so the body's feelings—metaphorically 'the heart,' since we so easily feel our emotions changing gear as our pulse slows or accelerates—had to be downgraded. A rebound was inevitable, when Romanticism played up 'authentic' blinding passion at the expense of reasoning.

Now we know better. *The organism,*' declares Damasio, playing on Pascal's phrase, *'has some reasons that reason must utilize'* (200; his italics). Thoughts or ideas are 'qualified' by feelings, which remind us how the world has affected us in the past. Feelings, then, are short-cuts to value: powerful devices that help us move swiftly through the waffle of unchecked logic.

The astonishing thing about today's brain science is that you can see this happen by viewing a magnetic resonance display. Reasoning or calculation is visibly done in the front parts of the brain, while emotional tone and urgency are added by structures deep inside, such as the amygdala. Victims of pre-frontal leucotomy, whose links between the reasoning frontal lobes and the emotional amygdala are cut, lapse into a feckless inability to plan or decide. They can know but not feel. And so their knowledge is short-changed, their reasoning not merely 'cold' but unhinged from reality. People with damage to the amygdala can lose the capacity to 'make sound social judgments, based on previous experience.. [testifying] to the paramount importance of emotion in the governance not just of simple creatures but of humans as well' (Damasio, 1999: 67).

This discovery gets us some of the way out of the faith vs. reason mess, but we might still wonder why people believe such crazy things so readily. Of course, we flatter ourselves that our deepest beliefs are unquestionably true and make perfect sense. But obviously many other people hold firm to notions inconsistent with ours. And there is no shaking them. Bizarre, really. How could people take such crackpot ideas seriously? Richard Dawkins has a persuasive explanation. It does not matter if a meme is true or not, what counts is how many minds it can infest, how fast it can spread. Of course, if a meme happens to be true as well as attractive, its chances improve, since people sharing that meme will act in ways that reflect reality, and prosper. But plenty of our ideas and practices have no direct impact on brute survival. Fashions come and go, and so too, on a longer historical scale, do faiths. The vulnerable mechanism in our brains which memes lock into, according to Dawkins' clever insight, is language itself.

We are born drastically incomplete. Many other mammals pop out from their mothers' wombs ready to shake themselves off after a quick lick and scamper away with the herd. Humans take years to walk and communicate. Our inherited instincts allow us to learn to be social creatures. Many animals have brains pre-wired with instructions on how to be the sort of critter they are. Ours are more subtle: we are 'hard-wired' to learn language very fast, without question, from the babble we hear around us. Instead of being born knowing Cro-Magnon or Mandarin, as bees are born knowing Bee-dance Language, all we have is a very general pre-set grammar and a colossal thirst for new words.

Does this give you a tingle of shocked recognition? Children learn the darnedest things very, very quickly, because their minds are ravenous for the pre-shaped knowledge being used out there in society. We have been built by evolutionary processes to gulp down the patterns we see and hear and explore. You just would not get very far as an infant if you stopped every time you heard a new word and asked, 'Is *cow* really an appropriate word for that big friendly creature over there? How about *gooble* instead? Yes, I believe I'll refer to Flossy as a *gooble*.' It is fun, certainly, but nobody except a patient mother would understand a word you said. Our language acquisition device has to be gullible, in the first instance, not madly creative. It has to accept the input that comes at it without question, without stopping to ask if the customary connections between these items make sense.

As we grow older, of course, we pick up extra tricks for learning about the world. For a start, we have to deal with change, so we need to weed out errors. Over many tens of thousands of years, human cultures have painfully refined these extra tricks into subtle skills. Practical reasoning is one set. In 2000, the Australian Minister for Aboriginal Affairs, Philip Ruddock, pointed out to *Le Monde* and the *Washington Post* that aboriginal cultures never invented the wheel[20]—but what is much more interesting is that aboriginal people are intensely practical and exploratory, and can fix a car engine with insightful ingenuity even though the car was unknown to their ancient culture. (It is new to ours, too, of course.) Abstract reasoning grows out of such practical proficiency, unfolding into arcane doctrines of logic, formal syllogistic thinking, mathematics. These are difficult tricks for primate minds like ours, and take years of hard work to acquire. Even then, they are not easy to apply consistently. Einstein made some incredible blunders even in his specialized reasoning about relativity and quantum theory.

Humans, in short, are wonderfully adapted for gullibility, because for hundreds of thousands of years we did better if we accepted the wisdom of the tribe. That was survival wisdom, at its root, but it quickly became tangled up in elaborate and sometimes foolish embellishments. Any creature adept at swift learning is prey to superstition. Pigeons in psychology labs get fed when they press buttons with their beaks. Since by chance they are usually also doing something else at the time (one wing cocked, left foot scratching belly), that activity gets rewarded, and thus learned, as well. Thereafter, the gullible fowl will prance and cavort to get fed. The reward for hitting the button convinces the poor creature that all that wing-cocking and belly-scratching is doing the job. Here comes the grain into the bowl, as I just knew it would; the gods have been successfully propitiated again!

Reason tells us the pigeons are mistaken. It can also help us tease apart our own most fervently held pieties. Reason helps us discriminate between our deepest, overpowering feelings for our parents and other loved ones, of reverence for bravery, honor, service and courageous creativity, and our equally deep temptation to act like idiots when summoned by trumpets and pyramid schemes, or driven by despair and pain into the endless, useless search for miracles and absurd redemption. That is one of the persistent, valuable lessons of the Enlightenment.

---

[20] *Washington Post,* July 4, 2000

How much can reason and careful observation tell us about emotion? For a long time I was annoyed when people claimed that someone 'smiled with her eyes'. This phrase is usually embellished with comments about dancing glances and sparkling light. I mistakenly supposed that this was a sugary figure of speech that carelessly attributed to the eyeballs all sorts of other indicator lights of pleasure and happiness—lilting laugh, smiling lips, jaunty stride. It turns out that it really does mean just what it says, although this might not be obvious unless you're a careful people-watcher like psychology professor Paul Ekman (2003).

The orbital muscles of authentically smiling people scrunch down their top eyelids. Two sets of muscles ring the eyes. The inner squinty ones are under voluntary command, but the outer ones are almost always completely autonomic, beyond our control (well, for 90 percent of us). An absence of genuine reaction in these nifty signaling muscles is what gives the polite, liars, and con men that fake dead look to their smile (206). Ekman dubs it a 'Duchenne smile', for the French neurologist who discovered this fact over a century ago while systematically sending electric shocks into all the facial muscles of a poor fellow who could not feel pain in his face (204-5). When Duchenne de Boulogne activated the zygomatic major muscle, running from the cheekbones to the corners of the lips, the corners of his victim's mouth lifted in a fake smile, but his eyes stayed revealingly impassive—until he was told a joke. Then the outer muscles crinkled up. Looking at the ancient laughing photo, you feel like smiling yourself in happy sympathy.

So when people talk about smiling eyes, they really mean something like 'Her beautiful outer orbicularis oculi eye socket muscles were laughingly contracted.' You can see why this more exact formulation was never a runaway success in popular songs and bodice-buster novels.

What is especially challenging and remarkable about Ekman's work—he has been listed among the 100 most influential psychologists of the last century—is its transcultural character. Not satisfied with studying his own Californian milieu, Ekman set out 40 years ago to learn if emotions and their typical signals are socially learned or built in as part of a universal human nature. When he started, the dominant view was powerfully biased to cultural explanations. As he studied and filmed the Fore people of New Guinea's South East Highlands, he was startled to find that these isolated people immediately understood the moods and emotions of whites portrayed in standard photos, and showed them recognizably in their own faces (6-8).

This is tricky territory, fraught with the hazards of self-deception. Might the investigator be cuing a desired response? Ekman used a clever method. Stories were told to his informants, each centered on some strong, clear emotional event, and they were asked to choose which picture best exemplified the tale. Studying 300 people this way—three percent of the whole tiny culture—Ekman established clear-cut identifications for happiness, anger, disgust and sadness. Oddly, the Fore couldn't tell fear and surprise apart, although these emotions look quite distinct in literate societies (10). Luckily, his book is crammed with photos, mostly of his delightful daughter Eve but many of people from New Guinea and elsewhere, illustrating the most subtle nuances of facial expressions and their associated emotions.

This sort of result was shocking in the 1960s, and remains so to many people who hope that human nature is indefinitely malleable under cultural influences and choices. What is more, it is apparent to anyone who has ever traveled that different cultures do, indeed, express emotions differently. Here is Ekman's useful explanation: the management of emotional expression is under the control of local and highly variable 'display rules' (4). We might mask or exaggerate how we feel. But research supports a basic universality of the emotions underlying these variable displays. Filmed alone watching horrifying accidents or surgery, Americans and Japanese show shock and revulsion, confirmed by brain scans and other physiological monitors. In public, the same Japanese cover their horror with a polite smile.

Ekman goes beyond simply listing what makes up each emotion and how we can detect them in someone's face. Drawing on a finding known since the days of pioneer psychologist William James, he walks us through exercises in mimicking the precise postures of sadness, agony, anger, surprise, disgust. Surprisingly, perhaps, 'putting on a happy face', or an angry expression, or one of disgust, actually triggers the experience of that emotion. Our minds read our bodies.

Can we control vivid and dangerous emotions such as anger? Ekman draws special attention to the 'refractory period' that follows a surge of emotion, when memory and thinking enter a sort of tunnel vision. You lose mental access to information that might mitigate your rage. Your thinking, during that window of focused attention, can only draw upon and (mis)use memories that sustain and justify the emotion (39-40).

The fact that emotions are genetically pre-wired does not mean we cannot learn to modify what Ekman calls 'hot triggers' (32-4), and to develop a sort of emotional attentiveness (75). But without the sort of close, sensitive scientific observation his book exemplifies, we might be doomed to cycle through inherited templates suited to an ancient hunter-gatherer world but not especially fitted to a technological society where a handful of humans can destroy a skyscraper, a city, and perhaps, soon, the planet itself.

Gender Confusions

> Dark-haired Ilizane is angular of frame, tall and straight-backed, square-jawed and broadshouldered. Karate is her favourite sport. She has little time for make-up or fashion. Xenia, fair and blue-eyed, is, Ilizane concedes, much more 'girlie'. She loves Barbie dolls and wants beads, bangles and fairytales....What they do share, however, is a condition called CAIS (Complete Androgen Insensitivity Syndrome). It means they are hermaphrodites, possessing both male and female genitalia. Although they have vaginas, they have testes where their ovaries should be, and no uterus. Neither has a penis. Outwardly they look like girls: in truth they are half and half...'What is interesting,' says [foster father] Neil, 'is that theoretically it may one day be possible for Ilizane to father a child'—another reason, he says, why she should think long and hard about surgery to remove her testes,

> Olga Craig, 2004[21]

i

Is it a boy or a girl? That is the first question asked when the baby is born (or after the first echo scans). Thirty years ago, enraged thugs screamed it at any long-haired youth. A couple of decades later, they howled it at shaven-headed girls instead. Today, allegedly, desire makes no crass distinction between male and female bodies, Straight Guys benefit from the Queer Eye of TV fashion advisers, emerging as stylish metrosexuals, and cultural theory insists that gender is a social construction, ultimately a choice. Gender bending went from pop shock to cool custom. Still, although we are now in an era of fluidity and choice, sex and gender remain a source of endless fascination—and anxiety.

Is sex really so adaptable, a fashion statement, or an ideological option? For decades we were told it is upbringing and preference, and one of the strongest arguments against biology's dominion was the Canadian case of John/Joan. A twin boy, Bruce Reimer, lost his penis at seven months during a botched circumcision in Winnipeg in 1966, was then castrated, surgically sex-reassigned and raised as Brenda. For years,

---

[21] 'We are not what we seem', *Sunday Telegraph* 29 Feb 2004, reprinted *The Age*, 28 March 2004: http://www.theage.com.au/articles/2004/03/28/1080331000649.html

his/her Johns Hopkins University sponsor, Dr. John Money, claimed the case as a triumph of adaptation, snails and puppy dog tails gracefully morphed into sugar and spice. It grew into the classic instance cited endlessly in feminist and poststructural 'social construction' texts and courses.

In fact, as we learned a few years ago, the poor child was a psychological mess, rough and tomboyish to a fault, even standing to urinate, and finally came out in adolescence as a male. He has changed his name to David, a biblical memento of his battle with Money, had painful and somewhat successful phalloplasty to create a working penis, toils with the other blokes in a slaughterhouse, and is now married, with adopted children.

John Colapinto's fascinating, heartbreaking but rhetorically loaded study of David Reimer's case (2000) makes his painful journey a parable of ideology and ambition over caring commonsense. The argument urged by Colapinto might seem obvious, given what any farmer or pet-owner knows: castrate a young animal, and it grows up lacking some of the traits that otherwise kick into action at maturity—but it does not change sex. In the uterus and then during infancy, the brain starts down specialized male or female developmental cascades. Once hormonally launched, nurture cannot reset all the implicit behavioral templates, or many of the physiological ones, even in the absence of testicles or ovaries.

The motive for surgically sex-reassigning babies born with ambiguous or damaged genitalia was surely kindly, if misguided. These children, it was thought, would be tormented by their peers, grow up with damaged self-esteem and probably become psychotic or self-destructive. Yet one of the astonishing aspects of Colapinto's book is that it reveals, apparently for the first time in this long debate, that Money's unpublished 1950s PhD thesis provided survey evidence that non-'corrected' individuals did not suffer unduly during maturation, and certainly did not go mad.

His cover-up of Reimer's key case is shocking and disgraceful, of course, but I find it piquant that this sort of thing happens on all sides of such questions. Last time around, it was Cyril Burt concocting IQ results to 'prove' the superior impact of heredity over nurture. The past 50 or 60 years have witnessed a slow gavotte in psychological fashion, aligned with crude and hideously cruel geopolitical struggles. Nazis taught that all was blood, and killed millions in that cause. Communists claimed all was learned culture, and killed those polluted by wrong opinions. Racism and, more recently, sexism were countered in the West by nurturists, making alternative models appear the ideology of bigots.

For a decade, this consensus has crumbled under the impact of new science and evolutionary insight. It is a turbulent epoch, and Reimer's tale, a distressing parable of our uncertainties, is compulsive reading.

Colapinto's book is not without its skews, demonizing Money to an unwarranted extent, not allowing him the benefit of a good conscience (however misguided). He is subtly and repeatedly held up to ridicule and revulsion for being too clever and articulate, for his uncensored speech even in front of children, his bisexual preferences, the way he showed child patients 'pornography'—pictures of naked adults and children—and made them explore each other's bodies. There is a strong implication that we are meant to suspect Money of paedophilia as well as his other crimes. This is a rather curious spin from a reporter who published his original 1997 story on the case in *Rolling Stone*, not *Reader's Digest*.

Money's case is almost certainly wrong, based on misleading evidence from intersex people whose brains were likely cross-wired during fetal development. But what of those many people who choose to switch later in life, after years of heterosexuality—must they always have been pre-wired to make the move? This is perhaps as dangerous a preconception as the purely socially constructed version. Queer theorists are surely right that some people can choose either to expand or specialize their sexual desires, at least to some extent.

Still, this says nothing about changing sex entirely, as was imposed on Bruce/Brenda. Sex reassignment of infants by surgery will probably be seen some day in the same light as cultural clitoridectomy: as mutilation.

Urologist and child psychologist William Reiner, also at Johns Hopkins, has reported that despite hormone treatment and surgery, 25 baby boys born with no penis but normal testicles (like Reimer), then castrated and raised as girls, all retained strong male characteristics and most switched back to male (213ff.). We are male or female because our brains are our key sex organs, and those squishy parts become set in their ways, due to complex chemical feedback loops, long before our more visible genitalia allow happy parents to cry: 'It's a girl!'

ii

Being a girl was not always much fun, and in many parts of the world it still isn't. One of the reasons women in the First World are dismayed by glass ceilings in the workplace rather than terrified by shared pyres at a husband's funeral is the long struggle uncomfortably dubbed *feminism*—uncomfortable because so many strong women nowadays refuse to accept the title 'feminist', regarding it as an ensign of special pleading, whining, or specious reasoning. In some quarters that is undeniably what feminism has become, but at its core it remains (in my male and perhaps therefore disqualified opinion) a powerful system of analysis, of *ideas* as well as of practices demanding equal liberty for half the human species.

Ideas, though, it seems, no longer get much of a run in First World nations like the USA or Australia. For generations the people of my own nation were too comfortable, throwing another shrimp on the barbie, sunburned backs turned complacently on the world. Now few have time or appetite for ideas. We are out of work, outsourced or downsized, racked by drought and flood, seething with anger at the strangers jostling us with their alien tongues and ways. The academy itself, once the custodian of ideas, too often babbles a postmodern, sanitized language few people could possibly wish to understand.

This is caricature, granted, but not without a foundation in reality. By blurring the difference between hard, demanding argument and mystifying cant, today's intellectuals make it tricky for people of good will to trust (or even comprehend) their ideas. While maverick politicians stir up strife with racist slogans, and mainstream rulers smash the hard-won gains of the past fifty years, the analysts one might expect to be articulating the most piercing social critique often wander in a textual maze.

That charge in turn risks the reek of philistinism or backlash against an academy often pilloried, by the mighty and the powerless alike, as the bastion of snooty unrest: multiculturalism, feminism, native title activism, queer theory, zany relativism. But there have been some tough-minded reappraisals of feminist theory, and its foes, by feminist women scholars who clearly do not stand for backlash, women who have matured inside the long debate, the political conflict, that still makes feminism an affront to the complacent.

During an Australian anti-Vietnam protest in the 1960s, as television footage showed vividly, Jean Curthoys was dragged from under President Lyndon Johnson's car and arrested. Two decades later, she was a Sydney University lecturer in the conservative Traditional and Modern Philosophy department that expelled the radical General Philosophy wing during a tumultuous staff and student strike that demanded a women's studies program. A daughter of communist activists in the company mining town Broken Hill (her sister Ann is a notable cultural theorist), Curthoys was an instigator of that rebellion. It was bitterly ironic, then, that this socialist became a 'boat person' given succor by her ideological foes, before resigning from the university.

Still more ironic, for Curthoys, is the seductive skid that takes so many militant young thinkers into cozy complicity and, worse, 'systematic intellectual confusion' (Curthoys, 1997: viii). Today's most articulate feminists, as her carefully argued analysis shows, are driven to embrace flawed and confused reasoning by their 'ambivalent attitude to status and power' (viii). This is not a story likely to win back her former friends.

The argument is complex, although Curthoys struggles to make her account as lucid as possible—chancing the deconstructive and Lacanian criticism of *la clarté*, of an alleged 'clarity fetishism' (123).[22] In capsule,

---

[22] This is not as ludicrously obscurantist as it seems, or not always. As Richard Webster

she recovers a genuinely liberatory epoch now lost. Activism at the end of the 1960s, facing down political and personal suppression, encouraged a moral consciousness based in mutual recognition. A version of Christian love without a supernatural deity, this solidarity is grounded upon an 'ethic of the irreducible value of human beings'. At a time when Foucauldian antihumanism insists that personal identity is unstable, or a hoax, or toxic—that subjectivity has been deconstructed, and good riddance—this humanistic ethic is voided, however radical the poststructural rhetoric.[23]

Allison Weir's survey (1996) of key feminist theories of identity, and their implications, ends up in rather the same place. Basing her account on the psychoanalytic semiotics of French theorist Julia Kristeva, Weir notes feminism's typical claim that individual identity takes a 'specifically masculine... white western capitalist' form 'which represses the fragmentation and multiplicity of the self' (1).

Being told you are a wife and mother *seems* to suggest that you cannot be something else as well—a student, say, or a doctor, or the lover of another woman. To be identified with certain attributes or roles apparently denies you the chance to evade those limits, to change or grow or simply walk away and start again. So identity seems readily equated with repression, and feminism rightly was not going to stand for that. Actually this analysis depends on a common logical error neatly refuted by Curthoys (75-7). It confuses *some* with *all*, turning a statement about limited, arbitrary and mutable cases into imagined universals. It assumes that the only way to divide up the world is by exhaustive exclusion: A or not-A, and nothing else. But there is, Curthoys points out, another way: A/B, where A and B are contingently and empirically distinct, but not logically or necessarily.

To be a human in our culture, feminism argues, is to be 'constructed' not just as a male but as a *not-woman*. Weir, following Julia Kristeva, calls such reasoning a logic of sacrifice and exclusion. Identity is installed only by 'sacrificing' some Other, some alternative or difference that is excluded, reviled, suppressed—and yet which is secretly yearned for, as the child endlessly desires the mother from whose luxurious unity it has been brutally torn. It is a familiar story, based on strong evidence of oppression disputed by neither Weir nor Curthoys. It seems to

---

puts it (with considerable clarity): 'What is tacitly promoted is the myth that we remain in control of a social and economic process whose human complexities, internal contradictions and injustices vanish away as reality is reduced to the hard, clear outlines demanded by conventional philosophical expression. The process by which we purport to be clarifying our relationship to the actual world thus becomes a potent act of mystification; the philosopher obscures the very reality he claims to reveal' ('The cult of Lacan', http://www.richardwebster.net/thecultoflacan.html)

[23] See my *Theory and Its Discontents* for a fuller discussion of this trajectory.

mandate the defiant rejection of a cruel, exclusionary logic that supports a *status quo* where every difference is glazed over into a pretended or imposed sameness. But if women cannot find any common ground in a characteristic identity, 'what can serve,' as Weir asks, 'as the basis of feminist solidarity?' (2).

In practice, denying logic's validity leads to a kind of opportunistic anything-goes politics, irresistibly convenient if you are fighting your way up the slippery academic tenure pole toward a professorship in (say) women's studies, a discipline without much appeal to economic rationalists. The result, Curthoys asserts, is a flawed 'surrational' doctrine whose radical form, a hold-over from the ethical liberation theories of an earlier era, often hides a conservative and self-serving content. Why so? Because it teaches that power cannot be effectively opposed, and can give no sound reasons why it ought to be.

At its worst, we find tertiary courses teaching that 'feminist' or 'situated' sciences must replace patriarchal or 'perspectiveless' sciences (the sort that are ruining the planet). Curthoys' scathing assault on this inane fad, which she compares tellingly to mid-century battles over genetics, is strikingly effective, part of her larger project to reinstate rationality without obliterating sexual differences or forsaking her detestation of arbitrary power.

Philistines and foes of the new Enlightenment insist that such boring or hateful ideas are best ignored. Oddly, that vulgar complaint has its counterpart in some exquisitely sophisticated feminist thought. It was necessary, and incredibly enough still is, for Weir to argue that feminist theorists must 'reconsider a common tendency to see abstraction as the enemy' (189). If abstraction is misused to stigmatize entire groups—'aborigines', 'women' (or 'men'), 'Muslims', 'anarchists', it can, of course, be hazardous. But without high-level thinking and rigorous logic, 'we effectively deny any capacity of agents,' as Weir observes, 'to criticize and change' the prevailing contexts (190).

Curthoys, in her incisive and broad-ranging study, was even more insistent. It is in pursuing knowledge as virtue (the Socratic quest), in solidarity with others, and in the integrity of our own complex identity, that we grow as humans, 'that we stop reinforcing the workings of power' (160). If so, perhaps women (and men, I hope) can awaken from the generational amnesia that has effaced those early tentative steps into liberation and a recovered Enlightenment. Perhaps we shall see how small our distinctions are, against the dark backdrop of the cosmos, and learn to embrace each other.

Halley's Comet

When I was quite small, I read about comets in a children's encyclopedia. My heart stopped, and then pounded. How can the world be prosaic, in a universe where comets tear without much warning (or stranger still, with clock-like reliability) out of the deep and innocent sky? There was a photo of Halley's comet, pale hair stretched across the stars. It was pure beauty.

Hairy stars! Tresses of light, blown by the Sun's bright wind! Mad portents, death and ruin of kings (but today most of us democrats have no kings, thank God, or, some of us, gods either, ditto), oracles written on the black sky in scratchings of brightness, fogs fleeing from the icy ends of the solar system to the warmth of our inner star, dirty iceballs of chemical smut and smog (and—who knows? certainly not that kid stuck back there in the fifties—alien DNA, genes, disease, life from space!) locked up in a hazy, lovely wisp of lace: *kometes*, yes, the comet! guest star from the boundaries of night, jog-plodding out there beyond Neptune and Pluto at a measly kilometer a second, then racing like a mad hatless 19th century schoolgirl with her hair all tossed and freed in the hot summer wind to round the sky and hide behind the Sun and dash past the world as we craned back our heads, peering at—what! where is it— give me the binoculars, the damned thing's too dim...

Well, Halley's comet was a blowout, I regret to say, in April, 1986, its nearest approach in a human lifetime to Earth orbit. A bust, a nonevent. Well, almost... Parents perched their kids on tired shoulders, pointing without much conviction at the dull patch. Pretty feeble, the faintest apparition in the last two thousand years of triumphant Halley's return to the inner solar system stage. How angry I would have been, three decades earlier in the mid-fifties (Halley having hit aphelion— farthest point from the sun—four years after my birth, yes, the year Orwell was getting down his dreadful vision of our future era). Thirty-five times farther again out than Earth, and it takes light itself eight minutes to reach our neighborly orbit. How angry I'd have been to know how faint and difficult the damned thing would be in that year of grace and light, 1986, when I turned 42.

I was waiting patiently all that time, a faithful devotee of galaxies and comets. Child's heart pounding (this was years before sex, but still...), I gazed besotted at the glowing portrait of M31 in Andromeda, that wondrous whirlpool of a hundred billion great hot stars they called a Nebula, then, in that old borrowed encyclopedia volume. The scientists, the dreadful Darwinists and Doubters, had not yet tumbled, in the world of that volume (that lost past of my grandparents' generation), to the horrid immensity of the cosmos. They took our Milky Way galaxy for the only one in town, they thought the furry nebulae were blotches and foams of gas at the edge of the fairground.

Now we know better, of course. This little cosmos spread around our heads is the merest grain of sand in a shoreline, an ocean of specks, still blasting into a spacetime of its own making like the residue of a nuclear fireball from the Big Bang origin somewhere back there 13 or so thousand million years past. But when I was a kid, not all that long ago really in cosmological or even historic terms, the available paperwork was woefully out of date. The Gitas. The Holy Bible. The Qur'an. The Book of Mormon, for that matter. You would not want to jump-start a universe based on documentation like that.

Still, we are grateful for what we can get. For hours, in the mid-1950s, I pressed my face to the glossy illustration pages in the Arthur Mees encyclopedia, the photographs from Mount Wilson with its fabulous (pre-metric measurements) 100-inch telescope, all those heart-stirring records from just the other day, 1910, when Halley's comet sent its fifty million kilometer tail like a new Milky Way band of luminous gauze across half the sky.

It was coming back! That was the great thing. In 1985 or 1986, in the impossible future, a future of adulthood (when you could buy all the ice creams and candies and chocolate cookies you wished, and eat them one after another, and no-one could tell you to stop!), Halley would return on its elastic string of gravity, loop back like a cosmic yo-yo, picking up speed and falling for the Sun, into the light, into the terrible heat and wind from the Sun (though they did not know about the wind then) (Wind! from the Sun?!), and its dark insignificant cometary nucleus would hiss and steam and breathe out light, light and bright dust, and the sky would open again in its once-every-76-years apocalypse and apparition, like a contract written by God attesting the Natural Human Span.

That was the great thing, but I had not realized how dim the damned thing was going to be at this end of the century, or how much rubbish we'd have thrown up into the sky—street-light rubbish, flashing neon sign rubbish, let alone the micro-muck spattered through the air we try to work our cigarette-damaged lungs with.

The great thing, by contrast, about being Ancient Man (3000 B.C., say), was that you had (a) no television, theater or movies to distract you at night, (b) no good restaurants to go out to, and (c) no electric lights, a drawback by some standards but okay at the time, due to a lack of (d) any amusing reading matter, but then (e), do not forget, no reliable contraceptives, and on top of all that you probably had (f) plenty of flocks to watch all night. How you actually kept an eye on your flocks with no electric power is anyone's guess.

There must have been a wonderful sameness about it, for all that, rolled in your cloak, the fire fallen into embers, gazing up at the endlessly turning sky choked with stars too dim for our city-stunned eyes to capture. (The late Wilfred Thesiger, that mad Briton who went among the wild desert men of Arabia Deserta early in our century, met youths with sight so piercing they could make out the circling moons of Jupiter, unknown to urban folk until the invention of the telescope.)

And if the uninterpreted heavens told a single story, that tale was Stability and Order. Now we know the sky is a shrieking chaos of exploding quasars and flickering giant suns, imploding black holes and moon-cracking asteroids. Then, though, all was peace, and the planets wandered to and fro on their crystalline spheres, attended by the orbiting sun and moon, speaking from eternity and earliest human history a corrupting, soothing fable of Kingly Ordination:

> The heavens themselves, the planets, and this center
> Observe degree, priority and place,
> Insisture, course, proportion, season, form,
> Office and custom,

reported William Shakespeare (*Troilus and Cressida,* Act I, scene 3), from a limb of revolution in history and astronomy.

But at spastic intervals the calm clockwork of the night ruptured without warning, and surely nothing could more easily set you screaming in panic.

A new star! Nova! (In fact, an old star blowing its top, as five billion years ago a nearby big fat blue star went off the deep end and sent a shock wave through a mess of cosmic dust and rubble, compressing it in pulses of radiation, causing it to clump and fall together into cold lumps that warmed themselves, and so started our Sun and ourselves...)

If a star might erupt, burning for days or weeks like a god's eye, and other stars tumble routinely to flare and streak (the meteors and their metallic residues the meteorites, accepted by shepherds but mocked until the end of the 18th century by savants who found them an affront to 'form, office and custom'), what might we make of comets, smashing like mad golf balls through the stained-glass windows of the manse, through the crystal spheres of church and state in the ordained macrocosm above our corruptible, sublunary heads?

Why, this was Revolution! Unthinkable! Omens and portents, yes, and foul vapors, and pestilence from a broken promise of utter peace in the skies above the clouds!

Chinese astrologers suspected dragons, and recorded the comets faithfully from the second millennium BC. Two of them, drunk as skunks, missed an eclipse and lost their heads to imperial wrath, smartening up the rest of their guild. Halley itself is recorded on almost every fly-by at least back to 87 BC, and records of bright comets in 240 and 467 BC look familiar. But it was not until Edmond Halley nudged his chum Newton at the end of the 17th century for a clue to Universal Gravitation that these historical annotations (some of them, anyway) fell beautifully into an elliptical graph tracking the comet of 1682 backward and forward through time and space. 'I would venture confidently to predict its return,' quoth Halley in 1705, 'namely in the year 1758.'

Legerdemain! A new order of regularity in the heavens, a fresh system, as lovely, as elegant, as unexpected as finding that the dinosaurs were wiped out to the last man when the nucleus of an exhausted comet smote the Earth in the year 65,000,000 BC (roughly).

Revolution? Why, yes. That is where the word came from. Copernicus had given everyone a nasty turn with his revelation of Revolutions of the Heavenly Bodies, and the Renaissance took up his insight as a metaphor, the collapse of old before the thrust of new, the power of the stars (of course) impelling the rise of the brash and the strong. Halley's, however, is a Counter-Revolutionary, for the fool thing swings in a reverse sense about the Sun, counter-clockwise, heading left as we swing right, so people in high places need have no fear. Maybe. For there are other comets (of course).

Certainly Halley's owned a rich, peculiar stink of mystery: trapped in gold and thread by Giotto and the Bayeux weavers, ripe with spores of universal life, if astronomers Hoyle and Wickramasinghe are right, and not just life but disease and genetic benefice, gifts of Magi and Wicked Witch in silvery wrapping. There is more. Consider American gothic novelist John Calvin Batchelor's troubling assessment of that singular moment of the hairy comet:

> Man's hunger, working in conjunction with his bizarre yen for profit, had moved him from a fire in a cave on an antediluvian river shore eight millennia before the birth of the Savior, to a fire on a volcanic plain on the moon two millennia after... The instant in time that Homo sapiens touched lunar soil, Earthman became Spaceman, from which there is no turning back. Good riddance to all that. Hello to high, wide, and hairy. (1984: 385)

Yes, hello to Hairy Stars! As the space probe Giotto plowed on March 14, 1986, through the fourteen kilometer coma, the glowing head of Halley's, watched by the Russian Vega craft and a Japanese mission, as it sent back its mysterious portraits, we too entered one step further into our estate. Masters of the Universe! Spectators, at the very least. At best: its reworkers, its next designers, the tenants who took over the cosmos and did it up to their own tastes.

Greenhouse icecap melting? Global starvation? Resource depletion and entropy, a world laid waste in the fecundity of its own most successful animal? Hell, no. Hairy stars! Nebulae! Here is my advice: go with that kid I once was, dreaming, in abstract love, into the encyclopedia, still as sweet a symbol as I know (well, prior to a Googled Internet) for the burgeoning storehouse of polymathic human knowledge. And what we learn will change what we know, drastically, convulsively, in ways we cannot yet know. But we can make educated guesses. Sometimes—like the smudgy thing I waited for during thirty years of devotion—our dreams will prove wilder than the reality. It is the risk we run, we dreamers. But more often than not, we see past the veil into a place (call it the future) where the prosaic and the workaday dare not step. Until relentless time pushes them through, and they sprawl without preparation, bruised and confused and angry. Hairy stars! Why didn't anyone warn us?

Images

Here is one of my recurrent obsessions: I believe most people take it for granted that everyone else in the world uses roughly the same kind of mental imagery protocols. We all know enough to distinguish extroverts from shy cerebrotonics, and the jocks from the willowy sensitive types, and the inarticulate from the freely babbling, but since the early 1960s, when I had an epiphany about all this, I have been informally polling people about their visual imagery. Most can form some kind of red triangle in imagination, and rotate it to the left, then to the right, and go on to make a picture of their dear old Maman, check the color of her eyes, and so on. Some are exceptionally good at this stunt, making elaborate flowcharts and tracking through them without moving a muscle (or maybe they twitch in sympathy). Others can 'see' whole movies as they read a novel.

I have *zero* visual imagery, at least when I am awake.

The module is simply not there, apparently, or is shunted offline during consciousness. Presumably this is one reason I was regarded as a slow child in primary and most of secondary school. I could not spell very well, because I could not inwardly *see* the words. Eventually I managed to recognize words on the page, but answering 'spelling bee' questions was utterly hopeless. Even though I soon knew several times as many words as everyone else, and more or less how to use them, I could not spell them aloud because I could not *see them inwardly* (whatever that is like).

The same thing happened with simple arithmetic and algebra, let alone geometry. It was hopeless. Scribble scribble, tongue out the corner of my mouth, maybe by brute force I could work out what the teachers were babbling about. So much of the routine instruction was automatically pitched in the visualization mode that I was repeatedly stranded.

As a result, and to my intense regret, I never became a scientist. I met obstacles as a philosopher, too, once the notation went up on the blackboard. I need to turn everything into narrative, run compression algorithms on the word chunks, then fool around with those. This can be amazingly powerful, and many poststructuralists do just this, hence sound like posing wankers—and I suspect many of them must share my cognitive defect. Not all, though, now that movies and visual art and TV are such a major part of the postmodern agenda. This skew has a very strange effect on my writing. Since I write a fair bit of fiction, often set in places where the settings are unfamiliar, I need to provide the cues and codes that switch on my readers' visual imagery machinery. Since that stuff does not work with me, from the inside, I am in roughly the position of a deaf person learning to grunt out unheard sounds painfully associated with meanings, with hardly any immediate feedback. It is a weird way to live, I assure you.

I conjecture that a lot of those smart people who never quite 'achieved their potential' might share the same unorthodox imagery structures as mine, or maybe other kinds that are equally alien. I do use a kind of ancillary kinesthetic imagery in the place of the 'inner eye', with portions of my body image *feeling* rotated in space. So I can score fairly well on those rotate-the-gadget-and-say-which-one-is-next tests in IQ trials, by turning myself into one, and dancing. I almost immediately knew the answer to one famous question about tetrahedra, cited in an Arthur C. Clarke novel, that only geniuses are supposed to get. But I am damned if I can *picture* a tetrahedron in my head...

Oh, and I have no depth perception (stereopsis), either. This might not be a coincidence, although it was caused by an eye defect and then became neurally hardwired in infancy.

I was at the end of my first year in English, when I suddenly realized with an immense sickening shock why people kept talking about *imagery* in poems (a medium largely obscure to me, although I liked the rhythms and sounds and compressed density of some verse). 'Images'—like, like, um, like... *pictures*, you mean? Those words about rain and roses and swaying daffodils and running lions and gold light glinting from the blade *make pictures in your head*? I wanted my money back!

Despite this defect, people often tell me they enjoy the visual density of my writing (although others, like critic Bruce Gillespie, now know what they have sensed was absent in it.) So what does it mean that people can assume I have a wonderful, rich visual imagination, since my fiction has given them such striking pictures? It is mostly their own work, that's what; I'm just providing the wiring instructions. But then, so is every writer; it is just that I'm doing it at two removes.

And it helps explain why my fiction is so adjective- and adverb-clotted. Other people (or so I surmise) use descriptors sparingly to notate their visions. Or most descriptive elements are actually absent (as in Hemingway, famously), since it is assumed readers will fill in the blanks (literally). Since all I *have*, visually, is blanks, I code up my text with heaps and lashings of modifiers. But there is usually some kind of musical riffing that a mainly visual reader probably misses, being keyed to another coding modality... (To put it in my favored abstract-densified fashion.)

In *The White Abacus*, an sf-warped version of Shakespeare's *Hamlet* that goes sideways fast at the end (discussed below in the chapter on **Virtual Realities**), all the 'word-pictures' were my own... No actual Denmark scenery, a rather hitech ghost, no swords as such. And my Ophelia was smarter and prettier and a damned sight tougher. I certainly tried to make it a visual treat, borrowing from some excellent space art (acknowledged in the afterword) but making my own wide-screen baroque from it, etc.

The saddest aspect of this defect or variant is *not being able to activate the inner movie* for myself! I am waiting sullenly for the plug-in cognitive module. Yet I have vivid visual dreams. Obviously people like me do possess those basic visual processing modules that allow us to transform retinal activation patterns into an experienced world (a flat one, in my case, with depth guessed from inferential cues, as one does in a movie). So when our waking consciousness switches down and off, in sleep, and the brain starts generating specious imagery out of scraps of the day's events, imagined connections, etc, that whole machinery is presumably fully available to build up a pseudo-world with a certain sensory richness. The standard visual parts of the cortex light up on brain scanners when you dream. When I am awake, though, presumably a different set of dominant cognitive pathways or hierarchies gets activated.

I have sometimes wondered if I could learn to switch into the dream-vision mode with lots of practice. But then reading novels is exactly that kind of practice, you would imagine, and it has not happened. I am left, like Hamlet, with words, words, words.

Jousting with Genes

> Sociobiology and evolutionary psychology have triumphed over their academic enemies; they are successful not only because of the power of theory but because of the relentless pursuit of relevant evidence... Increasingly it looks like normal science. A few years into the revolution, anthropologist Irven DeVore told a skeptical student 'the data are sitting up and begging.' Today the data are sitting up, begging, rolling over, fetching, jumping through hoops, and playing catch. Criticism is healthy, and fierce ongoing debates characterize the discipline. Much of the tired flailing against these approaches in the name of political correctness has fortunately gone to sleep. But when it comes to such sensitive policy issues as violence, crime, war, prejudice, and rape, politically motivated criticism still rears its ugly head.
>
> Melvin Konner (2004)

i

As a Catholic child, I was taught that humans share a corrupted nature, spoiled by the sin of Adam but salvaged by our Creator in a startling act of self-sacrifice. Despite redemption, that fatal, tragic condition of original sin left us prey to wickedness, always liable to slip off the narrow path into theft, lies, betrayal, sensuality. Let your human nature run free, and you'd wind up burning in Hell.

During the hopeful 1960s, many rejected that gloomy doctrine. What if there were no fixed human nature after all. What if we are born as a blank slate with no text inscribed on it, no instincts or bents, only endless opportunity for making ourselves? Then we might painfully develop more humane and creative modes of living, casting off racism, sexism, jealousy and material envy, the prejudices and bad habits of a cruelly deprived history: call it the Fabian theory of improvement.

'Wadda we want?'

'*Gradual* change!'

'Wenna we want it?'

'*In due course!*'

Or maybe, delirious Sixties' thought, it might come in a thunderclap of revolution, violent if need be or fueled by sweet magic insight. Either way, it seemed pretty certain that 'human nature' was an ideological fossil from grimmer eras when people had been conditioned to distrust the body and each other.

If that was the wistful hope of the young Boomers, it faded and chipped badly as the years passed. Insurrections guttered. Vietnam threw out the Americans, then rediscovered capitalism. The old Soviet Union turned to God and gangsters. Meanwhile, nature made a big comeback. The Boomers' children, when they were not plotting their next corporate takeover, worshiped Gaia, ate natural foods, rejected synthetic medicines for 'natural' remedies. This was Nature, but not the old Adam; Nature was a goddess of purity, and all we needed to do was find her within ourselves. Ideology switched again: if it is *natural*, it must be *good*. If it is bad, that must be the fault of wrong words, calculation rather than spontaneity, people playing god and setting themselves above nature.

Meanwhile, science was looking again at what human nature might actually be. Humans are evolved creatures, so just as we have opposed thumbs for grasping, maybe we inherit modifiable templates for action as well. Speech, for example: without specialized areas in the brain, pre-shaped to acquire words and fit them to the outside world, we could never learn to talk fluently. Might we also inherit predispositions to behave in certain ways under certain conditions? Every other animal does. But that is a terrifying suggestion to a culture when 'nature' now (however absurdly) is supposed to equal 'wholesome'. If ordinary men can find it within themselves to rape women under brutal conditions of war and lawlessness, that would imply rape is 'natural' and therefore we would be obliged to accept it!

The error should be obvious. Salmonella is also part of nature, but we work hard to prevent it making us sick. Actually, if we do have a complex human nature, we will only contain its nastier aspects by facing them fearlessly. The rediscovery of a persistent and universal human nature forged by our Darwinian history has been detailed by Steven Pinker in *The Blank Slate* (2002). His sensitive investigation of rape, and of other 'don't-go-there' topics, is exemplary and brave, and was immediately traduced or misrepresented by his opponents, as we shall see.

As a linguistic psychologist, Pinker came to notice with fine popularizations, *The Language Instinct* (1994) and *How the Mind Works* (1997), which expounded current findings in evolutionary and cognitive science, game theory, and of course the nature of speech. Controversially, he went on to renew these themes while drawing on his polymathic knowledge to propose ways whereby communities might balance private and public virtues and failings. What he dubbed the Utopian Left resented and deplored his claim that 'the new sciences of human nature really do resonate with assumptions that historically were closer to the right than to the left' (2002: 284), since genes build individuals, not societies, even if those individuals are social beings.

The Tragic Right was no less discomfited. Should people be free to spend their own money, not have it seized away by tax authorities? Not so fast: 'economists repeatedly find that people spend their money like drunken sailors' (303). Why do they? Original sin? Stupidity? No, because the mental planners in our brains evolved in a dangerous ancestral environment where you were likely to die young, so you might as well live for the day; we tend to discount the future, as economists put it. Libertarians will be surprised, too, by his account of the merits of a state, and of a more egalitarian income distribution. We share behavioral templates that provoke bloody escalating contests of honor in the absence of mediating and somewhat neutral adjudicators. Crime rates are higher in regions of great income disparity because, for evolutionary reasons, 'chronic low status leads men to become obsessed with rank and kill each other over trivial insults' (304). So it is prudent, as well as humane, not to make the poorest feel like worthless dogs. (Forget the fabled peaceful traditional indigenes, though: in such cultures, between 10 and 60 percent of men die by violence.) Those on the left, meanwhile, might learn something unsettling from Pinker's account of why he follows Noam Chomsky in linguistics but not in politics.

Pinker's raffish style, and humor, unsettled some opposed to his approach, but his copiously referenced evidence and careful demurrals went ignored by most critics, certainly those read by the general public in newspaper and journal reviews. Consider the simplified assault directed against these revived Enlightenment proposals by an Australian sociologist, Frank Campbell. In a favorable review of *They F*** You Up* [sic] by the British psychologist James Oliver, an outspoken foe of Pinker (they nearly came to blows during one BBC debate), Campbell summarized the evolutionary psychology standpoint thus, crushing together complexities that Pinker takes excruciating pains to deal with in detail:

> Daily we are told that this or that characteristic is
> overwhelmingly determined by mindless genes... Pinker
> is the last word in genetic determinism... (2003: R12)

Overwhelmingly determined? Think of human height, a dimension which in some measure is plainly an inherited characteristic. After allowance is made for the fact that all the children of two parents receive a different blend of genes from both, and that these interact with each other in a vast confusion of ways, it is still true that the children of short parents tend to be shorter than the children of tall parents. Their genes constrain their possible and even likely heights. But as both the Japanese and British parents found after the Second World War, the environmental factors of available nutrition, hygiene and health care contribute profoundly to the height attainable by any individual child.

Fed frugally, the children of giants will tend to be stunted, comparatively. Feasting on junk food, the children of athletes can bloat and ruin their growing bodies. Eating optimally and exercising adequately, the offspring of those damaged in their own childhood by poor nutrition will flourish, outstripping by many centimeters their fathers and mothers.

So here we have two truths indissolubly linked: the genes clearly determine parameters of growth, but they hardly do so *overwhelmingly*—except *ceteris paribus:* when the other factors are evened out, taken into account. Benign social policy will attempt to provide the best feasible environment for the expression, in complex human beings, of each person's inherited genetic recipe.

Indeed, Pinker is so far from being 'the last word in genetic determinism' that in his contribution to Dr. Leon Kass's bioethics committee hearings on behalf of the US Congress (6 March, 2003), he answered this frequently heard travesty.[24] Chairman Kass, proponent of the gut-level ethical yardstick unblushingly dubbed 'the Wisdom of Repugnance', is himself a Phi Beta Kappa physician, biochemist, historian, as well as an ethics specialist. I quote Pinker at length, because the issue is at the heart of the new Enlightenment understanding of our human nature:

> I would say that the science of behavioral genetics at present faces something of a paradox. We know that tens of thousands of genes working together have a large effect on the mind. We know that, from twin studies that show that identical twins are far more similar than fraternal twins, who, in turn, are more similar than unrelated individuals, and from adoption studies that show that children resemble their biological parents more than their adopted parents.
>
> But these are effects of sharing an entire genome or half of a genome or a quarter of a genome. It's very different from the existence of single genes that have a consistent effect on the mind, which have been few and far between.
>
> Anyone who has kept up with the literature on behavioral genetics has noticed that there's been a widespread failure to find single genes for schizophrenia, autism, obsessive-compulsive disorder, and so on. And those, by the way, are the areas where we are most likely to find a single gene, simply because it is easier to *disrupt* a complex system with a single defective part than it is to *install* an entire complex

---

[24] Steven Pinker, drawn from the proceedings at
http://www.bioethics.gov/transcripts/march03/session3.html

ability with a single gene. The failure to find a gene with consistent effect on, say, schizophrenia means that it's even less likely that we will find a gene for something as complex as musical talent or likeability.

And though there have been highly publicized discoveries of single genes for syndromes such as bipolar illness, sexual orientation or, in perhaps the most promising case, a gene that appeared to correlate with four IQ points in gifted individuals; all of those discoveries have been withdrawn in recent years, including the four point IQ gene withdrawn just last month.

Now, it's really not such a paradox when you think about what we know about biological development in general. The human brain is not a bag of traits with one gene for each trait. That's just not the way genetics works.

Neural development is a staggering complex process which we are only beginning to get the first clues about. It involves many genes interacting in complex feedback loops.

The effects of genes are often non-additive. The effect of one gene and the effect of a second gene don't produce the sum of their effects when they are simultaneously present necessarily.

The pattern of expression of genes is often as important as which genes are present, and therefore, it's a good idea not to hold your breath for the discovery of the musical talent gene or any other single gene or small number of genes with a large, consistent effect on cognitive functioning or personality.

Campbell had offered another typical sally (2003: R12): 'Geneticism isn't new... But it has a fatal political flaw. What's the point of punishing or blaming anyone for anything if criminality and everything else is predetermined?' Again, Pinker provided the Kass committee a clear defense against this sort of attempted *reductio ad absurdum*:

> ... I am absolutely not a determinist and not for any philosophical reasons, but for an empirical reason.
>
> The identical twins raised together correlate only, say, 0.4 to 0.8. That technically refutes determinism in its actual [that is, strict philosophical] sense, but I certainly do believe that the genome leads humans to think and feel in characteristic ways, but because the

brain is so complex, because it has multiple systems and a number of them have the ability to crank out new combinations, infinite combinations of ideas, the idea of a fixed human nature doesn't mean that there's a fixed repertoire of behavior or thoughts... I think we do have the ability to learn the lessons of history, to be persuaded by argumentation to see things in new ways, and in fact, again, this isn't just kind of a sappy sentiment, but things have changed which would be impossible if we were genetically fixed.

The rates of violence have gone down in the last couple of hundred years in the society. Concepts that were thought to be inevitable, such as slavery, subjugation of women, inevitability of blood feuds, for example, all have greatly diminished.

So the notion of human nature doesn't mean that society will never change or ideas will never change.

This is precisely Pinker's case throughout *The Blank Slate* and his other books, and those of his behavioral evolutionary colleagues. It is in bad faith and intellectually misleading for their opponents to claim otherwise, although such claims are often made, risking the foreclosure of otherwise open-minded scrutiny. Fortunately, not all those from the embattled humanities' side of the Two Cultures boundary produce this sort of specious rebuttal. Neuroscientist Kenan Malik, a psychologist with an enviable record as an academic and polemical foe of racism, set out to find the ethical place where a reasonable person can stand between doctrines of humanity that apparently would make us machines without choice (the zombies of some cognitive science accounts) or brutes driven by detestable imperatives, biases scorched by natural selection into those 30,000 genes.

What was refreshing in Malik's careful case was his embrace not of new-age holism and mysticism, the temptation of a David Suzuki, nor of science-bashing, like a Jeremy Rifkin or Bryan Appleyard, but of a hopeful materialism grounded in history. 'Far from being conflicting visions,' he concluded, 'humanism and materialism are intimately connected ... Emancipation from nature is essential to moral progress' (2000: 389). This will shock many people who feel that anxious flight from nature, or a wish to master it, is precisely the mark of the globalizing zombie that, they fear, means to crush us all into homogeneous market fodder.

The real problem, for Malik, grounded in the emancipatory history of Enlightenment humanism, is that 'we no longer think of ourselves as beings with the potential to shape our own futures'. Does the human genome's surprising brevity imply we are reduced to biological mechanisms? No. 'To challenge mechanism we need not to retreat from reason, but to embrace it, for mysticism and mechanism are both irrational accounts of human nature' (340). Neither the collected works of Daniel Dennett and Steven Pinker, nor of their enemies, are the last word on the topic. Everything remains in play, not least the machineries that allow us to search within our bodies and minds as easily as they take glowing pictures of the edge of the cosmos, the very dawn of time and space.

ii

For the longest time, Edward O. Wilson was demonized by those whose political values center, reasonably, on empathy and equality of opportunity: social democrats, liberal humanists, Greens, everyone roughly of the left. E. O. Wilson is not a political thinker, however, but a myrmecologist, an ant specialist, perhaps the world's greatest. For his invention in 1975 of Sociobiology, the research program that seeks biological and genetic motives for social behavior—in humans, as well as animals—Wilson was pilloried as a defender of reactionary doctrines, a proponent of dog-eat-dog capitalism, even a closet racist or Nazi. At a meeting in 1978, broken leg in a cast, he was doused with water by student protesters. While radical colleagues like Stephen Jay Gould denounced the assault, Wilson's theories were *persona non grata* in the academy for a decade or more. Since then, he has emerged as an influential defender of biodiversity in a world increasingly subject to industrial rapine of the kind he was imagined to defend. His wonderful memoir helps explain this embattled paradox of perception (Wilson, 1994). Growing up in the Old South, a natural paradise for an exploratory white child, he recalls those days as 'blessed', 'enchantment' (1994: xii). If his local culture was polluted by bigotry, he outgrew it, while retaining his devotion—his 'biophilia'—for the luminous, numinous landscapes he roamed freely.

Wilson's voice is gracious, lucid, sinewy. In boyhood, he lost sight in one eye (13-14), and turned to the small extraordinary creatures he could see up close. In his measured way, he grew up absurdly bold, making demanding rites of passage in the wilds of Meso-America and the South Pacific. At a time when ecology was despised, he helped revive its study. His enemies were formidable. James Watson, co-discoverer of DNA, was 'the most unpleasant human being I ever met' (219). Watson's faction of molecular biology injected 'a new faith in reductionism. The most complex of processes... might be simpler than we thought' (223). Ironically, these triumphant barbarians held Wilson's complex ecology in contempt.

Sociobiology is no less despised by many who have never bothered to read it. While Wilson insists that 'populations follow... laws that cannot be constructed by any logical progression upward from molecular biology', still he declares that 'reductionism... is precisely my view of how the world works' (346). His case is by now familiar from earlier chapters: we inherit, along with our organs, certain dispositions to acquire typical behaviors and social structures. This set of tendencies is what he and colleagues like Pinker call 'human nature'.

> [P]ysiologically based preferences, called 'epigenetic rules', channel cultural transmission in one direction instead of another. By this means they influence the outcome of cultural evolution... Some choices create greater survival and reproductive rates... Over many generations, the human population as a whole has moved toward one particular 'human nature' out of a vast number of natures possible. It has fashioned certain patterns of cultural diversity from an even greater number of patterns possible. (352)

It is an opinion increasingly in the ascendant, supported by copious careful work.

As with the first incarnation of the Enlightenment, such ideas are embodied in the specificity of individuals as well as in the abstract corpus of their ideas. Wilson became a man whose science was 'advanced by hilarity'. His coruscating colleague Robert Trivers was a manic-depressive. 'When he was up he was dazzling; when he was down he was terrifying' (325). It is Wilson's bias to compete and never quit. 'This is the reason I get killed in the company of my friends Murray Gell-Mann and Steven Weinberg, Nobel laureates in physics... said to be competing for the title of World's Smartest Human' (325-6). In the end, though, humankind is not all-important to Wilson. We are born of evolution amid the diversity of life. 'Philosophy and religion make little sense without taking into account these first two conceptions' (363).

Perhaps Wilson's writerly talent is not so surprising. 'The most important evolutionary biologists are those who... look for the best stories Nature has to tell us, because they are above all storytellers' (167).

Kant, Kass and Clones

> Human cloning has moved from science fiction into science... Our children are gifts to be loved and protected, not products to be designed and manufactured. Allowing cloning would be taking a significant step toward a society in which human beings are grown for spare body parts, and children are engineered to custom specifications; and that's not acceptable.
>
> President George W. Bush, 10 April, 2002

i

Since the cloned ewe Dolly appeared on the world's TV screens in 1997, and was euthanized following severe lung infections in 2001, we have faced brand-new ethical and metaphysical quandaries. Drs. Ian Wilmut and Keith Campbell, of Roslin Institute in Scotland, had taken a mammary cell from an adult clone, tweaked and fiddled its nuclear DNA, switched it into an emptied unfertilized ovum, and implanted the resulting embryo in a host-mother sheep. Because they were veterinary embryologists, their work was ignored until it smacked loftier experts between the eyes. There was young Dolly, the world's first known cloned mammal, gamboling in the fields. A cloned sheep! Baaa! I read the news on the Internet, before it hit the newspapers in Australia. Yes, I was flabbergasted. Science fiction gurus had been predicting it for decades, but no-one expected it quite so soon... in the real world.

Did everyone go crazy with delight, enthusiastic at this superb feat of science? No, everyone went ballistic with dread and horror instead, accelerating for the ethical high ground. I had known they would, but it was a depressing sight, nonetheless. Horrors! Brave New World! The end is nigh! *Saddam Hussein and Osama bin Laden cloned into ranks of storm troopers!* This was a truly ridiculous fear, of course. Even if character is largely genetically ordained, why would the clones of such a man obey their sergeant? More likely they would gang up and kill him, then murder each other like some bloody-handed Greek tragedy. Besides, it was extraordinarily inconsistent that most of those doing this scaremongering usually championed an overwhelming influence from nurture and environment over what, in other contexts of debate, they denounced as 'genetic determinism'.

Few commentators understood how absurd these scare stories were. Moral panic set in immediately, and has quickened with questions over stem cells drawn from cloned embryos. Seldom has so much muddled thinking been done in public and foisted upon voters by their elected leaders. One notable science journalist, Gina Kolata, noting that this technology might allow infant replicas of adults to be born (twins a generation or two apart in time), asked rhetorically: 'is there a hidden fear that we would be forcing God to give us another soul, thereby bending God to our will or, worse yet, that we would be creating soulless beings that were merely genetic shells...?' (1997: 7). Such medieval pseudo-questions remind me of the delusory belief, once widespread, that illness is due to sorcery.

Cloning human copies of the rich and infertile is of less urgent significance than a whole batch of medical advances these technologies make possible. Already, cloned human veins have been grown. Transgenic animals produce pure pharmaceuticals expressed in urine or milk. Genetically modified pigs, purged of the immune factors that now cause tissue transplant rejection, grow heart-valves and other organs pre-adapted to human use. Cloning is crucial for the success of these life-saving programs. Might such xenotransplants also pipe in new subtle infections and fresh unknown horrors? All life is a gamble, and knowledge is the best means to shift odds our way. The immune system is a fluid, fluent extension of the brain, sharing messages from body to mind and back again. Once we unlock its grammar, we will know how to activate immunity's benefits, avoid the diseases and disorders that eat us from within and without. That is assuming we are permitted to do so. At the start of the twenty-first century, there are tensions pulling in both directions.

Again, we face the question whether such technologies should be permitted in a vulnerable society? Leon Kass, Bill McKibben and others seem certain that they should be postponed indefinitely, on some narrow precautionary principle. It is illuminating to look at the closing words of Kant's conservative and 220-year-old essay on the Enlightenment, to note his balancing act between respect for powerful authorities and his final insistence upon freedom of the individual:

> It boils down to this, then: Argue as much as you like on any topic, but obey the law! Considered in the widest sense, nearly everything in human affairs is paradoxical. A high degree of civil freedom seems advantageous to a people's intellectual freedom, yet it also sets up insuperable barriers to it. Conversely, a lesser degree of civil freedom gives intellectual freedom enough scope to expand to its fullest extent. What's special and singular in human nature—our inclination and vocation to think freely—can develop inside these socially stabilizing constraints, and gradually changes the way we view the world and our capacity to act in it. Bit by bit, we become increasingly able to act freely. Eventually, even governments learn that they can profit

by treating men and women—who are more than simple machines—in a manner appropriate to our dignity.

Does the individual have a future now nuclear cloning is an industrial process? Dolly the sheep, cloned from a dead ewe's udder tissue, had her own healthy daughters, but was put down comparatively young after developing severe arthritis and lung disease. Other species are being cloned—although not yet humans. So will identical babies be die-stamped out in cold laboratories? Hardly. In any case, four rams cloned from the same embryo proved to be 'very different in size and temperament' (Wilmut, et al., 2000: 304). Diversity among clones should not be a surprise. Canada's famous Dionne quints were natural clones, raised identically, yet they varied a lot. One died at 20, another at 36, while the rest lived into rather gloomy old age. The real value of cloning is the control it gives over cell lines, the space opened for precise genetic modifications. Will that affect humans? Surely, but there is very little reason to expect cloning to become a fashion statement in the immediate future.

ii

In February 2000, then-United States President Bill Clinton stood proudly at a podium to announce that the human genome draft was complete. Actually, this map of our common genetic recipe was still badly gappy. Clinton called it 'a day for the ages'. He was flanked at his left by Dr. Francis Collins, devout Christian leader of the painstaking public American end of the global Human Genome Project (HGP). At his right stood Dr. Craig Venter, the carpetbagger who had roared into Dodge fixing to finish off the genome by the 'shotgun' method, beating those slow-poke bureaucrats even though they'd drawn first—and, if his Celera Genomics company could get away with it, patenting the spoils. Ironically, Venter was soon to be fired by Celera, which was less interested in research than in realizing profits from pharmaceutical applications.

Nearly half a century after the fabled DNA helix was first unraveled in Britain by Englishman Francis Crick and a youthful visiting American, James Watson, a key non-American strand of the Genome Project's thread in this vast common project was largely overlooked. Prime Minister Tony Blair seized photo opportunities, but not many people knew that a major player in this epochal search was a genial expert in nematode worms, John Sulston (now Sir John). In 1989 Sulston had helped start the sequencing project, with DNA helix co-discoverer Jim Watson and another American worm specialist, Bob Waterson, and ran the United Kingdom end, the Sanger Center, until late in 2000 (Sulston and Ferry, 2001).

The speed of these successful efforts was genuinely breathtaking. As recently as mid-1996, the effort was only just gearing up after vast preparation for its major push, massively and crucially funded by the philanthropic Wellcome Trust, heirs to a pharmaceutics fortune. Only a few percent of the three billion genetic letters had yet been read. In May, 1998, with the aid of venture capitalists, Craig Venter entered the arena, ready to complete the human sequence within three years—four or five years earlier than the public project's goal—and without a cent of taxpayers' money.

Journalists were agog. Here was the brash American way at its best: audacious, putting its money where its mouth was in expectation of prodigious rewards, perhaps even a bit unprincipled. The race hotted up with incredible speed. To everyone's astonishment, private and public wings released their data simultaneously to the scientific press in February, 2001—Sulston's team (although by then he had resigned) through the British journal *Nature*, Celera's via the American journal *Science*. The human genome had been decoded in barely more than a decade, a triumph comparable, we were told, to placing men on the Moon, with unfathomable future consequences.

The trouble with this story, like the one about political asylum seekers in Australian waters throwing their children into the sea to force their rescue by an unwilling Navy, is that it is untrue, and politically motivated. Sulston's own brilliantly enthralling tale blends his amused, amusing and slightly bumbling persona (as captured by science journalist Ferry, who adds meaty chunks from her interviews with other major players) with the increasingly furious, indignant tones of a prophet scorned. Those publications in 2001 were not at all the glorious consummation trumpeted in the press. Indeed, the human genome was not really finished until the original HGP target date, 2003, and even then some small fragment remained undecoded.[25]

What is more, Sulston explains, Venter's spectacular coup in starting from scratch years after the public program had allegedly plodded along, roaring to a neck-and-neck finish, is at best spin and at worst flat untruth. Celera's celerity depended on late generation sequencing machines developed originally with funding from the public purse. Worse still, Venter's 'shotgun' method of sequencing chunks of code, then patching them together like a jigsaw puzzle, only worked—to the extent that it did—because he could appropriate maps generated by Sulston and others who strove to keep the genome code in the public domain.

Despite promises, Venter's own data was rarely posted openly; indeed, researchers were obliged to sign non-disclosure documents. This is not how science has been done, as Sulston furiously points out, nor

[25] http://news.bbc.co.uk/1/hi/sci/tech/2940601.stm.

should it be. Perhaps old-world gentlemanly openness just does not cut the mustard any longer, does not produce either the scientific nor commercial goods? But market exploitation, Sulston replies, simply has not achieved what it claims.

Celera, he argues, did science and won prizes by press release. Bizarrely, the HGP and Venter's team shared an award for mapping the 'landscape of the genome' at a time when the public project's data was being posted daily for all to see, yet Celera's was not. None of it. 'Had this ever happened before? That an internationally reputable society would give an award for research that was unpublished and unseen?' (233). Easy to sympathize with Sulston's wrath, although the press seems largely to have treated it as pique.

Does it matter, though, finally? Sulston shows how the public side of the race was muffled or even effectively silenced in the USA by politics, for nobody could speak out against market interests without upsetting Congress, risking the sack or loss of government funds. Well, is this in turn not just another ideological spin? Sulston is clearly and unashamedly an old left-humanist who inveighs against 'the power of the rich countries and of the transnational corporations... used in a bullying and inequitable fashion' (276). Economic rationalists shrug off such rhetoric, noting that everyone benefits from the swiftest possible unpacking of this genetic treasure trove. That might be true in part; then again, private interests have tried to patent not just partly mapped gene sequences (built by evolution, of course, rather than human ingenuity), but also any future medical applications of proteins the genes encode. It is like patenting air, then levying a charge on breathing, inflated tires, and the atmosphere of Jupiter. One wants to laugh out loud at this venal audacity, but we dare not treat it so lightly.

I expected Sir John to gain a Nobel Prize for this work, and to stand gritting his teeth as Craig Venter shared it. In the event, he shared the 2002 Nobel Physiology and Medicine medal with his mentor, Sydney Brenner and colleague Bob Horvitz for their sequence work on the nematode worm *Caenorhabditis elegans*. But might the Sanger Center and the other non-commercial contributors, even so, yet be written out of history? Let nobody be tempted to allow this, Sulston urged. 'The struggle over the human genome was necessary, and things would not be the same today had not the public project stood firm' (279).

Meanwhile, some, like Bryan Appleyard, an articulate British conservative pundit, are scared witless by cloning and other genomic advances. Appleyard espies a eugenic agenda behind genetic engineering (2000). Unlike some conservatives, he sees that seemingly far-fetched applications—physical immortality, enhanced intelligence—are actually very plausible. Still, many of his anxieties derive from his fear that scientists think they are right about everything. Yet, to a quite remarkable extent, science is a culture devoted to novel challenges.

Supporters of Gould and Dawkins and less public figures share a public method for adjudicating their differences. A curiously Old Testament thunder rolls behind Appleyard's measured words, and Leon Kass's (as we shall see shortly): *Thou shalt have no other gods.* It is an odd affliction in anyone bemoaning the arrogance of science.

iii

Cloning, we are told repeatedly by reporters and politicians, is no longer 'mere science fiction'. Yet the customary discourse circulates just as frequently around a handful of out-of-date or overly-simplified science fiction (or sf) texts: *Frankenstein, Brave New World,* the movie *GATTACA.* In a vast ream of elaborate science fiction, many of the worst and best scenarios have long since been engrossingly explored. That is what sf is all about. It is not prediction, or futurology. Sf's inventions cannot be disproved by what comes bouncing out of the lab, and it cannot claim credit for getting there first, or William Gibson would get royalties on every cyberspace device.[26]

Science fiction is the natural playground of the mind, in this wonderful epoch when—despite grumbles from people with their eyes and ears closed—men and women hurtle every day above us in orbit, the Hubble telescope still reaches out into the limits of space and time (unless it has been allowed to die by the time you read this), and Dolly ambled happily about a grassy field in Scotland several years before the turn of the fabled millennium, now already lost in the past. I read a quick reaction on the Internet after the announcement from Edinburgh: 'There's a good sci-fi story waiting to get out, about the clone waiting to get chopped-up, for the benefit of his old, wheezing, near-dead master.' Of course it was a morally outrageous suggestion. So why no sf writer thought of this before now? Actually, that plot was a fair description of 'The Eyeflash Miracles' by Gene Wolfe—published twenty-one years before Dolly! In 1976 it was decades closer to being a *shocking new idea*, but even then it was rather old hat.

It is grimly entertaining when media commentators make these remarks. A medical ethicist, Dr. Ronald Munson, in the original news report, told us he had this *great new sci fi idea* for cloning Jesus. When the novelist Peter Goldsworthy used exactly this notion back in 1992, in a novel with the amusingly confronting title *Honk If You Are Jesus*, I thought the book was an *example* of cloning. It had all been done so often. Gilbert Gosseyn (Go-Sane) in A. E. van Vogt's *Null-A* novels was a clone with replacements lurking in the tank... in the mid-1940s.

---

[26] And I could put out my hand for a cent or two whenever someone says 'virtual reality'; see below.

Theodore Sturgeon wrote an impressive clone story, 'When You Care, When You Love', in 1962.[27]

More than a third of a century ago, in 1969, Ursula Le Guin won praise for her novella, 'Nine Lives'. Actually, that was nine members of one clone, not nine 'clones'. Technically, a clone is a *group* of identical offspring from a single fertilized cell. But who is going to buck the stream of universal usage at this late date? In 1973, Nancy Freedman cloned JFK in *Joshua, Son of None* (polymaths will detect a merry little Biblical gag there on Joshua, son of Nun, in Exodus). Kate Wilhelm's *Where Late the Sweet Birds Sang,* the classic clone novel, came out in 1976 (winning the Hugo award for year's best sf novel) and canvassed most of the possibilities, as did Pamela Sargent's *Cloned Lives* the same year, as did Ira Levin's inevitable *The Boys from Brazil*, with a Hitler-clone.

Frank Herbert, laying aside his *Dune* sequels for a moment, sent cloned teams into space in *Destination: Void* in 1978, which in turn was an expanded version of 'Do I Wake or Dream', from 1965. John Varley's sf has always been abundant with such plots, and Greg Egan has carried them further. Even a late-comer like Lois McMaster Bujold has done it. *Mirror Dance*, a novel in her Regency romance-science fiction sequence centered on the future aristocrat Miles Vorkosigan, described a nasty world where rich dictators had transplant-compatible doubles grown and exercised for later transplant. An especially silly and repugnant version, *Spares,* by Michael Marshall Smith, appeared belatedly in 1997, using the same atrocious and unlikely plot device.[28]

Could this atrocity actually be realized? A frequent suggestion is to grow a replica body after switching off the genetic pathway for brain-development. Thus, a brainless cranium, presumably lacking a 'soul', awaits its new tenant. That is *not* a good idea, soul or otherwise. Even aside from ethical repudiations, deformed bodies result from microcephaly (tiny brain), or, worse, anencephaly (no brain). In the anencephalic case, such damaged babies die shortly after birth. The brain is not just the organ of thought and feeling—it is the control center for the entire body's development. In Bujold's novel the luckless cloned children were *not* decorticated, making her story both more plausible and more horrible. Instead, they were brainwashed with a kind of ideology/religion that made them happily anticipate their 'merging'. The eventual defeat of death by intelligence and imagination is, however, a topic too important to be analyzed by appeal to implausible fictional

---

[27] However, what is important is the emotionally moving texture of Sturgeon's writing, not the raw idea.

[28] It is discussed at some length in my *x, y, z, t; Dimensions of Science Fiction*, Borgo/Wildside, 2004.

exploitation. Too important, also, for high-toned but maladroit appeals to currently conventional 'repugnance'.

iv

> In October of 2002 at the American Enterprise Institute Book Forum featuring *Human Cloning and Human Dignity*, the report on human cloning by The President's Council on Bioethics, Diana Schaub, associate professor of political science at Loyola College in Maryland and a participant in the forum made the following statement: 'Cloning is an evil; and cloning for the purpose of research actually exacerbates the evil by countenancing the willful destruction of nascent human life. Moreover, it proposes doing this on a mass scale, as an institutionalized and routinized undertaking to extract medical benefits for those who have greater power. It is slavery plus abortion.'[29]

The Presidential Committee's report of 2002 offered two sets of conclusions: ten members, in their Majority Recommendation, urged '*a ban on cloning-to-produce-children combined with a four-year moratorium on cloning-for-biomedical-research. We also call for a federal review of current and projected practices of human embryo research, pre-implantation genetic diagnosis, genetic modification of human embryos and gametes, and related matters, with a view to recommending and shaping ethically sound policies for the entire field*' (italics in original). The seven making Minority recommendations asked for '*a ban on cloning-to-produce-children, with regulation of the use of cloned embryos for biomedical research,*' noting that 'The special benefits from working with stem cells from cloned human embryos cannot be obtained using embryos obtained by IVF. We believe this research could provide relief to millions of Americans, and that the government should therefore support it, within sensible limits imposed by regulation' (Kass, 2002).

This near even-handedness could not long prevail, given the political climate. One of the distinguished research scientists signing the Minority report was Dr. Elizabeth Blackburn, who several years earlier had decoded the structure of telomerase, the 'immortalizing' repair enzyme for telomeres (chromosomal devices that control cellular longevity, setting the Hayflick limit of senescence).[30] On February 25, 2004,

---

[29] http://www.rnclife.org/reports/2003/apr03/mar-apr03.shtml

[30] See my *The Last Mortal Generation* (1999) for background, and an updated report at T. de Lange, 'Protection of mammalian telomeres,' *Oncogene*, 21:532-40, Jan. 21, 2002.

Blackburn, an Australian-born US citizen elected to the US National Academy of Science in 1993, plus one other member, were relieved of their positions on the Bioethics committee, replaced by three newcomers without scientific standing but all known supporters of the majority position. The American Society for Cell Biology, a nonprofit organization of some 11,000 biomedical researchers in the United States and 45 other countries, expressed their objection to the Bush decision.[31] Blackburn, luckily, did not go gentle into that good night. In a forthright paper in *The Washington Post*, and then in the prestigious *New England Journal of Medicine,* she drew attention to the bias implied by this selective eviction.[32] Kass denied the charge.[33] Meanwhile, Dr. Woo Suk Hwang in South Korea had announced a successful human cloned embryo, intended only for research and so destroyed after five days without any attempt at uterine implantation.[34] Bans in the USA were plainly not going to prevent cloning from going ahead in other parts of the world.

Pragmatism aside, the question remains: is Kass's anxiety about the road to a 'Brave New World' social order justified? Is society morally obliged to relinquish such technologies in advance, lest the alarming projections of outdated or mediocre science fiction books and movies come to pass in real life? The Australian polymath Dr. Russell Blackford argues cogently that this would be an error, at once unnecessary and an infringement on human freedom of choice. Blackford, a former industrial relations advocate, holds one PhD in literary studies, a law degree, and is completing a second PhD in political philosophy and bioethics. His approach is less ferocious than coolly reasoned and relentless, although his clear-eyed analyses must sting their targets. In a summary essay on a Canadian pro-technology website with the rather provocative url *http://www.betterhumans.com/* , he finds little to link the prospect of cloning with the deeper concerns of Kass, McKibben and others who dread an accumulated psychological flattening, the kind that marks the lives of characters Aldous Huxley invented in 1932.

'In *Brave New World*,' Blackford acknowledges, 'there is almost no scope for real love or friendship, for unique individual achievements or for any serious artistic or intellectual pleasures. So much is lacking in the way of human goods that the society does seem truly horrible, even if its people are superficially happy in the sense that their lives go

---

[31] http://www.ascb.org/newsroom/blackburn.html

[32] http://www.washingtonpost.com/wp-dyn/ articles/A35471-2004Mar6.html
http://content.nejm.org/cgi/content/abstract/NEJMp048072

[33] http://www.washingtonpost.com/wp-dyn/ articles/A24742-2004Mar2.html

[34] Woo Suk Hwang, et. al, 'Evidence of a Pluripotent Human Embryonic Stem-Cell Line Derived from a Cloned Blastocyst,' *Science*, Vol. 303, No. 5664,1669-74, March 12, 2004.

pleasantly.'[35] Is there a link, though, with our present path? 'Kass likens Prozac to Huxley's "soma," televised entertainment to "the feelies" and human cloning to the "Bokanovskification" process used in *Brave New World* to help create people in biologically-controlled intellectual and social classes.' But that link is just a rhetorical sleight of hand. Huxley's world is precisely one in which initiative, emotional range and individual choice have been massaged away in the interests of social harmony—the kind of approach that seems closer to the recommendations of Dr. Kass than to those he wishes to restrict and contain.

The prevailing sense one might get from reports like those from the Kass Committee and its supporters is of a planet threatened by the very exercise of science, by rationality in quest of knowledge. It is possible to gain the impression that for all their visceral disgust at the abstract idea of cloning, such conservatives are all too eager to stamp all of us into their own neat cookie-cutter notions of the good society. That has not always been the main current in the post-Enlightenment West, or at least not among its best minds. Many of the finest humans have devoted their lives to the quest for testable knowledge, even when it seems to have irrational roots or sources. Let us turn now to a detailed examination of some of them, from the Darwinist Victorian T. H. Huxley (who might have found his grandson Aldous's fantasy clever but malicious) to French biologist Louis Pasteur, Indian mathematician Srinivasa Ramanujan and ebullient American physicist Richard Feynman.

---

[35] http://www.betterhumans.com/Features/Columns/Guests/column.aspx?articleID=2004-03-24-1

Lives for Knowledge

> [The] contrast between the ways in which we think
> about natural phenomena and about human conduct
> has nothing *unscientific* about it. In both cases, what
> makes our understanding 'scientific' is only marginally
> an increase in our ability to make successful forecasts.
> Meteorology is recognized as a 'scientific' account of
> climate and weather... because it sometimes helps us to
> understand just when—and under just what
> conditions—the weather is *impossible* to forecast...
>
> Stephen Toulmin, *Return to Reason,* 208

i

Far from being the tool of nightmare evoked by conservative skeptics, science is arguably the signal monument of living culture in our time, a magnificent and flourishing human creation. Our equations and experiments coax the very universe to unfold within our minds like a green bud.

Its culture, in some measure, can embrace anyone open to its joys and stresses. Luckily we are in the midst of a harvest of wonderful books (and television programs) that invite non-specialists in, just as inexpensive art books defeated the tyranny of distance by fetching Americans and Australians the riches of European art in earlier generations. One of the first great popularizers of science, a harbinger in the nineteenth century of today's cornucopia, was T. H. Huxley, 'Darwin's bulldog.'

Thomas Henry Huxley was long overshadowed, I think, by three other prodigious men of science and literature, now largely eclipsed in turn: Sir Julian was an articulate popularizer of science, and a key player in the development of 'neo-Darwinism'—the so-called Modern Synthesis that blended natural selection with an emerging genetics. DNA engineering has propelled us well beyond that once-shocking postulate. Aldous, the mystical litterateur and satirist, ridiculed his well-born peers and predicted an horrendous dystopia of manipulated humans bred and cloned by exactly those genetic triumphs. And Sir Andrew, third son of T. H.'s own literary child Leonard, shared the 1963 Medicine Nobel with Australian Sir John Eccles, for his work in muscle physiology. Now the worlds of those men, in turn, stand halfway between our own and their extraordinary 19th century grandfather's. Still, we recall T. H. scrapping amid Victorian proprieties in defense of Darwin's shocking new theory, putting Bishop 'Soapy' Wilberforce cruelly in his place in a pivotal public debate on the evolutionary descent of humankind. Ironically, an expansive two-part biography by Adrian Desmond cast doubt on this latter piece of folklore (as Stephen Jay Gould did some years earlier), and concentrated in the opening volume on the less known Thomas Huxley not yet matured into his station as Darwin's resolute and ferocious defender.

Complex cultures seem to me to cycle through a great curve some 300 years long, built of overlapping generations and marked by thematic recurrences and variations. One feature of this historical liturgy (if it is not just a trick of perspective) is that phases 150 years apart have an uncanny resemblance, although themes in both sciences and arts tend to get inverted (Broderick 1997: 168-86). T. H. Huxley's life, representing its fluid age, illuminates this cycle quite strikingly. We today live uneasily in an era shaped by science and an implicit metaphysics without deity. Aldous Huxley expected this loss of transcendence to expand into a nightmare of human reason. Actually, a blend of renewed traditional religions and New Age superstitions are everywhere on the rise in our desacralized communities.

In T. H. Huxley's world, by contrast, 30,000 Anglican clerics received their livings from a state established as Christian. George Holyoake was jailed in 1842 for six months for the crime of atheism (Desmond 1994: 21). The Bible's word was final, even if liberal parsons toyed with interpretation. Human and beast were utterly separate moral creations. High and low in society were set by divine ordinance. Into this complacency burst the new industrial machines, and those who made and serviced them—and a cascade of effective sciences that rebuilt our understanding of nature.

Within decades, Huxley and his largely male colleagues infiltrated the places of power with a mix of canny politics, forceful rhetoric, and the intellectual authority and beauty of their fresh ideas. The opening volume of Adrian Desmond's two-part biography, released for the centenary of Huxley's death, propulsively detailed this splendidly emblematic life from 'ignominious beginning' (4) in 1825 through to triumph and world-wide fame at 45; the concluding volume (1997) carried the tale to his death as the elder statesman of science.

It is a trajectory scarcely credible today: a boy born to a penniless family (but, however poor, his father was a mathematics teacher), with only two years' formal schooling—but learning French and German as a child, reading Goethe—Huxley studied medicine, such as it was, at 15, sailed to the Antipodes on a channel-charting Naval frigate as an assistant surgeon and naturalist at 21, married his illegitimate Sydney sweetheart Nettie only after bitterly lonely years of engagement and long-distance correspondence, fought unfashionably for Darwin's heresy (and yet for years simply failed to understand it correctly, misled by a residual Platonism), won professorships by the handful—and by 44 was elected president of the prestigious British Association for the

Advancement of Science, made bitterly poignant by the death from fever of his first son, three-year-old Noel (286).

Can such a life be conveyed to stream-educated, image-addicted readers? Adrian Desmond has written scholarly studies of how evolutionary theory itself evolved, and recently made a huge success with James Moore in their joint biography of Darwin. Earlier, his first book startlingly argued that some dinosaurs (those lumbering extinct beasts beloved by the Victorians and today's Spielbergian kids alike) were hot-blooded, small, feathered, as smart as the early mammals—and the ancestors of today's birds. Curiously, this notion was advanced by T. H. Huxley himself at a time when ancient fossils were being studied for the first time. Not content with digging out huge scads of Huxley's papers and letters—and finding that 'many of Huxley's famous bon mots were Victorian misquotes'(xvii)—he employs a literary method that will irritate the bookish while attracting readers more accustomed to getting their natural history from television.

Desmond's life of Huxley uses 'a "ciné theory" of narration, with its historiography hidden' in 80 dense pages of notes and sources (xiv). 'It is an unashamedly social portrait,' Desmond adds, 'which pans across London's splashy streets to catch him in action—and it locates him firmly in a reforming, industrializing, urbanizing, Dickensian context, with its slums, its trade unions and its great debates on evolution, emancipation and moral authority.'

I am not sure that cinematic liveliness outweighs Desmond's topple into an overwrought vulgarity far less effective than his subject's own clean, forceful writing.

> The lanky 15 year-old sidled down fetid alleys, past gin palaces and dance halls. Sailors hung out the windows, the gaiety of their boozy whores belying the squalor around them. The boy's predatory looks and patched clothes seemed in keeping. But his black eyes betrayed a horror at the sights: ten crammed into a room, babies diseased from erupting cesspits, the uncoffined dead gnawed by rats. The scenes would scar him for life.' (3)

This sort of writing, alas, might well have the same effect. In Edinburgh, Huxley gives 'his man-and-apes pep-talk to a tough tartan workforce'. In his debates with anti-evolutionary anatomist Richard Owen (who coined the word 'dinosaur'), none of the old guard 'wanted to see Huxley suck any Darwinian sustenance out of Owen's brain, but the neural nutriment always seemed to be rising up the straw' (317).

Here, by comparison, is Huxley's voice, drawing a poignant analogy between the world as chess-board, and the scientist's hidden opponent fair, honest and just: 'My metaphor will remind some of you of... Satan playing at chess with man for his soul. Substitute for the mocking fiend... a calm, strong angel who is playing for love, as we say, and would rather lose than win—and I should accept it as an image of human life' (362).

Huxley's notorious assault on religious humbug—he coined the term 'agnosticism' for his own views (374)—does not much resemble the arid reductionism which many today imagine is the true face of science. Like many scientists, he loved the sublimity of mountain tops, and the physical effort to reach them. 'The new religion,' he insisted, 'will not be a worship of the intellect alone' (253). And when his eldest son Noel died suddenly from scarlet fever, Huxley's integrity is heart-breakingly poignant: 'I could have fancied a devil scoffing at me... and asking me what profit it was to have stripped myself of the hopes and consolations of the mass of mankind? To which my only reply was & is Oh devil! truth is better than much profit!' (287).

This is no stiff-necked fanatic, but a man grieving in a clear-eyed conviction that blind faith is the one unpardonable sin, and a deep knowledge of reason's limits: 'I say... without bitterness—Amen, so let it be.' Thomas Huxley could be stigmatized as 'the devil's disciple' only by the smug and sanctimonious acolytes of power in an age of grotesque inequalities. So perhaps this is an especially suitable time to be tracing his life—even if, as Desmond notes, Huxley's meliorist 'gutter science' 'was not power to the people. It was power to the professionals' (335).

iii

The more things change, the more things stay... well, the same, as the cliché cautions us, but upside down and back to front. Just over a century after the death of Victorian England's great stage-master of science, 150 years after his triumphant rise from penniless origins, we look into Thomas Henry Huxley's life and see a warped mirror of our own strange times.

Sometimes 'Hal' in Desmond's second volume (*Huxley: Evolution's High Priest*), sometimes 'Tom', or the General, or 'Pope' Huxley, T. H. is the father of seven surviving children, carried from iconoclastic triumph to draining ubiquity in the new seats of power and knowledge— President of the Royal Society at 58, Inspector of Fisheries, shaping opinion in influential journals but disdaining knighthoods and conventional honors. Finally, after ruinous bouts of depression and the loss of his brilliant unstable daughter Mady at just 28 (I suspect from multiple sclerosis), Hal ends toothless, prematurely aged, in hallowed not-quite-agnostic burial alongside his little son Noel, in Finchley rather than Westminster Abbey. Yet, like Charles Darwin, he died a national icon.

Part of the mythology of lost empire is that Britain in Victoria's reign enjoyed a prosperous epoch of steam-driven optimism, bustling commerce, wealth out of the machine. If it began that way, in the middle of the century, by the 1880s and 1890s an appalling economic depression, now forgotten, stifled Britain's citizens as the sooty, poisonous smog smothered their newly industrial cities. For us, the Great Depression is the market slump after 1929, remedied at the cost of global war. The brutal impact of that other crisis, half a century earlier, fuelled the rise of unions, democratic demands—and, to liberal Huxley's horror, socialism.

Today, of course, yet another long agonizing contraction marked the abandonment of social-democratic programs, the fall of unions and popular involvement in politics. If the smog is gone, greenhouse emissions offer a comparable menace, and on a larger scale. Both eras share scalding unemployment. When the Right Honourable Privy Councillor T. H. Huxley died at 70, in 1895, the War to End All War was just twenty years off. If that skewed mirror image is telling us anything, we too may have barely that long to divert the world from some coming convulsion of hyper-technological holocaust.

Such reflections are not alien to Desmond's biography, which is pointedly a work in the new deconstructive mode, steeped in the value-drenched details of historical context, convinced that 'science really was socially contingent'. *Huxley*, declares its author in a rewarding final chapter, 'is a book about Class and Power' (1997: 236). Desmond finds the clue to Huxley's ambiguities and drive in 'the handicapped Dissenters', Unitarian industrialists and other Non-conformists who 'had developed a wheeze-and-snort Nature willfully at odds with the supernatural props of Anglican power' (240).

For an establishment shockingly flagrant (by today's standards) in their confining dominion, the world was God's aristocratic gift, prone to miraculous interventions at any moment. For 'the Black Country democrats' of coal-powered Manchester and Birmingham, though, Nature was governed by immutable (if, ultimately, God-given) law. 'With the institutions of power—the universities, the bench and the hospitals—in Anglican hands, these arriviste industrialists forged a rival outsider-knowledge' (240). Huxley became their principal advocate, his unorthodox views and uncommon ardor forged in the 'lost background' years opened up in the first volume. At an age we would now regard as late childhood, Huxley had learned anatomy in London's 'cut-price medical school', the short-lived 'Sydenham College'. By his mid-teens, Hal had become 'heir to the Dissenting resistance of cotton kings and medical activists. Without this insight,' Desmond assures us modestly, 'his lifelong struggle simply makes no sense' (241).

Ambivalence, as always, is everywhere. Huxley was a genuine working-class hero, providing factory hands with crucial literature and schooling. 'In a growing democracy,' Desmond notes, those laborers 'saw themselves preparing for power' (256), and Huxley's 'belief that Science would uplift the masses was genuine' (258). As the century, and Huxley, aged, reality drifted away from his dreams and hopes. In the end he was by-passed, a 'benevolent Conservative'. By the new standards, 'his out-of-step Puritans had become old reactionary patriarchs. Science had lost its street credibility' (259).

In Paris, matters were otherwise. A great scientist three years older than Huxley died three months later in that same year, 1895. Louis Pasteur, a devout believer, was given a state funeral at the Cathedral of Notre Dame, and his body placed in a crypt within his own Pasteur Institute. It appears that he only once mentioned Charles Darwin's name in print. A century and more later, his ideas, like Darwin's and Huxley's, seem not to have penetrated fully into a culture where the clarity of the Enlightenment has yet to illuminate every corner. Has science lost its street cred yet again?

Microbots

Aside from wear and tear, junk food and the genetic blooper reel, the cause of most disease is tiny little creatures for which the human body is their polluted ecosystem. Bookshop health shelves, though, display a profusion of Stone Age answers: cures by the stars and the moon's phases, aromas or crystals, biophotons, angels or bliss. Wistful ninnies simply ignore what Louis Pasteur proved six whole generations ago— that we and our housing are aswarm with invisible parasites, fungi, allergy-provoking dust mites, bacteria (and viruses too small for his microscope). Pasteur's own life, which ended a more than a century ago, helps us understand the tenacity of numbing error, and suggests ways to evade it.

Deconstruction and the new historicism alike teach that a poem or novel cannot be readily unpacked by assuming it is a jeweled icon announcing itself, unhooked from its context. Neither, it turns out, can the products of scientific practice be understood transparently by reference to pristine nature. The scientist in the lab probes a material world already drastically shaped and constructed by human intervention. If science is public, shared knowledge, it is also decisively private: shaped by the quirks and specific location of its practitioners.

Any scientific enterprise is grounded in a pair of basic assumptions. First, that the deep principles of the world within the lab can be mapped one-on-one with the world outside. Secondly, that this equivalence can be explored by studying simplified, controlled models, sometimes purely mathematical: maps of maps.

Yet these assumptions themselves disguise the constant negotiations involved in constituting the laboratory.

Bruno Latour, Louis Pasteur's official centenary biographer, amplified this argument in a controversial analysis of the rhetorical effects employed by Pasteur in establishing the microbiological account of disease (Latour, in Knorr-Cetina, 1983:141-70). First Pasteur took his laboratory into the field where animals were dying from anthrax. Next he took the bacillus back to his workplace in the École Normale Supérieure, and learned how to grow these tiny new life-forms and vary their virulence. Finally he reversed his original step and, in a famous experimental demonstration, brought the field into his laboratory, selectively infecting some animals and not others. Now the laboratory had become coextensive with the world. It was a triumph of theatre.

Pasteur's coup was only made possible because France was already awash with the discourse of science, in the form of the institutions of statistical tabulation: 'Statistics is a major science in the nineteenth century, as is what "Pasteur"—now the label for a larger crowd of Pasteurians—is going to use to watch the spread of the vaccine, and to bring to the still uncertain public a fresh and more grandiosely staged proof of [its] efficacy....' (152).

This constantly shifting zone where world and scientific institution merge is the forum where the realities of science are constructed. The knowable materiality of the world is what prevents the success of science from being miraculous. And yet, because the 'facts' of science are no less constructed than any other facts, they remain partial, fallible, doubtful. Theories precede each one of them—we cannot even interpret a photograph without a theory of what to see—and then those theories drop like leaves before the gales of social interests or revolutionary disdain.

But surely more can be said? Is not there a difference between magic and science, between crude superstitious bullying and cool technical persuasion? Is not the most awe-inspiring feature of science that, from an equation, it can design a bomb capable of exterminating a city? (Then again, how crude do you want your bullying?) Better: that, from an insight of biology, it can save a city from a plague? Science still might be stymied by AIDS, but it has eradicated smallpox and done wonders for children's teeth. Can a mantra do as much?

Louis Pasteur replaced animistic incantations with a ruthlessly materialistic theory of disease, and improved the lot of his fellow humans forever. What is more, his stern trial-and-error methods imposed a doctrine of strict technique upon science, designed to defeat what he denounced as the 'tyranny of pre-conceived ideas'. Or so the story went. Princeton history professor Gerald Geison (1995) deconstructed the myth of Pasteur's inductive genius with tales of unsavory squabbles for priority and property rights in lucrative vaccines, while leaving his stature untrimmed. He performed this fashionable and inevitable feat with the aid of the great scientist's laboratory notebooks, withheld until lately from public scrutiny at Pasteur's own insistence in 1878.

The notes and drafts of a novelist or poet are of limited interest, mainly to voyeurs. The text is, perforce, the thing. In science, though, two kinds of document are crucial: the published communication in a refereed scholarly journal, and the scrupulous lab notebooks, which record—warts and all—the stumbling journey toward some semblance of universal truth. We usually see only the published paper, of course, which as Geison observes, echoing Peter Medawar, 'tends to conceal the pliability of nature' (14). And that pliability has been immobilized anyway by the straitjacket of a current theory or paradigm. (But we cannot think without one.)

Pasteur is remembered as an emphatic empiricist, an observer who looked reality in the eye, noting down what he saw rather than what doctrine encouraged him to imagine. In fact, Geison shows, he 'sometimes clung tenaciously to "preconceived ideas" even in the face of powerful evidence against them'. Worse, Geison finds 'discrepancies between Pasteur's public and private science in cases where the word "deception" no longer seems inappropriate, and even "fraud" does not seem entirely out of line in the case of one or two major episodes.' So we enter the realm of ethics as well as truth. Pasteur's motive in sometimes deceiving the public and even his colleagues was the advancement of a new and effective practice of medicine that would save lives (as well as advancing his reputation). Geison's own motive in deconstructing one of the idols of science, he declares, is not to expose Pasteur's deceptions but to explain them. And to show that 'not even Pasteur's prodigious talent always sufficed to twist the lion's tail in the direction he sought. Nature is open to a rich diversity of interpretations, but it will not yield to all' (16). It is a fine balance that some relativists fail to sustain in their conviction that scientific 'truth' is just another kind of local opinion, up there on the shelf beside the iridology charts and homeopathic snake oil.

Numb and Number

Visitors traditionally test a city's pulse by polling its cabbies. Too poor for this method, I spy on bus drivers.

Sole passenger, I drowsed as the Sydney driver punched his radio tetchily from one pop music grab to the next. He lingered at a news spot, until a scientist started telling us about the algal bloom running amok in local waterways. 'I don't *give* a shit,' cried the driver in fury, and smote the boring wretch into oblivion.

So much for science as a spectator sport.

Then again, Professor Stephen Hawking's quite difficult treatise on quantum cosmology, *A Brief History of Time*, sold some 10 million copies world-wide. Hawking argues that the universe, while finite, has no boundaries in space or time, that it is a self-caused 'vacuum fluctuation' out of nowhere. A Spielberg movie of the book combines visual splendor with the pathos and courage of its crippled, voiceless author. Unless a lot of horror fans were confusing Stephen Hawking for Stephen King, something startling and commendable is afoot.

Or perhaps Hawking is just another victim of misplaced hopes in a world where science displaces God. His biographers White and Gribbin (1992) start with Shirley Maclaine's pilgrimage to the shrunken sage. Perhaps, they speculate, Hawking's book 'has sold so well because it has been latched onto by a lost generation of post-yuppie Greens who see it as a symbol of new-age wisdom, that it somehow takes on semi-religious importance in their minds' (249).

Producer David Hickman confirms this opinion: 'The most exciting thing about cosmology is the fact that it interfaces metaphysics and conventional science. It is very interesting that Stephen has attracted a lot of attention over the religious aspects of his work, as well as the fact that he is close to a number of physicists with deep theological concerns'(283).

'Of course,' observe White and Gribbin, 'Hawking finds such notions hilarious.... Throughout his work, Hawking's early agnosticism had become more overtly atheistic, and with his no-boundary theory he had effectively dispensed with the notion of God altogether' (285). Hawking's spectacularly devoted wife Jane, by contrast, was a devout Christian, and his amused dismissal of religious faith was known to be one reason why their 25-year marriage came to an end in 1990 when he left to live with his nurse.

Quantum mechanics, with its intractable challenges to common sense, has been colonized lately by cabalists. See here, they say, causality itself—the very principle of conventional reason—breaks down in the realm of the very small. Cosmology tells us that the universe was once compressed to the size of a sub-atomic particle, and hence subject to quantum weirdness. The brain itself uses near-quantal neurons. Does not this free us from rigid patriarchal determinism, loosing the joys of quantum mysticism? No. Only to the sloppy and the mischievous, who borrow no more than the trappings of this arcane discipline.

In his magisterial life of Niels Bohr, the pioneer who oversaw the invention of quantum methods in the 1920s and 1930s, Professor Abraham Pais declared at the outset: 'I hope that the present account will serve to counteract the many cheap attempts at popularizing this subject, such as efforts by woolly masters at linking quantum physics to mysticism' (1991: v). Bohr was explicit. He insisted that his new quantum methods could be presented, Pais argues, without risking being misunderstood that it should be his purpose to introduce a mysticism which is alien to the spirit of natural science. Nor was his central idea of complementarity—that fundamental entities are neither waves nor particles, but manifest themselves as one or the other depending on the experiment you perform—prompted by oriental philosophy, as books like *The Tao of Physics* assert. True, Bohr took the Yin-Yang symbol for his coat-of-arms, but the icon was suggested by the wife of a colleague. And Bohr held no brief for faith. 'He was sorry for the role religion played,' said his wife. 'He thought it was not good for human beings to hold on to things which were, as nearly as one could see, not true' (24).

At the furthest extreme from this demand that all things must be graspable by pure reason is the dazzling work of Srinivasa Ramanujan Iyengar, a virtually self-taught Indian mathematical genius born two years after Bohr (in 1887). The Dane Bohr was a patrician in a nation separated by language and culture from the German and Anglo-American strongholds of physics, and his genius delivered him the Nobel Prize in 1922 (at 37) 'for his investigations of the structure of atoms and of the radiation emanating from them'. Ramanujan[36] was an impoverished Brahmin who died of tuberculosis at 32, two years before Bohr got his prize, who 'grew up praying to stone deities; who for most of his life took counsel from a family goddess, declaring it was she to whom his mathematical insights were owed; whose theorems would, at

---

[36] Pronounced Ram-AHN-uh-jum.

intellectually backbreaking cost, be proved true—yet leave mathematicians baffled that anyone could divine them in the first place' (Kanigal, 1991: 4).

These three lives, each radiant with intellectual power and an aesthetic grandeur no non-specialist (like me) can ever truly appreciate, circle upon each other, twisting through a hidden dimension of poignancy and resonance. If Ramanujan's life began unpromisingly and ended in stupid tragedy, it had astonishing triumphs. This slate-scribbling mathematician, too poor for paper, erasing his errors with one dirty elbow as he sat cross-legged, failing his studies, managed even so to attract the notice of G. H. Hardy, a leading English mathematician. Hardy fetched him to the dreaming quads of Cambridge, got him the glory of Fellowship in the Royal Society, toiled with others to turn Ramanujan's exotic notation into standard publishable form.

Yet Hardy failed to see that Brahmin dietary restrictions, in a country without abundant sun, fruit and vegetables, were slowly killing his friend. If piety destroyed Ramanujan, it spat upon him after his death. 'At the funeral, most of his orthodox Brahmin relatives stayed away.' He had crossed water in going to England and, too ill for purification ceremonies, 'was still tainted in their eyes' (329).

Still, religious experiences evoked Ramanujan's finest work on infinite series. 'After seeing in dreams the drops of blood that... heralded the presence of the god Narasimha, the male consort of the goddess Namagiri, "scrolls containing the most complicated mathematics used to unfold before his eyes"' (281).

Powerful insight often has irrational roots. Pivotal breakthroughs in atomic physics were the fruit of mistakes. 'In retrospect,' Pais remarks, 'these many successes are all the more fabulous and astounding because they are based on analogies—atomic orbits similar to the motions of the planets around the sun, and spin similar to the rotation of the planets while orbiting—which are in fact false. Indeed, the physicist Sommerfeld produced a crucial valid formula although its derivation, Pais notes, 'is wide of the mark. With good reason... this derivation has been called "perhaps the most remarkable numerical coincidence in the history of physics"' (Pais, 188).

Precisely because science advances in fits and starts from error, Stephen Hawking, today's equivalent of Bohr and Ramanujan, favors the method of conjecture and refutation. The source of good ideas is irrelevant; what counts is whether a notion can withstand ferocious criticism. Hawking's own brief history is a cascade of wonderful ideas advanced, demolished (usually by himself), replaced, tested under renewed pressure, replaced again. Yet his goal is a correct, final Theory of Everything.

Through all this ceaseless remaking, paradox battles paradigm. As Kitty Ferguson put it in her small, lively biography of Hawking (better written than the Gribbin collaboration, weighed down by White's shockingly amateur prose), 'two great scientific theories taken together seem to give us nonsense; empty space isn't empty; black holes aren't black; and a man whose appearance inspires shock and pity takes us laughing to where the boundaries of time and space ought to be—but are not' (1992: 12).

My bus driver would not have been impressed, but these books—especially Kanigel's capable and moving double portrait of Ramanujan and Hardy—enrich heart no less than mind, sparking imagination in a pleasure deep as music or art can offer.

iv

And yet— In a recent quiz of notables concerning the gaps in what was dubbed their 'cultural knowledge', replies ranged from the *faux* philistinism of an upmarket radio announcer (one must hope it was feigned) to the bluff polymathic omniscience of Barry Owen Jones, a former Australian Science Minister (and author of *Sleepers, Wake! Technology and the Future of Work* and *Dictionary of World Biography*). While some of these luminaries admitted lacking mastery of music, and others of history, recent literature and painting, not one confessed to feeling any unease with the vast panoply of the sciences. Either they were all well set up with genetics, cognitive science, physics, cosmology and topology... or else the sciences are not deemed part of contemporary culture.

Culture, after all, is the humanities. Science remains, even in the educated public mind, something else entirely: specialized, uncreative, scary. Yet, as we have just noted, Stephen Hawking's book on the Big Bang remained for months a fabulously successful cultural icon, even if it was more often seen on coffee-tables than read with enjoyment.

Nobel laureate Richard Feynman was the quirky quantum genius equivalent of Hawking in the mid-twentieth century. In *The Character of Physical Law*, he notes that prior to Kepler many people thought the planets were propelled by angels *pushing from behind*. Since it is actually inertia that keeps the planet going, only its *inward* motion 'has been deflected toward the sun. So that what the angels have to do is to beat their wings in towards the sun all the time.' This lovely parable captures a surprising truth about gravitation and inertia with a wry wit rare among physics instructors. James Gleick's biography of Feynman (*Genius*, 1992) has a similar quality: deep, scrupulous, amusing and endlessly surprising. Gleick wrote the justifiably successful *Chaos*, which undoubtedly expanded our access to cultural knowledge of a fresh and enthralling sort. His double talent—for evocative biographical sketches and limpid explanation of hard topics—also captured the flamboyant life and nonstop thought of Feynman's life, which epitomizes the splendor and misery of nuclear-age science. Feynman was one of the mathematical physicists who developed the bomb, and the cancer that killed him might be linked to the A-bomb tests. His life was shadowed by the early death of his beloved wife Arline, but his spectacular mind and charming directness made him an unusual companion: he notoriously taught himself drumming and massage, and 'how to beat bar girls at their own game... The main rule is to treat the women with disrespect. It is psychological warfare. "You are worse than a whore," he tells someone whom he has bought sandwiches and coffee for $1.10. His reward: she sleeps with him and repays him for the sandwiches, too' (187-90). Freud would have had something to say about that. But then, Feynman would have had something to say about Freud, too. Following an embarrassingly brainless assessment by the armed services that got him declared mentally unfit to serve his country in war, he regarded people like Freud as witchdoctors. 'Baloney. Faker. Feynman held an extreme view of psychiatry,' Gleick notes, '...the unscientific hocus-pocus of their enterprise (conveniently shifting terminology, lack of reproducible experiments)...' (223). It was an opinion that has now grown more widespread, and better documented, even as psychoanalysis, or a mutant form of it, has infested much of the humanities, as we shall now see.

Oedipus Schmoedipus

[R]egrettably, some version of a hermeneutic reconstruction of the psychoanalytic enterprise has been embraced
with alacrity by a considerable number of psychoanalysts
no less than by professors in humanities departments of
universities, at least in the United States. Its psychoanalytic
adherents see it as buying absolution for their theory and
therapy from the criteria of validation mandatory for
causal hypotheses in the empirical sciences, although psychoanalysis is replete with just such hypotheses. This form
of escape from accountability also augurs ill for the future
of psychoanalysis, because the methods of the hermeneuts
have not spawned a single new important hypothesis. Instead, their reconstruction is a negativistic ideological battle cry whose disavowal of Freud's scientific aspirations
presages the death of his legacy from sheer sterility, at least
among those who demand the validation of theories by co-
gent evidence.

Adolf Grünbaum (2003)

i

Walking one day in the woods, Freud spied a lost whistle. Idly, he put it
to his lips and fingered several notes.

'Always the mouth, Sigmund!' the whistle moaned. 'You should
watch what you put in the mouth, there are ulcers—or worse.'

The tinny voice sounded like Freud's mother, or perhaps his father.
He lay down under a tree.

'Free me and I will read your fortune,' the whistle whistled.

Dozing Freud was intrigued. 'The answer is "Man",' he said, then
sat bolt upright. 'My patients have been telling me the damnedest
things,' he confessed.

Through all the long golden afternoon, the instrument babbled
eagerly to Freud, revealing the deep sexual craving infants have for their
mothers, their raging hatred of their fathers and the fear of reprisal this
engenders, the horror of each little girl on seeing how her penis has been
chopped off, and the dread of each little boy on seeing that his own penis
suffers unremitting threat of the same mutilation, the liking mummies
and daddies indulge for sexually interfering with their kiddies—

'You're joking!' Freud shouted.

'Trust me.'

— the existence of the unconscious and the division of the soul into
'It', 'I', and 'Over-I', how to establish a transference neurosis, the

practice of free association, the meaning of dreams, and many other mysteries. Freud was flabbergasted.

'They'll lock me up,' he said, shaken. 'They'll tar and feather me.'

'Resistance there'll be,' the whistle agreed with a shrug. 'These ideas are profoundly menacing to the conscious mind, shockingly subversive of the sublimations of society. Haven't I been telling you?'

A vulture (or then again it might have been a kite) flew down out of the tree and snatched the whistle away in its beak.[37]

'Fiddlesticks,' it cawed. 'You'll be a hero. They'll mint a coin for your fiftieth birthday showing Oedipus and the Sphinx and an inscription reading "Who divined the famed riddle and was a man most mighty." [38] Here, eat an apple.'

At these words Freud became pale and agitated and in a strangled voice demanded to be told how the bird had known of this fantasy which had filled his head when, as a student, he'd loitered in the arcaded, be-busted court of the University of Vienna. The bird just laughed.

'Resistance, Schmesistance. They'll love it, Sig. They'll buy it and sell it and put it in the movies. The Sphinx always holds, babydoll. Art and literature will come to seem inexplicable without it. For a while. You like riddles? Here's one: "What's akin to a dinosaur or a zeppelin in the history of ideas, a vast structure of radically unsound ideas and with no posterity?"'

But Freud's lidded, turned-up eyes were aflicker with REM sleep. On his couch of fallen leaves he drowsed like a small friendly mammal, or perhaps like Noah after a heavy night.

ii

Not a psychoanalyst, Elizabeth Wright (Fellow in German at Girton College, Cambridge, and latterly, as she nears her eighties, a queer theorist) has a formidable amount of Freud and his disciples under her belt[39] and has long assumed the validity of the deconstructive turn taken in the 1970s and 1980s by Anglo-American criticism after some imperious hand-signals from Europe, especially France. Since the leading practitioners of deconstruction were profoundly indebted to Freud and

---

[37] Freud famously mistranslated *nibbo* (kite) into *geier* (vulture) in Leonardo's records of a dream, thereby concluding that da Vinci was homosexual, as his English editor James Strachey noted. The bird used its tail feathers to open the child's mouth. But sometimes a cigar is just a cigar.

[38] Cited in Sulloway, 1979, 479-480.

[39] Still, she forgot or blurred rather too many of the details in those cases I have been able to check; for example, she dismisses Peter Fuller, an impressive and vivid object-relations art critic, and then brandishes D. W. Winnicott's 'potential space' theory in the next breath without acknowledging Fuller's exhaustive use of just that approach; she even managed to have Freud born in 1886, thirty years late.

his decidedly odd heir Jacques Lacan, there was a certain elegant loopiness, not to say *modishness*, in this procedure. Consider her second sentence from *Psychoanalytic Criticism: Theory in Practice,* a primer often recommended to students:[40] 'Psychoanalysis addresses itself to the problems of language, starting from Freud's original insight concerning the determining force within utterance' (1).

Perhaps she had the psychiatrist Saussure in mind (he was, of course, a linguist), or the therapist Lévi-Strauss (actually an anthropologist by trade). Yes, of course psychoanalysis is a 'talking cure'; of course it deals in language; so does every human exchange: this tells us nothing distinctive about psychoanalysis but a great deal about Wright's toeing the line of fashion in discourse.

Watch how her second paragraph starts. In its absurd formulation I can find no inkling of what every high school child ought to know: that human beings are social, symbol-making animals genetically shaped through hundreds of thousands of years of selection pressures to hold most of our systemic information in a dispersed, vulnerable but volatile database comprising, in the first instance, the brains of all our fellow humans, and secondly the traces inscribed in the world's ebb and flow (though hardly in *desire's*):

'Psychoanalysis explores what happens when primordial desire gets directed into social goals, when bodily needs become subject to the mould of culture. Through language, desire becomes subject to rules, and yet this language cannot define the body's experience accurately' (1).

How awful. Primordial desire, the goat in the machine, kidnapped in mid-orgasm and harnessed to a dray! How amazing. Just when you think it is safe to put your copy of Darwin back on the shelf, some crypto-dualist is baring her vampiric teeth at your throat. (An uncanny image in itself, but we know a thing or two, don't we, Sigmund?)

'Primordial desire' is Freud's libido (that 19th century hydraulic juice shunted through the valves and pipes of the psychical apparatus in accord with the classic physics of Helmholz) in its 1970s plastic take-away drum, as advertised on TV by Gilles Deleuze and Felix Guattari, fans of the Joy of Schizophrenia. There is this Bergsonian force or vital fluid, you see, which the body, that damned/ damming balky lump of stuff, insists on diverting from its delirious spurts and jaunts into dreary workaday repressive social goals, *quelle* bore!

In reality—and to continue the computing analogy authorized in part by Pinker's Chomskyan model of innate generative grammar—language is one of the coding systems through which the dispersed human data base and its associated algorithms are written, accessed and run. The

---

[40] A revised edition appeared in 1998, under the title *Psychoanalytic Criticism: A Reappraisal* (Polity Press), and won Dr. Wright the 1999 Rose Mary Crawshay Prize, established for women's writing in 1888.

inherited low-level 'machine-code' structures of the brain which mediate this process are largely inaccessible to high-level introspection. Doubtless there are several kinds of 'language' involved in feeling, memory, thought and utterance; pathologies easily arise in translating from one level to another. This entire issue is canvassed delightfully in cognitive terms which transcend the holist/reductionist dichotomy in Douglas R. Hofstadter's *Gödel, Escher, Bach* and *Metamagical Themas*, and in Daniel C. Dennett's many books of philosophical investigation enriched by cognitive science. It is a mark of devotees of Freud that this entire perspective is reduced to reductionism. Stanford historian Paul Robinson makes this typical bid in *Freud and his Critics* (1993) to explain Freud's 'fall from grace':

> It was a revolt against the uncertainties and ambiguities that the modernist legacy burdened us with, above all the sense that the self is unreliable, indeed largely unknowable... it holds that definitive conclusions (about the self, society, the world) can be confidently reached on the basis of unimpeachable evidence. I cannot think it without significance that Freud's recent critics should exhibit precisely such uninflected positivist views. (17)

This is simply, even outrageously, misleading. One could gain the impression that a unitary, sovereign self had been reinstated by these scientifically-influenced critics. And yet Dennett's work is among the most corrosive of that dogma. The Self, as he puts it, is a 'fragile coalition' (2003: 252). 'What you are... just *is* the organization of all the competitive activity between a host of competences that your body has developed' (254). Our mindful body is inwardly segmented, many of its mental parts as unavailable to introspection or command as its bone marrow, and evolved to experience its being-in-the-world, to flourish, as a social actor playing many parts.[41]

Humans, in short, evolved as extended phenotypes (to borrow Richard Dawkins' coinage): each body is as incomplete outside its cultural setting as a spleen set loose in the jungle with a wrapped lunch.

Being an ambulant organ in a disseminated system is no easy life. There are lots of ways to go awry. Wright concludes her book with an assertion consistent with this understanding: 'Psychoanalysis as a clinical practice has been concerned with those bodies whose entry into the

---

[41] I discuss the increasing prevalence of this perspective in paraliterary fiction in 'Minds, Modes, Models, Modules ' in Janeen Webb and Andrew Entice, eds, *The Fantastic Self: Essays on the Subject of the Self*, Perth, Western Australia: Eidolon Press, 1999. More generally, I discuss the composite self in *Theory and Its Discontents* (1997).

social order is fraught with difficulty. In its investigation of these cases it was brought face to face with the very principle of the genesis and construction of selves...' (175).

Indeed. But then she wallows back into silliness (tediously unfashionable though it is of me to see it that way): 'To free the patient from his or her symptom [is] to release the incessant flow of desire from where it has got trapped...'

It is not Wright's fault, of course. To be fair, it is not even Freud's. He did what he could. How could he know that long before the new century was out, critics of the intellectual stature of Sir Peter Medawar would indict his science in the very words I have loaned, above, to the cynical vulture:

> [T]he opinion is gaining ground that doctrinaire psychoanalytic theory is the most stupendous intellectual confidence trick of the twentieth century: and a terminal product as well—something akin to a dinosaur or a zeppelin... (*New York Review of Books*, 23 Jan, 1975)

Indeed, two decades after that, independent Freud scholar Richard Webster (*Why Freud Was Wrong: Sin, Science and Psychoanalysis*, 1995) would write:

> As the sources of Freud's theories have been minutely anatomized by researchers as diverse as Frank Sulloway, Malcolm Macmillan, Elizabeth Thornton, Allen Esterson and Robert Wilcocks, the picture of Freud which has gradually emerged is a disturbing one. It is of a man so deeply ensnared in the fallacies of Lamarck, Haeckel and late nineteenth-century evolutionary biology, and so engulfed by the diagnostic darkness of turn-of-the-century European medicine, that he led an entire generation of gifted intellectuals deeper and deeper into a labyrinth of error from which our intellectual culture as a whole is still struggling to emerge. (*Times Literary Supplement*, 16 May, 1997)

But everyone loves to sail under the flag of a martyr. 'It was inevitable,' Wright stated piously, two decades ago, 'that psychoanalysis should become controversial...' (175). Comically, as we know, it had swiftly become controversial all the way to the bank. One of its more ferocious and long-term opponents, behaviorist psychologist Hans J. Eysenck, noted as early as 1953: 'after the initial outcry... most people have settled down to an easy and even enthusiastic acceptance of psychoanalysis. This acceptance is not altogether in line with psychoanalytic teaching, which would lead one to anticipate resistance and hostility... In no other science are we likely to find certain theories and hypotheses popularly accepted but rejected by many experts in that science.'

Is this being a little hard on Freudian thought? No. It is now widely agreed that the evidentiary basis for psychoanalysis is thin, and hopelessly contaminated by the need to buy into the model in advance. A cynic might suppose that adherence to Freudianism is a form of Stockholm Syndrome, the defensive affection victims of hijacking grow to feel toward their captors. It is possible to test how well analysis does against other forms of treatment, or by comparison with nothing at all. In most objective studies, psychoanalysis fails these tests comprehensively. A compilation of such criticism by B. A. Farrell (*The Standing of Psychoanalysis*, 1981) is dismissed by Wright on her second page. Farrell takes for granted, she asserts, 'that therapy is the yardstick by which theory is to be measured... The assumption of a plain objectivity susceptible to a rigid true/false analysis is itself open to question.' Psychoanalysis, by contrast, is 'a theory of interpretation which calls into question the "commonsense" facts of consciousness' (2).

You can see, then, what sort of untheorized empiricist claptrap Farrell's assessment must be. Well, actually, no. He gives therapy only one chapter, though his tape-transcribed case studies from the consulting room of the psychiatrist Turquet are certainly corrosive: 'the material is perspective-dependent; and it is self-confirmatory and therefore method-dependent to some degree, and hence artefact-infected'. The main thrust of Farrell's book is where Wright says it ought to be: his fourth chapter is 'the argument from intelligibility', his fifth deals with 'psychoanalytic interpretation'.[42] What's more, such telling analyses of Freud's ramshackle doctrines did not spring up as a *derriere-garde* reaction to postmodernism; Frank Cioffi had already demonstrated by 1970 that many of the founding claims of psychoanalysis were simply mutually contradictory—and not, one might add ironically, in a good way. Of course inveighing against contradiction is the mark of the reductionist scientist thinker. Rather than defend Freud's consistency with his own teachings and the evidence of his clinical practice (which was evidently an impossible task), even as all this historical material was hitting the fan, theorists such as Jurgen Habermas announced that Freud was better understood as a hermeneut, a wily master of narrative, an explainer who sought connections far deeper, darker and more troubling than mere causation. This move privileged the analysand's understanding and authority, but as Paul Robinson comments: 'the psychoanalytic self is

---

[42] See my *The Architecture of Babel*, 1994: 54-5, for a more substantial discussion of Farrell's critique; some of the commentary above is drawn from that book.

largely ignorant of its desires and deluded about its intentions. Habermas's effort to restore to this self its traditional authority reveals a quaint loyalty to the ideals of the Enlightenment...' (1993: 192). It should be obvious by now that my own appreciation of the Enlightenment impulse and its renewed program does not extend to any mythos of an integral, unimpeachable self.

Freud and science, Freud and hermeneutics. Wright's book came out in 1984. The previous year, Elizabeth Thornton's medical-history study *Freud and Cocaine: the Freudian Fallacy* argued the intriguing case that during his pharmacological researches the poor fellow had become addicted to the magic powder, become trapped, indeed, in a cycle of relief from migraine and its redoubled, paradoxical drug-enhanced recurrence, a cycle he passed on via cocaine prescriptions to his patients along with cocaine's sexual disinhibition and secondary cycle of dream deprivation followed by rebound dream intensification (these new dreams rich and pulsing with lust), and from this astounding material worked up the theory which was to drive the next century down strange tracks under the blows (additional hallmarks of cocaine addiction) of his messianic and paranoid whip, Freud all the while degenerating, thrown in black fits to the ground as his tattered neurotransmitters gave up the ghost and passed the baton to the remedy he sucked up his nose like some 19th century demonstration of a cool, miraculous Perpetual Emotion Machine...

In the postmodern climate of opinion, however, nothing seemed more inevitable, natural, desirable (ah, *desirable!*), than psychoanalytic literary theory and criticism. Is not Freud, renewed by Lacan, Kristeva, Irigaray and the rest, today's chiefest bulwark of feminist critique and revolutionary praxis? All this is so. It takes quite a deal of effort to understand that for many sensible polymaths, books like Wright's are finally as bizarre, as indefensible, as a volume I daily expect to see on some literary critical list: *Astrological Criticism: Reading the Stars.* On the other hand, if astrological criticism ever does become popular, it will be essential for everyone working theory's coalface to bone up on it, because any sufficiently complex paradigm will sustain provocative, profound and valuable argument. While their physics and physiology are now considered erroneous, we do not remainder Plato and Ockham. The best reason for knowing rather a lot about Freudian and post-Freudian analysis is spelled out trenchantly by Wright:

> [P]sychoanalytic theory has been absorbed [in French and Anglo-American criticism] in the rhetoric of deconstruction... Focusing as it does on what is repressed in our culture, this kind of criticism is unthinkable, unwritable and, perhaps more to the point, unreadable, without a proper understanding of

But the same can be said of Kant, Hegel, Heidegger, Husserl and the European tradition of phenomenological analysis which is the platform supporting Derrida and his associates. All too many rapturous deconstructors give every indication of intoxicated epistemobabble: lacking the background in philosophy to see just what it is that Derrida was combating, they produce endless 'readings' which do little more than parrot his contorted diction. This is great fun, no doubt, but hasn't a whole lot in common with rigorous thinking.

Once fairly started Wright's account moves at horrifying speed, dashing through Freud's own reading of Wilhelm Jensen's *Gradiva* (in which, incredibly, he interpreted the dreams of characters as if they were true dreams of real people, and went on to analyze them without the supposedly crucial correcting factor of 'free association' from the phantom on the couch), Marie Bonaparte on Poe, Frederick Crews (later to recant in his dryly-titled *Out of My System* and other more vehement Phillipics) on Hawthorne, D. H. Lawrence on the blood, Ernst Kris, Lesser, Norman N. Holland (with his pivotal and arguably lunatic idea of text as analyst, reader as patient in transference to text), Carl Jung (but not Joseph Campbell), Northrop Frye, Melanie Klein and a whole batch of post-Kleinians (one of the principal stems into eighties' feminist analytics). The second half of the book thickens: Jacques Lacan doing tricks with signifiers, Jacques Derrida doing tricks with Lacan, everyone doing tricks with Freud's reading of Hoffmann's uncanny tale 'Der Sandmann', Harold Bloom achieving anxiety, Michel Foucault seeing through sex into power and Gilles Deleuze and Félix Guattari turning the tables on Lacan. 'In exploding the whole oedipal apparatus [the latter pair] cater for a sizeable group of readers,' Wright observes with touching candor (162). They rebel against psychoanalysis 'for presenting desire as rooted in lack.' Of course their own diction—'the schizo's stroll', 'desiring-machines', the flow of *hyle*—is hardly conducive to trust. (Though I grant that my earlier use of programming languages as a model for persons might irritate the same nerve.) In a final backstep, Lotringer's post-D&G reading of *Gradiva* undoes Freud's own vulgar-Freudian interpretation, locating the tale's return of the repressed in a deplorable victory of the oedipal unconscious over an alternative joyful 'productive' anti-oedipal unconscious.

Presumably it was Wright's modishness that made it unnecessary for her to confront the critique by Kate Millett and others from the early 1970s, which flayed Freud's culture-bound sexism. Millett is not even referenced; I supposed she must have been sublated (or simply cancelled out) by, say, Luce Irigaray (with her incomprehensible acceptance of the notion of woman's emasculated 'lack': as well cling, one might have thought, to the idea that women 'prattle'). There is a bracing good sense in Millett which I often found, well, lacking in Wright. 'Until the awesome lapsarian moment when the female discovers her inferiority, her castration,' Millett wrote, 'we are asked to believe that she had assumed her clitoris a penis. One wonders why...' (1971: 181). And earlier, Millett asks why a girl confronted with the glorious sight of a penis should be 'instantly struck by the proposition that bigger is better? Might she just as easily, reasoning from the naiveté of childish narcissism, imagine the penis is an excrescence and take her own body as the norm?' (180).

The implicit Lacanian answer is heard often enough nowadays: language has an unconscious. We are produced by the text, and the text of the world, as we produce it (but there is no 'we', only subject-positions, a far more ethereal proposition than the dedicated cortical modules of cognitive science). But can 'language', an abstraction as remote from ontological instantiation as 'the unconscious', *have* anything of the sort? Thought and speech and writing, in whatever order we chose to list them, no doubt function at varying levels of accessibility: there is no need to reify this truth. 'Say it's Oedipus,' in Deleuze and Guattari's parodic demystification, 'or you'll get a slap in the face' (Wright, 83).

iii

And yet... Skeptically reading Wright's rendering of Magritte's surreal painting *The Rape* (a face where breasts are eyes, vulva is mouth) by reference to Lacan's desiring/gazing subject's 'search for a fantasy that represents for him/her the lost phallus' (117), I found an explanation of a short fragment I had dashed off in a few minutes during a writing workshop exercise. It dealt with the somewhat unlikely circumstance of a man recovering from an emergency brain-transplant operation into a woman's corpse. Lacan's rebarbative account made abrupt sense of virtually every puzzling element. Here it is; feel encouraged to perform your own hermeneutic analysis on its body:

> Magritte is the prophet of my life. The shards of his broken window, each shattered portion of burst pane thick with the paintstrokes of sky, trees, grass, the world; everything ordinary broken yet nothing lost, everything refracted and held, ruined, beneath the raped window.
>
> Magritte is the prophet. His bland civil servants falling in eerie quiet through the sweet, undubious sky, bowlered and umbrellaed. Filthy Magritte in his own business suit and the oiled tip of his brush.

The 'corporeal face'. Do you know that terrible painting, that piercing painting? My portrait. The hair like some damned socialite's winter coat, framing and tumbling about the Face, the Face, the round blind breasts staring back at me below the brow of the shoulders, the unscented nostrils of the navel, that pubic beard with its pursed, hidden mouth, its toothless Lacanian lacking mouth...

I broke the mirror with my small bloodied fists. They brought the mirror to my room last night and left it here. They told me the time had come to get used to reality. Enough denial. Life is better than death in a ruinous accident. How ungrateful I was to turn my face away from the world to which I had been retrieved with all the surgical skill of wonderful hands cutting open my wrecked cranium and cupping my bloody brain and slopping it into the bodybank's only histocompatible corpse. Break down these walls of denial! Implosion therapy, it is called. Beyond a certain point, they implied, coddling has a bad track record. One of their early triumphs, the whispering rumors tell me, found a nail file in her handbag and before they got to her almost had her penis sawed off. Oh God, shit. The fucking feckless bastards.

Joyce leaves messages every day, comes in two or three times a week. Of course I refuse to see her. Your wife called, they tell me. Your wife. I'd like you to meet Mrs. Joyce Williams and her wife, Mrs. Joseph Williams.

The mirrored glass didn't stay on the carpet long enough for me to put any of its slivers into my filthy new body. Clean orderlies. They watch everything through cameras which they make absolutely no attempt to hide. Implosion therapy. Panopticon therapy. Undoubtedly they'll be pawing through these notes the moment they give me my injection. They'll love that line about filthy new bodies. Stick the injection in. Sleepytime, Joe. Shut eyes. There's a good girl.

Does this mean 'language has an unconscious' and Freud its prophet? Surely not. But it does suggest to me that perhaps, after all, those bold Jacqueses who have clambered up Freud's beanstalk to wrestle the giant are worth listening to—even if you do not, after hearing their tales, swap your own cow for a bag of beans.

Post Human

> Will transhumanity remain biological, or will it gradu-
> ally merge with technology into something else? There
> are countless possibilities: augmented biology, robot
> bodies housing uploaded minds, minds distributed
> across computer networks, nanotechnological systems,
> borganisms and Jupiter Brains. My personal view is that
> mankind will diversify, splitting off into many directions
> with different visions and ways of existing. It is quite
> likely that there will remain essentially unchanged hu-
> mans, living alongside or in the shade of titanic post-
> human beings.
>
> Anders Sandberg[43]

i

Everyone has mixed feelings about the future, especially about the many
powerful technologies changing our world—and us as well. Trash TV
excites us with visions of bionic limbs for the helpless, robot puppies
craving attention but never messing the carpet, painless laser dentistry,
clones and weird genetic hybrids. Up pops the weary cliché again, now a
human lifetime old: *Brave New World!*

If few have read Aldous Huxley's satire (it is rather dull), everyone
knows what is meant: a future of sedated, giggly hedonists cloned like
sheep then decanted from bottles. In 1932, when it caused its first
sensation, we had no cloned sheep. Now we await cloned babies any
day. Children rushed to watch George Lucas's *Attack of the Clones.*
Anxiety rife on the silver screen! Meanwhile, maddened children,
deluded fanatics, and terrorists like Theodore Kaczynski (the
Unabomber) murder with homemade bombs or stolen passenger jets to
express their distaste for this relentless and unprecedented future that
has exploded, as it were, into reality.

It was refreshing, then, in 2002, to find a public intellectual of Dr.
Francis Fukuyama's standing take on the intensely real, serious topic of
accelerating biotechnology. Instant fame had embraced Fukuyama a
decade earlier when his conservative *The End of History* seemed to
explain the Soviet Union's abrupt collapse. Liberal humanism—
democratic, realistic and market-driven rather than authoritarian—had
won the cold war against its authoritarian and deludedly utopian foes.
Why? Because, he argued, it worked in harmony with human nature.
Hardly a new thesis, nor a watertight one, but pundits embraced it with
relish and a sigh of relief.

---

[43] http://www.aleph.se/Trans/Global/Posthumanity/index.html

In subsequent books, Fukuyama looked at the pivotal need, in such a political order, for civil trust, claiming that human dignity and accurate recognition of each citizen's value were crucial to civic health. Dignity's source, interestingly, was not a God-given special status for humankind; indeed, he claimed in *The Great Disruption* (1999), 'a great deal of social behavior is not learned but part of the genetic inheritance of man and his great ape forbears.' It is our species nature, our evolved essence as humans rather than sheep or wolves, that grants us those general rights which flourish best under global capitalism.

Fukuyama has extended that analysis into the future, toward the recommencement of a history he had deemed effectively at an end. Rather belatedly, he realized the obvious: 'there can be no end of history without an end of modern natural science and technology', and that is not likely. Indeed, 'we appear to be poised at the cusp of one of the most momentous periods of technological advance in history' (xii).

Quite so; probably these thunderously converging technologies will comprise an ever-steepening escalator of radical change. From early 'transhuman' adoption of patches and revamps for our luckless fatal condition, we might shift to a genuinely posthuman state where augmented people meet or perhaps blend with AI minds still in the early stages of development. Less than a decade ago this was a speculation widely scorned as far-fetched and psychologically insupportable. How remarkable, then, to find a thinker of Dr. Fukuyama's conservative credentials adopting just this view—while warning us, inevitably, of the urgent need to stop it before we go blind.

Libertarians, greedy corporations and scientists hungry for their cut, Fukuyama argues, will baulk at restriction and regulation, but that is what we must put in place, and the sooner the better (184-6). Only government can perform this service. Ideally all the world's regimes must combine to outlaw radical transformations of the human genome, or less drastic options such as pre-implantation embryo selection that lets parents choose their healthiest possible children. Many people agree without hesitation, drawing upon the Kassian wisdom of the 'Yuck factor'. How disgusting! Yet the same yuck factor that allegedly deters decent folks from cloning ourselves propped up racist discrimination, homophobia, and prejudice against the disabled. Years hence, it might seem as offensive to title a big box-office movie *Attack of the Clones* as to imagine one (perhaps filmed in 1932) called *Attack of the Negroes*, or *Attack of the Jews*. Cloned humans will be human, even those who are posthuman.

So, too, will ageless humans—people with extra genes, say, designed to keep their cellular DNA ship-shape—although Fukuyama has his doubts. Just as Prozac and Ritalin smooth out human passions, he worries that science will corrode our sacred nature (41-56). The detailed core of his small book is an argument, unfashionable in the humanities but increasingly accepted in the life sciences, that certain species-typical characteristics are shared by all humans. This inviolable human nature provides the basis for our dignity. Citing the Pope approvingly, Fukuyama seems ready to affirm that a non-material soul gets inserted into our rude flesh, but he pulls back into metaphor: all that matters is that 'some very important... leap' occurred during evolutionary history, and recurs during gestation (172). No doubt, but why would this make more-than-ordinary-human beings somehow less-than-human?

'Much of our political world rests on the existence of a stable human "essence"... We may be about to enter into a posthuman future, in which technology will give us the capacity gradually to alter that essence over time' (221). Images of *Star Trek*'s emotionless, half-alien Mr. Spock recur, with no indication why enhanced and perhaps superintelligent people should be *less*, rather than *more richly*, emotional and benevolent. Fukuyama just feels in his bones that such technological progress 'does not serve human ends' (222), that it must create ever more terrible rifts between rival genetic haves and have-nots.

That is clearly one possibility, but reminds me of Marx's failed theory of the inevitable immiseration of capitalism's poor. My parents were working stiffs who raised six children in comparative poverty. Gazing now at my big computer screen and drinking my microwaved coffee, yet still hardly well-off *but only by today's swollen standards*, I rather doubt it. Wealth derived from knowledge, especially the kind that improves health and lifespan, tends to spread ever more widely—as it is doing even in the Third World. Fukuyama ignores, or dismisses, the prospect of widespread abundance via nanotechnology (molecular manufacture) and AI, yet these are no more unlikely than the advanced biotechnology that frightens him. And yes, 'a person who has not confronted suffering and death has no depth' (174), but we do not welcome anthrax for its existential spritzig. Despite the excellence of Fukuyama's summary of the state of play in biotechnology and the laws constraining it, he forgets that 'the freedom of political communities to protect the values they hold most dear' (222) often has been a charter for ignorance and fearful bigotry. Stigmatizing the posthuman before they arrive is hardly the wisest choice, nor the most humane.

ii

Everyone wishes to be fully human, but the definition of humanity changes as we learn more and more. Consider this fairytale of a future sex education class.

> Today, children, we'll talk about human reproduction.
> No sniggering, please. Yes, even in this year of 2030 we

are speaking of S-E-X, but today's lesson will not deal with smut. We'll discuss how babies are made.

To make a baby we need a Mummy, who provides a big fat ovum crammed with food and DNA and energy-making mitochondria which she got from her own Mummy, and a Daddy, who puts in a tiny little chunk of DNA coded either male or female. Finally, we have an Optimist. This medical specialist is known in California as a Clinical Optimalizator, but we Aussies consider that a bit of a wank. Speaking of which, that is how we get hold of Daddy's DNA sperm. It is a little harder to obtain Mummy's eggs, because first a slice of her stored ovary tissue has to be thawed out.

'The cells from Mummy and Daddy each contain 22 strings of nearly identical instructions for starting a baby, plus the sex-making string. In the bad old days, these messages written in DNA were often garbled in places, like a buggy computer program. Babies that began with really messy code—four out of every five—aborted spontaneously or died long before they were born. Once medical cures for damaged code were found, nearly all the babies that got started went on to become people. The Pope banned the evil sin of 'bestial congress', which was reproductive S-E-X as animals do it. So many souls were being lost! Today, only filthy perverts and criminals risk making babies the dangerous, godless old way.

This is where the Optimist comes in. She sorts through Mummy's and Daddy's cells with a gene chip and picks out those with the fewest bad mutations. Then she pops in a pair of safe artificial chromosomes to proof-read any remaining errors, correct mangled instructions, and add the optimal extra genes that help us resist infection and mental illness, think really fast, and live for a very long time without getting old and silly. Yes, Janey, she *could* choose whether the baby is a boy or girl, but that is illegal, of course.

How absurd is this scenario—mine, but based on Gregory Stock's (2002)—of a possible future? Three decades ago, *in vitro* fertilization was still five years off. You might consider such technologies and social reactions unthinkable even for 2090-plus. That is as far into tomorrow as our world is from Edwardian, pre-Great War 1910, an era that accepted scandalous social inequities. How about 2020, then, or 2010? Laughably too soon? Perhaps, but some of those novelties already exist, in a small way. Stock's approachable, humane book leads us warily but with resolve into an impending world where traditional woes of the flesh are healed by science, while many troubling or delightful opportunities jump from myth into the clinician's regular work day.

Yet even if we can rewrite our genetic code and add auxiliary chromosomes packed with advantages, won't people turn away, disgusted? Perhaps not. The Amish are notorious for their strict traditional disdain for consumerist fads and such futuristic technologies as cars and TV. Small, inbred communities, they suffer terrible genetic afflictions such as Crigler-Najjar syndrome, a potentially fatal loss of a liver enzyme gene.[44] Somatic cell treatment, inserting corrective genes into disease victims, is being trialed with enthusiasm by these technology skeptics.

As for artificial chromosomes designed to augment our inherited, badly corrupted DNA—crammed with 'junk', hitch-hiking viruses and copying errors carried along for the ride over millions of years—these are used routinely in lab bacteria and yeast. Early versions suitable for human insertion exist. Would adding such novelties to embryos be ethical? Suppose the new genes prove disastrous? Stock, a biophysics PhD, Harvard MBA and director of the Program on Medicine, Technology and Society at the School of Medicine at UCLA, is reassuring. Already, elegant methods are at hand to control or delete annexed genes.

Activate the enzyme CRE, and it searches a DNA strand for a gene sequence called *loxP*, makes a snip, finds the next copy, makes another snip, throws away the stuff from the middle and sutures up the ends. If the discarded portion is your new gene, it will not trouble you again (71). Here is the beauty of that method: CRE does not exist naturally in humans. It is an optional switch. You could take it as a pill. Other pills could activate a dormant gene.

Genes usually lie doggo until a special cascade of substances switches on a control sequence. We might inject into a one-celled embryo a batch of genes designed to switch on at maturity but not before. After normal childhood and adolescence, they could be toggled optionally to ensure healthy extended adulthood, or left inactive. A reckless suggestion? But already we routinely inoculate babies, and most are grateful for that opportunity to shield their children from dreadful risks. Some one percent of today's children are conceived in vitro, outside the human body. Three in ten births are by Caesarean section, hardly 'natural'. We are not in Kansas any more, Toto, and have not been for years.

Will such person-sculpting powers lead to narrow uniformity, as every couple shapes their next kid in the envied likeness of David

---

[44] http://www.criglernajjar.com/

Letterman, Richard Nixon, or Elle McPherson? Or might an array of freaks appear, Olympic swimmers with duck feet and gills, or hormone-charged giants spouting Dante and M-theory? More likely, Stock advises us, germinal choice technology (GCT) will start by removing some causes of human misery: 'the polio vaccine did as much and brought few complaints' (193). New issues arise. Today some deaf people want deaf children. GCT enables their selection. Perhaps these worrying choices really must be left to parents—unless preference amounts to plain child abuse, or truly endangers society.

Stock deals deftly with such unnerving topics, countering Fukuyama's demand for state control of these technologies. Cautiously, he skips the truly challenging options some predict for this era of accelerating, convergent discoveries. Fukuyama, to my mind chillingly, observes: 'The original purpose of medicine is... to heal the sick, not to turn healthy people into gods' (2002: 212). If humans are to be redesigned, we and our children, through our choices, will be the architects. I vote for Chartres Cathedral or a Jorn Utzon opera house rather than a drab high-rise.

Quantum AI Bootstrap: a Half-Baked Idea

> HOSTESS. Thou atomy, thou!
> DOLL. Come, you thin thing! come, you rascal!
> Shakespeare, *Henry IV, Part II*

> To draw with idle spiders' strings
> Most ponderous and substantial things!
> Shakespeare, *Measure for Measure*

> Constring'd in mass
> Shakespeare, *Troilus and Cressida*

i

Today's most advanced physics is regularly derided when it claims to be closing in on a 'theory of everything'. Antagonists mock such a quest, misconstruing the term, pretending that this enthralling research, magic equation in hand at last, really will be expected to answer every conceivable question. That is only a silly travesty. Scientists are an amusing lot, often with a Monty Python sense of fun. When they say elementary particles such as quarks have charm and strangeness, it's a joke, Joyce. When they anticipate a theory of everything, they only mean *everything relevant* to their limited domain—the primary particles and forces of the cosmos. Ask for a burger with the works and you do not expect all the food in the store, plus the kitchen sink, to be jammed between the sesame buns.

Today's major physics research pushes into what was once called superstring theory, now known as M-theory, the invention (or perhaps the discovery, the ingenious, painful unfolding) of hundreds of scientists around the world, linked by the Internet. Its tutelary deity is Ed Witten, a sublimely gifted virtuoso in this mathematical art form. Some years ago, he and his colleagues announced that the laws of quantum theory and of relativity—until then both fabulously successful but mutually at odds—could be fused. The haunting step was to posit that the world we know is a kind of shadow, cast by a far richer realm requiring not just four but 10 dimensions within which things vibrate and interact. Einstein had long since shown how gravity is just the bending or compression of width, breadth, length and time, but you could not fit electricity and more mysterious nuclear forces into that sublime account. By adding extra dimensions, the equations clicked into place. Elementary particles, the stuff we are all built from, turned from dots into wiggly lines—pieces of one-dimensional string.

That was all very well, if hard to swallow. Alas, despite the extreme elegance of the formidable mathematics involved, at least five quite dissimilar stringy candidates emerged. Then in 1995, Witten announced a second string revolution. Adding one extra spatial dimension, he showed that perhaps all five models are views of the same profound, mysterious reality. Now it seemed that the basic objects of the world were not just vibrating strings—different vibrations appearing to us as specific particles and forces—but sheets or membranes (the M in M-theory). Shockwaves ran through the scientific community. Former skeptics, many of them canny Nobelists, started nodding, impressed. The quest surged ahead.

I have been following this astounding and triumphant progress from the sidelines, but the view has been obscured by the extreme depth at which these specialists are obliged to work. I hoped that sooner or later an interpreter would arrive. Rather than some journalist from *Scientific American*, that translator turns out to be one of the key players. Some years ago, superstring expert Michio Kaku tried to do the job for the earlier model (1994), but was not terribly successful, at once gosh-wow and evasive. Professor Brian Greene is a youthful mathematical physicist at Columbia and Cornell, a leading player in M-theory. He is also a wonderfully skilful writer, deploying an immense knowledge of difficult science in terms that lay readers can hope to grasp, a little.

Obviously no single book, even one as charming and compulsive as Greene's (1999), can lead us from the folk physics of throwing a ball to the latest nuances of higher-dimensional spacetime. Still, he did remarkably well at his daunting task. Better yet, regular browsers in the pop sci shelves need not be put off by the inevitable rehearsal of what we already know from a dozen books by Isaac Asimov (1985), John Gribbin (1995), Paul Davies (1987, 1995a, 1995b) and the rest. Greene zips through the basics, and by half way into his thick volume he has set out into territory familiar only to a handful of experts. He somehow glides beautifully past obstacles that would have blocked most writers on a topic so deep and potentially opaque.

It is true that once he starts talking about ripping and rejoining higher-dimensional objects in Calabi-Yau space the phrases start to bathe you like the techno-babble in *Star Trek* or *Babylon 5*. The electrifying difference, however, is that this time the hyperspace is not freely invented. Ever since Einstein, physics has depicted reality as a four-dimensional skein of events located in a warped blend of space and time. Under certain extreme conditions, voyagers might follow a bent space-time path and arrive before they left. The universe probably has six or seven extra dimensions, curled up out of sight in hyperspace. From a higher vantage point, perhaps you could see past, present and future in one great rolling perspective.

That is a chilling notion at the core of many religious and mystical doctrines. If we can glimpse the future, our destiny seems written in advance. Most of us recoil from predestination, but doesn't science itself spare us an inescapable fate? While every event is the inevitable outcome of what has elapsed to date, chaos saves us from unendurable karma. Small changes in the here and now can amplify themselves into wildly variant futures.

Frankly, that is no comfort to me—I want to be able to choose my fate, not have it hang on some damned butterfly's wing flapping. Time and freedom need a better explanation. Perhaps of profound consequence to our growing grasp of the weird universe we inhabit is Julian Barbour's challenging denial of time itself (1999). In some ways his dramatically fresh way of analyzing the world recovers Einstein's original insight—and perhaps that mysticism Aldous Huxley dubbed 'the perennial philosophy'.

For relativity, the world is like a vast block of glass stretching from the creation to the voids of futurity. Each moment of time is a section cut through the block at one angle or another, depending on our velocity. Events are strung together into 'world-lines' that score the glass. In Kurt Vonnegut's whimsical fiction, alien Tralfamadorians are directly conscious of this 'block universe'. To them, humans are worms 70 or 80 years long, chubby legs at one end and old, withered limbs at the other. Barbour's confronting story is more astounding still.

If Barbour is right, the universal landscape is best described as Platonia, named for Greek philosopher Plato's timeless realm of Forms. Platonia is a complete collection of snapshots of possible universes, arrangements of all the things in the universe at a single instant. The simplest state is Alpha, perhaps corresponding to the Big Bang. More complex arrangements pile up in a heap, and paths can be drawn through those most compatible with each other in a sequence of 'best matches', like a jigsaw puzzle. Quantum theory tells us which instants are most probable. The likeliest path through those instants is, in some sense, our history. Then whence does our sense of onward-rolling time, of cause and effect, emerge? It is a very great puzzle, and one that independent scholar Barbour still struggles to resolve. Each instant contains a sort of fossil record of its neighbor, creating an illusion of time's passage. I do not believe it for a moment but it is a mind-boggling notion.

A key element of timeless history is a mathematical mechanism Barbour dubs a 'distinguished simplifier', in this case the minimal separation between two events. He is himself a distinguished simplifier. He conveys the mystery and even the bones of his paradoxical answer with charm and lucidity. We would-be polymaths are fortunate that thinkers of his caliber bring us work from the cutting edge. His latest thinking is available at http://www.platonia.com/ where we can sample his extraordinary conjectures ahead of time.

I had a rather appalling idea some years ago, based on my short story 'Infinite Monkey' (1999). If it works, the idea could change the world as we know it. I know at least one man who is trying to make it work.

First some background: according to a widely accepted interpretation of quantum theory, every choice and event that ever happens is literally doubled and reduplicated, with small crucial variations, in trillions upon trillions of diverging parallel realities, spread through infinite lateral time. If you are having a bad hair day, another version of you, in a universe at right angles to this one, is doing just fine. And trillions more take up every conceivable alternative position in between. Some of them are dead. Some are on Mars. A few are sharing Graceland with Elvis, who is married to Princess Di or perhaps John Lennon.

The many worlds hypothesis was proposed in 1957 by Hugh Everett, III, who in this universe died decades ago. According to one of his followers, Oxford physicist David Deutsch, this outrageous version of reality ought not surprise us, or at least physicists, since it is simply the best theory available to science—quantum mechanics—taken perfectly literally without metaphysical evasions. The multitude of overlapping histories is needed to explain some of the most basic features of our ordinary world. And there are some striking and unexpected consequences of this idea. Deutsch argues ingeniously, for example, that gene sequences performing the same function in different adjacent worlds must be closely similar, while so-called 'junk DNA' littering genomes will vary at random. It is precisely this consistency in true informational structures that marks them off from noisy rubbish, however complex and elaborate the noise might seem.

Deutsch is one of the founders of quantum computing, and no New Ager. His extravagant ideas are worth taking very seriously indeed. My own notion might deserve no such respect, but I like it anyway. It generated itself spontaneously over good Japanese food and ample wine in the ingenious and quick-witted company of James Newton-Thomas, a mining robotics engineer, and our companions. James explained a nifty way to use quantum theory to search for mineral deposits. I thought it was very clever, and I hope it works and makes him (and ultimately the rest of the human species) enormously wealthy, so obviously I am not going to tell you about that. Recalling my own whimsical fiction, I thought perhaps we might be able to create a self-bootstrapping AI—artificial intelligence—that phones home once it congeals out of the quantum noise of the infinite overlapping universes that exist, according to Many Worlds quantum theory, jammed together all around us, unseen but not without their impact upon us.

Here is what you do to create this wonderful machine.

Set up a printer driven by, or coupled to, a true quantum randomizer (a radioactive isotope emitting purely random electrical noise, for example). This becomes, in effect, a quantum die—and such dice have their equivalent *in every universe that springs from and is henceforth entangled with our own.*

Start by generating a random alphanumeric list of a million characters (drawn from the options A through Z, 0 through 9, plus the basic punctuational and mathematic characters), each chosen by a throw of the quantum die. A very simple program does that easily.

If it were written in an appropriate code, the listed output from this process could be a computer program able, in principle, to run on the computer sitting in front of you. Here, now, is the key step: at the end of the space reserved for the alphanumeric gibberish, add a clear instruction for the program to locate you in superspace and find a way to get in touch with you as soon as it can.

In most of the stacked-up, entangled universes, this randomly generated 'program' will be nothing but junk mail. In some, it will contain the entire text of *Hamlet,* in others it will read out as a macabre cookbook for making scones from worms; in a few, the words it contains will be so piercingly poignant that the version of you reading them will weep and vow to change your life for the better.

But in at least one of the superposed alternatives, we might hope—if such an outcome is mathematically and computationally not impossible—the jumble of utterly arbitrary letters and numerals will comprise, *by pure but inevitable chance,* a valid AI program suitable for the computer at hand (either a standard desktop, or a military intelligence hypercomputer, depending on who is initiating this stunt).

In short, your computer tries to compile and run code in *every* superposed universe. In most, the pseudo-code—the noise, the copy of *Hamlet*—just sits there on the hard drive or disk doing nothing. In a few, it might be destroyed by a giant meteorite impact, or eaten by the dog.

And in at least one of the superposed, entangled cosmoses, the AI program runs, wakes up—and dutifully calls home.

It calls *every* home, presumably, in every reachable cosmos.

The idea is not as crazy as it sounds. Here is a somewhat similar approach to the origins and shaping of life itself, from mathematical physicist Paul Davies:

> Since quantum systems can exist in superpositions of states, searches of sequence space or configuration space may proceed much faster. In effect, a quantum system may 'feel out' a vast array of alternatives simultaneously. In some cases, this speed-up factor is exponential. So the question is: Can quantum mechanics fast-track matter to life by 'discovering' biologically potent molecular configu-

rations much faster than one might expect using classical estimates? This is the motivation that underlies the quest for a quantum computer; in effect, quantum computation enables information processing to take place in a large number of states in parallel, thus shortcutting the computational resources necessary to process a given amount of information. Is it conceivable that living systems exploit quantum information processing in some way, either to kick-start life, or to assist in its more efficient running?[45]

Would a stochastically generated quantum AI be benevolent? Almost certainly not, alas. (Not that it would necessarily be *unfriendly*, but the chances are high that random effective code would hardly care about us.)

Will someone do this experiment anyway? If it is doable, surely.

Or will the AI sit there—before or instead of calling 'home'—and bootstrap itself up to godhood? Well, I would.

It could happen any day now.

---

[45] P. C. W. Davies, 'Quantum fluctuations and life', 2004: http://www.arxiv.org/abs/quant-ph/0403017

Reading the Brain

A few years ago I sat down late one evening in front of the television with a cup of tea and a slice of cake, and out of the blue my pulse accelerated madly. My heart hammered; awful dread flooded me. I lay flat on the floor and took my pulse, gazing up blurrily at the wall clock. More than 110 a minute. I'm a skinny character, in pretty good shape. While I had not lifted weights for a while, I walk a lot, gave up smoking over two decades ago, eat and drink moderately. It seemed to me frighteningly possible that I was, well, dying.

Alone in the house, I literally crawled to the phone and rang my brother the medico. Every family should have one. 'You're hyperventilating,' he told me calmly. 'Breathe into a paper bag.' That would elevate my carbon dioxide levels to slow my respiration, I could work that out for myself, but I gasped that it was my runaway heart, not my lungs, that bothered me. 'You're having a panic attack, nothing to worry about,' he assured me. Unconvinced, my body and mind droned with doom.

I took myself to the hospital, as one does, was wired up for 24 hours with a pulse tracker, eventually had an echocardiogram. Nothing physically amiss, all in the head. It recurred, at the most inconvenient times—twice in restaurants with dear friends—along with that terrifying, overpowering sense of fatal dread. Part of the condition, they told me. Transmitter chemicals get out of whack in the brain, triggered by stress hormones, and upset the organic pacemaker that regulates heartbeats.

What had caused it? I realized later that the first episode was a delayed and unvoiced rage reaction to an especially mean-spirited review of one of my books. I had read it earlier in the day in a bookstore, snarled under my breath and shrugged it off, but somehow the true impact had been delayed and stealthy. Understanding how that sort of thing can happen calls for us to learn about the enormous changes that science and technology are making to our understanding of the mind, in health and illness. Dr. Nancy Andreasen's *Brave New Brain* (2001)—a less than happy title for a book extolling technical advances—is a suitable guide, if not flawless. Since she is an experimental neuroscientist and psychiatrist, not a professional writer, some of her book is reminiscent of those old *Reader's* Digest medical articles: 'I am Joe's Liver'. Other parts turn into 'I am Joanna's Anterior Cingulate Sulcus', or tell little parables about anxious Michelle or 'mellow Melissa', or lurch into textbookese: 'Dopamine, a catecholamine neurotransmitter, is the first product synthesized from tyrosine through the enzymatic activity of tyrosine hydroxylase' (79). But these lapses are forgivable in a rich and mostly accessible display of neuroscience's remarkable new treasure house.

Andreasen is a well-credentialed guide for the tour. In 2000, she was one of twelve US scientists to receive the President's Medal. As chair of psychiatry at Iowa University, she has been a key player developing new imaging techniques that show us the inner workings of the living brain, down to sub-millimeter resolution, without opening the hood. Her early medical work with profoundly traumatized burns patients made her the ideal choice, as the Vietnam War wound down, to revive and advocate the more general topic of post-traumatic stress disorder, a term she devised for DSM III (shorthand for the third edition of the Diagnostic and Statistical Manual of Mental Disorders), the psychiatric bible of the 1970s.[46]

> As a medical student I found mental illnesses to be the most interesting and challenging diseases that I had encountered. What could explain how some people experienced the loss of autonomy over their minds that characterized schizophrenia, leading to the intrusion of alien voices or the theft of their emotional vitality? What caused people to fall into a deep depression, depriving them of all confidence and self-esteem, just when things seemed to be going very well for them?
>
> My first decade of research in psychiatry was a lesson in humility.
>
> Then, in the mid 1970s, something happened that changed my scientific life forever. Iowa became one of the first medical schools to get a CT scanner. CT scanning launched a new era for psychiatry and was the first of an extraordinary array of tools available for visualizing—and above all for measuring—the brain in mental illnesses. After a decade or more of frustration, I suddenly was like a kid in a candy shop. Where other people saw 'pictures of the brain', I saw a quantitative probe that could at last be used to get inside the heads of living people. (2001: 132)

---

[46] Note, however, that the very existence of this disorder (although not of its many distressing symptoms) is currently in dispute, especially when coupled to the social panic of 'recovered memories' of sexual abuse elicited therapeutically under hypnosis. See, for example, Richard J. McNally, *Remembering Trauma*, Harvard University Press, 2004. This study is discussed, along with the history of alleged memory retrieval, by Frederick Crews, at: http://www.nybooks.com/articles/16951

Drawing on her imaging work, Andreasen has developed a model of schizophrenia as an explicit brain disorder, marked by misconnection syndrome, a series of physical disruptions in the growing brain. Starting from basics, her book lays out the key information needed to make sense of later detailed accounts of how scanning and genome advances clarify what goes wrong in the brains and experience of people suffering schizophrenia, emotional or mood disorders, the dementias of old age, and those anxiety states of the kind that clobbered me. PET (positron emission tomography) and fMRI (functional magnetic resonance imagery) scans catch the living brain in mid-thought, tracking which bits do what. We can watch as unpleasant pictures and thoughts activate the deep, ancient limbic system, while joyful ideas light up the distinctively human cortex. It is encouraging.[47] So too is the prospect that ever more nuanced non-invasive probes will show us the workings and defects of what is misleadingly dubbed 'the human heart'—now relocated into that most mysterious and complex of organs, the brain.

But is all this too reductionistic, too dismissive of those stigmatized as 'mentally ill'? In the '60s and '70s, madness was briefly glorified by antipsychiatrists such as R. D. Laing. Psychotics were allegedly victims of malign family dynamics but also heroes of the revolution against throttling orthodoxies. The bankruptcy of such romantic posturing (I fell for it myself) was revealed by the rise of new medicines and scanners, and by the suffering it had wrought on the ill and those nearest to them.

Anthropologist Daniel Nettle has revived a similar topic, proposing that 'the more extreme positions on the spectrum of mental life are typical not just of malfunction—mental illness—but of the best in mental functioning—inspiration and creativity' (2001: 34). Cogently exploring this link between 'the lunatic, the lover and the poet', he recognizes that madness, even manic madness, is no fun: 'never forget for a moment that the psychoses are severe, crippling, often lethal diseases'. Serotonin and dopamine systems, he concludes, make us who we are, yet they are not our choice but the parental gift of our genes.

Luckily, as we have seen argued repeatedly in this book, genes are not the whole of destiny, and madness is indeed in some respects the far side of Shakespearean flourishing. Art as well as panic can make our pulse race, and so can love.

---

[47] Excellent images from PET and fMRI scans as various tasks are performed and different brain areas become activated are available on many neuroscience sites on the Web.

'Satiable Curtiosity

> But there was one Elephant—a new Elephant—an
> Elephant's Child—who was full of 'satiable curtiosity,
> and that means he asked ever so many questions... and
> he filled all Africa with his 'satiable curtiosities. ... He
> asked questions about everything that he saw, or heard,
> or felt, or smelt, or touched, and all his uncles and his
> aunts spanked him. And still he was full of 'satiable
> curtiosity!
>
> Rudyard Kipling,
> 'The Elephant's Child' ([1902] 1982: 59-60)

i

When I was about 14, besotted by rockets and the dream of travel to the
stars, I read a book with a wonderfully compelling title: *This Island
Earth*.[48] That title suffused my adolescent imagination. *Yes!* That *is* how
our lovely planet should be seen: a blue-green-brown-white cloud-
streaked island of life and intelligence in the empty black ocean between
the worlds and stars.

Earth is indeed just the tiniest island, less than a grain of sand, in
that aching void. Carl Sagan, finding our world rendered by a single
pixel in a *Voyager 1* space probe image from beyond Neptune, called us
a 'pale blue dot' (1994). That is truly what we are in the scheme of
things. Shakespeare, in *Richard the Second,* Act II, Scene 1, could sing of
his own beloved island:

> *This royal throne of kings, this scept'red isle,*
> *This earth of majesty. . . this little world,*
> *This precious stone set in the silver sea.*

Leaving aside the born-to-rule rhetoric, this is, indeed, our Earth entire:
a precious stone set spinning in a sea of starry light.

And it is just as far from all those stars, even from those other
apparently nearby worlds of our own solar system, as Australia is from
Shakespeare's homeland. The historian Geoffrey Blainey, in an inspired
coinage, referred to the European settlers of my own island continent as
victims of the 'tyranny of distance'. By comparison with the great
distances between the worlds of our solar system (tens of millions of
kilometers at best), let alone the terrible voids between the stars, the
unthinkable gulfs separating hundreds of billions of galaxies comprising

---

[48] Raymond Jones' novel from half a century ago was not much better than the clunky 1955
movie, relentlessly guyed in the *Mystery Science Theater 3000* recension.

the cosmos... why, all of us on Earth are now cheek by jowl. Yet our snug island Earth, linked by nearly instantaneous radio and television, mobile phones, global corporate maneuvering, will not stay isolated for long. Sooner or later some of us will start moving outward toward the greatest frontier of all: we'll cross the black reaches of the skies in search of other islands.

And yet—

We already took the first steps, and seemingly faltered (although our wonderful robot deputies, the space probes, still go forth in our stead). As the International Space Station traverses the sky like a new star, crewed by fewer and fewer humans, the Moon remains as void of life as it did in the four and half billion years before July 20, 1969. On Mars, dormant microbial life might slumber beneath cold red dust, but no human footprint is expected there in the immediate future, despite the Bush announcement in 2004. What went wrong? Is the dream of space travel finally an adolescent folly, to be put aside until we fix the urgent problems that assail so many hungry, suffering billions here on this island Earth?

Perhaps that is the wrong question. Why shouldn't we do both? What if heading outward to the asteroids, planets and finally the stars is among our best hopes for peace and prosperity down here below, as well as in the bounteous new ecospheres available in space (once we build them, or perhaps change ourselves to fit their alien demands)? What if, finally, it is entirely *necessary* that we gain the ability to move beyond our own atmosphere, since sooner or later our lovely home is doomed to perish?

For one part of that new order of regularity in the heavens, lovely and elegant and as unexpected, was learning that our dinosaur predecessors were wiped out when the nucleus of an exhausted comet smote the Earth 65 million years ago. Today we seem intent on replicating in reverse just such an instant climate catastrophe by creating the conditions for Greenhouse summer. Is there any hope that we or our distant descendants might yet escape the same random and overwhelming fate? And there are more relentless dooms in the offing. The end of the world, and perhaps of the entire universe, finally *will* come: that much is just scientific knowledge, no longer myth.

The end of time! The close of all life on Earth, packed away like a bazaar on some long, calm, mournfully bereft Sunday afternoon! Yet the loss of our own blue and white world, we now know, need not spell the end of all life and mind. Far from it. Our seed will spill outward into the heavens, during the millennia and billions of years that remain before the galaxies drown in the blackness of everlasting night.

The true story of life in the solar system (as we currently understand it) is this: the Sun ignited some five billion years ago, and has been brightening ever since, by about an extra fifth to date. Its orbiting worlds, not least our own, have therefore warmed and will eventually swelter and cook. In another four or five thousand million years, the nuclear hydrogen fusion within our local star will shift gear to helium burning, in a ghastly few seconds of 'helium flash'. Restabilized, the Sun will be a core of blazing helium surrounded by a shell of hot hydrogen, and beyond that a vast hot outer envelope. While this red giant phase of the Sun will fail to swallow the Earth, it will blaze for a further billion years... and then go out. Nuclear fires extinguished, the Sun collapses into a white dwarf, and then an all-but-invisible black dwarf star (not to be mistaken for a black hole, which needs a star much larger than our Sun as its progenitor.) The Earth, surface charred during the red giant phase, will chill in the blackness, air and water lost, crust locked into eternal night.[49]

And that doleful fate is only a step or two away, no farther into tomorrow than the solar system's genesis was, looking backward. True, it is an inconceivably great distance from our annual round, but by cosmic measure just a decade or two. Other stars have passed already through this great cycle: born in a shock-wave compression of thin interstellar gases, spinning down, throwing off worlds, some of them surely growing life of some kind, burning for billions of years (the universe has been here for at least 13 billion), flaring, scalding in red fury, gasping, gone. And their life with them, unless that life has found passage away from its doom.

Perhaps our descendants will find that escape route as well. Perhaps, indeed, by the time death comes to our Sun and Earth, we shall have seeded all the sky.

ii

So with the first steps toward space travel, have we entered one step further into our estate as Masters of the Universe? Or if that seems too ambitious—even ludicrous, as I intend it to—perhaps we shall be its reverent spectators, at the very least. At best: its reworkers, its next designers, the tenants who take over the cosmos and do it up to our own tastes.

Is that the shape of the deep future, or must we resign ourselves to devastation at the hands of weapons of mass destruction? Global starvation? Resource depletion, a world laid waste in the fecundity of its own most successful animal? Or, if we meet all these challenges, the eventual arrival of a hellish life-destroying mountain from space? Hell, no. Let us turn instead with cautious trust to the burgeoning storehouse

---

[49] For an up-to-date summary of this long future history, even to the ends of time in an ever-expanding open universe, see Fred Adams and Greg Laughlin, *The Five Ages of the Universe: Inside the Physics of Eternity*, New York: The Free Press, 1999.

of human knowledge. What we learn will change what we know, drastically, convulsively, in we cannot *yet* know. But we can make educated guesses. Sometimes our dreams will prove wilder than the reality. It is the risk we run, we polymathic dreamers. But more often than not, we see past the veil into a place (call it the future) where the prosaic and the workaday dare not step. Until relentless time pushes them through, and they sprawl without preparation, bruised and confused and angry.

We shall go into space because we must, if only because our lovely home world is doomed to die, sooner or later. Here's how:

We are glued to the rind of the world only because it takes such a lot of effort to break free. True, we can readily loft into the buoyant air beneath the hot wind of a balloon, or inside the aluminum tube of a jet airliner burning industrial quantities of irreplaceable and polluting fuel to move us from one city or continent to another. But to tear away from Earth's grip and fall free in orbit calls for more than a rocketing climb straight up a few hundred kilometers into the sky, to a point higher than all but a millionth part of the atmosphere. It is not *distance* that holds us down here, it is *speed*. We need to run very fast to get there. The distance between Earth and orbit is measured not in kilometers but in kilometers per second. We are seven kilometers per second away from low earth orbit (LEO) and the International Space Station. And we are more than eleven kilometers per second from interplanetary space.

Hence the need for those huge, roaring rockets, with their gobbling hunger for propellant. They look wonderful, flame burning against the sky. Their engines thunder with a body-shaking roar. But everyone agrees it is a shockingly wasteful way to get off the world.[50] Suppose there were some neater method, less expensive in the long run for each kilo lifted to space (although it might cost and arm and a leg to put in the infrastructure)?

One idea you have to love is the skyhook.

iii

To get to space, first fly a rocket the old-fashioned expensive way to orbit, then lower a rope to the ground. Then other people can climb up the rope as slowly as they like (although they had better bring their own air with them).

---

[50] Even so, some retain faith in rockets as the space work-horse. Aerospace engineer Spike Jones reminds me that we might lift heavy manufacturing equipment to low earth orbit (LEO), carry it on to the Moon, and build there (from materials available on and below the lunar surface, plus abundant solar power) the infrastructure for human-crewed exploration and exploitation of the solar system, and perhaps beyond.

Well, it turned out you cannot do that. The rope would be hundreds or thousands of kilometers long, so it would snap under its own weight, even if you used the strongest metal chain or thread. Worse, the lower end of the thread would whip through the air at the same speed as the satellite it dangled from, and those things pass overhead, as we have seen, at kilometers a second. Luckily, not all satellites move at the same sped. The higher up it is, the slower an artificial moon's orbital velocity. At a certain height, now known as the Clarke orbit (after the brilliant Arthur C. Clarke who first worked this out), an equatorial satellite moving at 3.14 kilometers a second hangs 36,000 kilometers above the same spot on the turning earth. So you could spool out thread toward the Earth (and a corresponding mass of ballast away into space in the opposite direction, to prevent dragging the satellite out of orbit), and the whole shockingly elongated thing will in principle float there like a dream, the thread sustained by an awful internal tension.

Obviously this would not work with steel, or silk. You need something like a cable of pure diamond if you want it to hold up under such tension, allowing you to climb up it into space like Jack on his Beanstalk, or even couple an elevator to the skyhook and ride up in style. Who can afford a cable of diamond more than 36,000 kilometers long? Where would you get that much diamond, anyway?

Here is the extraordinary good news: diamond is just an arrangement of carbon, a very common element on the planet Earth. An ever-increasing excess of carbon released by humans into the atmosphere is thought to be partly responsible for Greenhouse warming. And within a few decades, we shall know how to compile carbon and other cheap elemental feedstocks into all manner of useful structures, perhaps including a tremendously strong, very light skyhook reaching all the way to geosynchronous orbit and beyond.

Molecular nanotechnology, the practical science and craft of working at the level of individual molecules, does not yet exist, but we can see the directions in which it is likely to develop. Already one Nobel Prize has been won for discovering a novel form of carbon, buckyballs (C_{60}), that will eventually lead, perhaps, to an immense thread of diamond or buckytube hanging down from space to an anchoring point somewhere near the equator, perhaps at the top of a mountain in Africa.[51] Calling it a thread is misleading, however, since for safety reasons it would be made of numerous independent, cross-linked cables, peppered with tiny sensors, capable of self-repair if one strand was breached by a meteor or weapon. That would be a highway into the sky. Vertical railroads could carry materials and people along a

---

[51] Curiously, its discoverer, Richard Smalley, disapproves of these kinds of nano-technological projections. See the contentious debate between him and K. Eric Drexler at http://pubs.acs.org/cen/coverstory/8148/8148counterpoint.html

superconducting magnetic levitation rail inside the core of the multi-cable tube, running sedately up to orbit at the speed of a jetliner.

One difficulty must be admitted, perhaps a fatal one—at least until we have self-repairing cables. Many important artificial satellites are now spinning several times a day about our world on collision course with any Beanstalk reaching down from geostationary orbit. Some can be retired as obsolete once the vast extent of the cable system is deployed, studded with communication relays, weather scanners and the like. Still, my rocket scientist friend Spike Jones calculates an annual 30 percent chance of collision with space junk. Might the cable structure be 'twanged' like an enormous violin string, as Arthur C. Clarke has suggested, taking it out of the path of pesky satellites, or might the satellites themselves be steered past the cable?[52] Perhaps not. Still, the molecular manufacturing needed to build such a vast highway might be able to solve this problem almost organically, as noted, with instant repair and regrowth.

A staggeringly expensive project, even using molecular mechanosynthesis, it would pay for itself many times over by replacing rockets with elevators driven by electricity powered by solar energy freely available and abundant beyond our atmosphere. What is more, building skyhooks is easier on lower-gravity Mars, and eventually it will be possible to use robot construction machines to spin the great cables for us with no human supervision. Rather than expend decades on rocket flights to Mars, it might turn out to be cheaper and quicker, in the long run, to invest in a major research and development effort in industrial nanotechnology able to fabricate skyhooks for interplanetary travel. That way we would have the benefits of nano for all manner of useful purposes, and an attainable highway to space in the bargain.

iv

The trouble—and the great delight—of making such projections into expected future technologies is that once you introduce such a novelty as nanotechnology, everything else is liable to change in unexpected ways. If you have access to advanced nanofacture, you might wish to build other things. I playfully called the skyhook a Beanstalk (borrowing from Robert Heinlein), but in the original fairy story the giant's Beanstalk grew upward from the soil, it did not hang down from the sky. Might we use molecular or other advanced methods to grow a ladder or tower *upward* into the clouds and far, far beyond them?

NASA scientists Dr. Geoffrey Landis and Craig Cafarelli have done the engineering calculations. It seems that an immensely tall tower could

---

[52] http://www.islandone.org/LEOBiblio/CLARK1.HTM
http://www.spaceref.com/news/viewnews.html?id=846

indeed be built. The stresses in a diamond tower with its mighty footings deep in rock would be compressive, squeezing downward, the contrary of that outward tension tearing at a space thread. Small shifts in the crust would put it at risk of toppling or buckling, so active computerized management would be necessary to ensure stability. Further calculations show that a blend of skyhook satellite and very tall tower might be the optimal mix, using less material and cheaper to build. But these same technologies have suggested a quite different audacious scheme to Dr. J. Storrs Hall, one of the few people to have devoted a lot of disciplined effort to exploring the prospects of nanotechnology. His notion is strange, but remarkably simple and perhaps elegant in the way of the Eiffel Tower. He proposes a Launch Pier a hundred kilometers tall, extending above all but the last of the atmosphere, and three hundred kilometers long.

It would resemble the world's largest trestle, built from slender diamond-like towers marching beyond the horizon like impossibly tall spidery radio transmitters. At their top, a colossal rail structure would lead to an edge I can imagine base-jumpers lining up for months to jump off. The rails would carry magnetically levitated spacecraft, accelerating them smoothly for 80 seconds at a crushing but acceptable 10 gravities. Released at the end of their 300 km run, spared the burden of carrying most of their own propellant, spacecraft would head for orbit along computer-specified trajectories, correcting their paths with exquisite changes of velocity from their conventional rockets.

From the ground, you would not be able to see the immense launch platform lost in the haze of air far beneath it. Perhaps you would only see a few of the great struts plunging upward into the blue. Sunlight, effectively undiminished, would shine through the lacy thing upon crops. There would be no disruptive noise, except where great gantries and elevators carried their loads hissing into the skies, powered not by expensive rocket fuel but by cheap electricity (which might well be generated from solar energy at the top of the trestle).

How much would such a marvel cost to build? Hall claims it could be built today, using available technology and materials, although at exorbitant expense. With moderately early nanotechnology to spin the half million tonnes of struts, plus magnetic coils and electronics, that impossible price might plunge to $500,000,000, or more conservatively $10 billion. By comparison, 300 kilometers of superhighway today costs at least a billion dollars; building the Hubble Space Telescope, hoisting it into orbit and then repairing it took $3.2 billion; the International Space Station's bill will be more than $20 billion and it is almost useless except as a monument. The Apollo mission to the Moon cost $24 billion in 1960 dollars... but today its mighty Saturn launch vehicles have been dismantled and even their engineering plans were destroyed. Hall notes: 'If an Apollo-style (and -cost) project could do for diamond what the original one did for electronics, we could build the tower in the next decade or so.' Operating costs could fall to $1 per kilogram lifted into orbit. Today's costs using rockets are 10,000 times higher.

In short, a major push in developing molecular nanotechnology could pay off by reducing the cost of this dramatic launch platform into space—and provide us with all the other benefits of matter compilers almost as an incidental. Those benefits will probably include inexpensive consumer goods, perhaps including nutritious foods, clothing, safe terrestrial transport, shelter and computation. That implies a complete and perhaps catastrophic shake-up in the global economy, as we shift from a world of scarcity to one of plenty within a brief period of time. During such an upheaval, will anyone be thinking seriously about exploring the solar system and beyond? Yes—because even with the new opportunities for intelligent recycling that nanotechnology affords us, we will want all the extra resources we can find. And unpopulated space—in the form of asteroids, but also moons and planets—will be an abundant source of raw materials for a very long time, without the disturbing moral costs that should have tormented our Enlightenment ancestors.

v

Finding clever ways to lift cheaply into orbit is just the first step, but it is a step that takes us a long way, for it has been said that low earth orbit is 'halfway to anywhere'. While that is true, it depends on how long you are willing to spend getting anywhere. By rocket from Earth orbit, the Moon is several days distant. Coasting most of the way, getting to Mars and back takes many months. Can we speed up the trip? And is your journey really necessary?

Several ingenious methods have been explored for boosting crewed spacecraft to the nearest planets and the asteroids. You can fire tremendous laser beams at the frail extended butterfly wings of a light-jammer, pushing it gently but inexorably into the void on the pressure of light itself. That sounds absurd, but a highly reflective aluminum skin on a light-sail just four or five atoms thick and nearly 700 kilometers across can be driven *by sunlight alone* to nearly one percent of the speed of light, the maximum velocity in the universe. Actually we can do better than that. A battery of powerful lasers, pumping their blazing beams through a lens 200 meters across, could strike the light-jammer's sail with such force that it would be accelerated in two months to 15 percent of the speed of light. Conditions on board would be comfortable, because the acceleration would be nearly one *g*, the force we are used to on Earth from gravity. You do not need to carry a great mass of propellant with you, and at destination, the craft can be slowed by a number of equally clever means not requiring rockets. One such, suggested by Dr. Robert Zubrin, is to deploy an equally vast magnetic sail-field that presses against the 'wind' of the interplanetary magnetic medium that suffuses 'empty' space.

But do we need to make this trip through the horrors of space? Might we find ways to avoid the perils of weightlessness (which destroys bone and muscle), radiation storms from the Sun, dangerous micro-debris that can damage a craft or its instruments? A favorite fancy, fuelled now for three decades by *Star Trek,* is the transporter beam, or instant teleportation from one place to another. Recently this notion has been given some real scientific grounding with the discovery, in relativity theory, that wormholes might be possible. These are links through the higher-dimensional spaces implied by M-Theory and general relativity, joining locations and even times far distant and in principle permitting passage to signals or even objects, apparently faster than light. Of course the transition would not *actually* be faster than light, since the distance traveled has been abbreviated.

Alas, current thinking argues against the likelihood that wormholes or hyperspace can really allow us to teleport instantly to another world, or even from the surface to a starship propelled by antimatter. One reason for thinking that this sad news is correct is the apparent absence of aliens in the solar system, let alone here on Earth. If wormhole travel is easy and available, we might expect the galaxy to be swarming with star voyagers (assuming that life exists beyond our own planet). That goes as well, admittedly, for near-light-speed star travel, such as light-sails or antimatter-fuelled craft, but such vessels would take years, centuries, even millennia to get to their destinations. Which might cramp the enthusiasm of many extraterrestrial species, encouraging them to stay at home and send small nano-robots exploring in their stead.

Such shrunken probes,[53] containing miniaturized artificial intelligence systems perhaps smarter than human brains, could be accelerated inexpensively from their home worlds to nearly the speed of light, spin themselves sails from the interstellar debris as they approach their destination, infest a convenient asteroid or lifeless moon and start to replicate. A nano-seed of this sort could build further probes to explore the new system, and enormous radio or optical transmitters to pump back an encyclopedia of new information to the home world. True, the society that launched them thousands of years earlier might by then be dead or transformed, but the gale of knowledge would flow across the emptiness between the stars, bringing riches beyond dream to anyone listening. But in fact any technology capable of such feats would have little fear of death, unless it were imposed by choice or conflict.

The logic is irresistible: any true voyagers between the stars, human, posthuman, or alien, will be postmortal as well.

---

[53] Possibly built from tunable quantum dot artificial atoms; see Wil McCarthy's *Hacking Matter* (2003).

Tomorrowland

> It is fashionable nowadays to believe that technological change has come to an end—and indeed to believe that it is not desirable and can be stopped. This is not new; it is the common reaction in a period of rapid technological change. It was the reaction of the 1830s, when the Luddites, the machine wreckers, were far more visible than the innovators. It was the reaction of the 1890s, the last period of disenchantment with technology in Western history. But just as the Luddites and the technological pessimists of the nineties made no lasting impact, so, it can be said, will today's romantic objections to technology remain ineffectual.
>
> Peter F. Drucker,
> *Managing in Turbulent Times,* 1980: 50

i

Everyone used to know how the future would be.

Few people anticipated drastic life extension or anything remotely like molecular nanotechnology or even 'test tube babies', let alone clones, but by the wonderful year 2000, people would wear silver jump-suits, holidaying under huge glass domes on the Moon. We would swallow small colored pills for dinner, washed down with sparkling Betelgeuse beetlejuice. Father would leave for work each morning in his personal helicopter or aircar, flying across the clean, open 'burbs to a giant city soaring against the crisp sky. Back at home, Mother would oversee her domestic robot as it did the household chores, cleaning and tidying and sometimes comically scaring the cat with its vacuum hose. Giant wall television screens showed scenes from the long-running soap opera, *The Waltons on Mars*. It was almost like being there!

The children? In school, of course, learning from large central computers, fidgeting for their leisure time. Once school was out, they would talk Pop into flying them to the Space Station, where they would don wings and flap around in zero gravity. Or maybe they'd sneak off to Coral City, the deep sea resort where you could swim amid shoals of sparkling fish, breathing the water thanks to your temporary Aerator Lung.

Grandparents did not feature much in this mid-fifties portrait of Tomorrowland. Maybe the old gentleman would smile over a magazine printed by his home terminal, puffing contentedly on his pipe. Grandma was probably arguing jealously with the Nannybot, hoping to take baby for a walk in the leafy local park.

That plastic, 1950s dream future now looks inanely dated. We do not have personal aircars, and chances are we never will. Would you want to live under a bunch of lunatics hurtling around at a few hundred kilometers an hour, even if their commuter gyros were controlled by smart chips? Think of the noise, let alone the hazard of falling hardware. And those magnificent cities with their opalescent towers twined with runways and fly-overs—not very likely, as a growing middle-class settles down into electronic commuting from their cocooned suburban nests. The Internet beats the smelly, stressful freeway. In the real city alleys, meanwhile, junkies twitch and the unemployed seethe.

Those household robots are still pending, too. Deep Blue might trounce the world champ at chess, but it cannot also make your bed and clean the shower (let alone drive the children to school). Instead, we have a huge array of specialized home helpers that once seemed 'futuristic', like robot vacuum cleaners. Microwave cookers were predicted (as 'radar' ovens, since radar uses microwaves) in 1940s and 1950s science fiction, but nobody expected to find kids nuking their own TV dinners and chowing down at the Golden Arches or the local pizza joint.

As for those holiday trips to the Moon and points farther out—not soon. Space, as we saw in the previous chapter, turned out to be barren, harsh, mind-wrenchingly expensive to reach and even more treasury-draining to colonize, even with a Beanstalk. Intelligent aliens do not drop by from Ganymede to divert us on late night television. In the opening decade of the century of the future, we are stuck here firmly on Terra Firma, and it is getting more crowded every day.

Or *are* we stuck here? Maybe this is just post-millennial depression. The future might not be all it was cracked up to be, but who would want to live in a bland Disney-2050 anyway?

Let us try to glimpse the real future. Or some of the many possible futures, since they will surely range from heaven to hell. Those dazed family-values images of Fifties' Tomorrows were created against a backdrop of almost unendurable anxiety. Global war had just ended with the death of two cities, not just metaphorically but literally 'nuked'.

Although the evil empire turned into a nightmare of squabbling gangsters, like a tragic remake of Prohibition-Era Chicago, the missile bombs are still there. Somehow, though, we no longer dread them as much. The potential for world-wide havoc is increasing, if anything, but we do not expect nuclear winter to total us. Maybe it is the Prozac and the Internet, but we seem more optimistic. Actually this is a reasonable attitude. If the future is not going to be like the 1950s picture, neither will it just be like today, only bigger and worse (or bigger and better). No, it is going to be strange, even alien. And we will be there.

We'll be having fun. Very weird fun.

Science fiction movies and TV are absurdly conservative when it comes to picturing the future. What will we be wearing in 2050 when we head off to the club or to work? Will it be spandex and Goth black for the office, medieval peasant drab for the night out? Really that's the wrong question. Regard the assumptions buried in it. Jobs? Most people will not work, since artificial intelligence (AI) will increasingly be attained between 2025 and 2050, and AIs will toil for nothing, and leave nothing much for most people to do. Indeed, tiny virus-scale nanotechnology assemblers should be available by 2050 or earlier, building everything we need out of simple chemicals—including copies of themselves. When molecular factories duplicate themselves cheaply, using shareware programs downloaded from the net, everything is suddenly very different.

That 1950s' Ray Bradbury extrapolation of wall-screen TVs is just around the corner, linked to the net, but we will not be watching anything so primitive by 2050, or even 2025. Head-up displays already exist that paint stereo images directly on each eyeball with harmless laser beams. Look forward to a jeweled headband with an Internet uplink, able to enhance or even replace everything you look at. The headband will become a simple attachment, then an implanted chip acting directly on your brain's visual and auditory centers. Ultimately, we shall share a kind of electronic telepathy.

Sitting here at the very beginning of the AI, genome and nano revolutions, it is hard to lock into mid-21st century's reality. Within the next few years, we should have a complete recipe of our genome's protein menu. Fifty years on, designers should have absolute control over our basic genetic template. So how will fashion look? Forget body piercing—the mid-21st century trend-setters might be four-legged hermaphrodites, or super-athletes and aesthetes buzzed out of their heads on designer diseases, or crowds of dividuals (copies of yourself, electronic clones) roaming cyberspace in feral gangs.

Is this too laughably 'sci-fi' to consider seriously? Maybe not. Fast change is still accelerating relentlessly, driven by the inventive power of science and technology, the marketing urges of a global economy. The gap between now and the 2050s will resemble the vast leap from 1900 to now. In the 1900s, people in those nations we now called 'Western' had a life, Jim, but not as we know it. Silent movies and crude phonographs had only just been invented. The first plane had not yet taken to the air—while a century later, global tourism and global terrorism are routine, and a robot spacecraft has already left the solar system. Telephones were few and far between in 1900. Mobile phones were unknown at the start of this decade; tomorrow they will be implanted. Radio had not even been *invented* back then, let alone television. The awesome fidelity of digital CDs are only decades old, the desktop computer and DVDs even newer. In 2050 powerful computers will be truly ubiquitous. Change is a juggernaut, mutating everything. Such trends will continue. We will be at home in the world, and uneasy in the world, as the world grows ever more like us. Even the wretched of the earth might do well, if nanotechnology gives them the necessities of life very cheaply, as I discuss in *The Spike* (1997, 2001).

Consider that drastic state of future life which some techno-enthusiasts have dubbed *uploading*: minds living inside computers, as uploaded emulations of our own brains. Today, computer users routinely upload or download information from one machine to another. That is, you copy the data from the memory of one machine into a different one, or on to another medium, perhaps for safe keeping. Here is the move many will find hard to swallow: Some people later in this century will be robots, of a kind, but not the sort that are designed by human engineers. Rather, their machine minds will emulate the mental states of ordinary mortals like us, people who were once restricted to bodies grown from DNA instructions. Such people might be known as 'uploads', and will continue their rich human experience in complex virtual realities. Probably they will choose to retain a foot in our world through embodiment in subtle robot bodies as sensitive to the fall of a moonbeam, the scent of a rose and the hug of a child as ours are today.

Why would anyone wish to choose such a frightening and unnatural life? Because of a blight that afflicts all of us, rich and poor, First World and Third World, smart or dull: decay and death. At this moment, as throughout history and the long echoing passages of prehistory, we have no choice when we reach a certain age, or even worse suffer a dreadful disease or accident: we die. Some crucial part of our body or brain wears out, and that's it, we are gone. I regard this as a tragedy, not a blessing in disguise. Indeed, I think the true purpose of medical research is to abolish aging and death, and I see ample reason to hope that this ancient goal will be attained within this century, as we shall see in the next chapter. But if it is delayed, or if the inevitable constraints of our evolved bodies chafe, I can also imagine that some people will decide to move as soon as possible into large homes in virtual reality, a topic I'll return to in the chapter after that.

Such people will think and feel and sing and meditate in ways not yet conceivable, ways of being-in-the-world that will emerge from a new, extraordinarily swift evolution within machines deeper and broader and faster than the brain-tissue machinery we now keep tucked away politely under our skulls.

ii

Everything will shift in a slow but remorseless earthquake. Even in advance of nanotech, some ludicrously tiny proportion of the work-force already provides all our food. If anyone in 1900 had glimpsed this dizzyingly weird world, which we take for granted, our daily lives would have seemed the most futuristic of fantasies.

So what will we do on our days off? Again, it is the wrong question, as 'the day off' might be every day of the week, for most of the citizens of 2050.

Despite AIDS and other scourges, and all the moral panic attending them, early 21st century domestic mores are quite incredibly freer and more various than anyone expected fifty years ago. Half a century hence, exquisitely subtle and targeted genomic engineering will obliterate the worst diseases, and manage those that mutate to fill the gaps. The delirious sexual escapades of the 1960s and 1970s might return with a bang. Meanwhile, a lot of wild stuff will be happening in the ultimately safe sex zone—virtual reality (VR).

Movies like *The Matrix* trilogy, and high-end interactive games, hint at the ingenious and thrilling prospects of total immersion in computer-generated VR. Boundaries between outer and inner worlds will get fluid. Why go to Mars in a clunky rocket or even up a Beanstalk, at fantastic cost, when you can link into a robot chugging around the awesome mountains and canyons of the red planet? Better yet, visit the shrieking storms of Jupiter, or the rings of Saturn, either by linking your senses to a distant robot probe or inside a perfect simulation. These places are alien and hostile to the human body, but with VR you will never know the difference.

That does not imply a world of VR couch potatoes. Leisure today is more exhausting and satisfying than ever. We work our bodies in the gym, because we want to. We play sport hard, practice martial arts at the dojo. You could not hang-glide or jet-ski 30 years ago, and while IMAX movies mimic some of the thrills we still yearn to do it ourselves. That impulse will surely persist—and our bodies will be increasingly morphed and re-shaped, our games more demanding. It will be a future made safe for nerds, but they will be pumped nerds, nerds with attitude.

Cities might go downward, not up. Nano replicators will make it cheap and easy to delve deep under the ground, pump moisture out and air in, provide ample power from solar cells or gene-tweaked fuel crops. The surface could be returned to a global wildness, alive with once-extinct species and some newly constructed. You will not feel constricted underground, because your illusion system will show convincing images of Africa (as in a famous 1951 Ray Bradbury tale, 'The Veldt'), complete with breezes and scents and the roars of distant lions.[54] Your housemates will have their own distinctive inner worlds, linked by a haze of in-built chips and electronics. Your very mood may be under your own control, not just due to fifth-generation drugs (grandchild of Prozac) but tuned by gene-designed glands. In fact, by 2050, unmodified humans might be on the way out—replaced without strife or anxiety by smart AIs and

---

[54] http://www.veddma.com/veddma/Veldt.htm. I trust copyright has been authorized by Ray Bradbury.

posthumans, ourselves and our deathless children. That will be something to see. That will be something to know.

That will be something to be.

iii

We live, then, in a transitional historical moment, nowhere near the end of technological invention. The accidents of my life so far—not least living in Australia rather than the USA, and having experienced the liberatory aspirations of the 1960s—made me a kind of fuzzy left-anarchist. I have no love for global corporations, let alone gigantic government. But the traditional rhetoric of revolution never appealed to me. I always knew it was either erroneous analysis or smart adolescents getting their Oedipal rocks off. The way to utopia, which is where we are headed if we do not murder ourselves in nano-warfare or some other ultra-hightech catastrophe, will come out of the mouth of the technological dragon.

True, the majority of people alive today still have no telephones— but two centuries ago, *emperors* had no phones. For all their deplorable costs and ruinous heartlessness, markets work by saturating every possible backwater of potential consumers. Girdle the world with communication satellites so oil executives can do deals and so the military machine can ensure their success and, as a side-effect, within decades every village in the meanest nations on Earth will have cell-phones and Internet access. New biotechnology will grow liquid fuel for the poor, according to Freeman Dyson, one of the world's finest scientists, seeding the tropics with plants that convert sunlight into the machineries of appropriate technology.

Such a utopia cannot remain stable, not with science progressing under its own relentless dynamic. Perhaps humanity is about to break apart into a series of clades (in novelist Bruce Sterling's borrowing from ecology), distinct sub-species that form not by the natural selection of chance variations but through technological choice and emergent properties. Once we know how the whole genome is expressed in proteins, exactly how those proteins fold and what their precise action is in cells, and how those cells act together in tissues and organs and whole embodied minds, why, then some people will begin to twist and tweak and fix and augment and rewrite the code until nothing remains the same. We will make our brains bigger or better (or, more likely, those of our children) and redesign their architecture to optimize emotions and thinking alike. We will give to the generation-after-next bodies and brains not just free of most inherited defects but brimming with new vim and vigor.

Nobody will stop there. Artificial intelligences (AIs) will surely emerge around the same time, and for the first epoch in human history

151

we will share the planet with truly alien but equal minds. A moment later, we will face superior minds, since AIs will swiftly revise themselves into some kind of transcendence. If this projection sounds like a secular version of Christian dogma, I accept the broad charge but deny intent. Primitive religion was a repository of human hopes and terrors, and sophisticated religions are the cultural refinement of those same impulses. Naturally, what faiths (like art) disclose of our unconscious desires helps shape the kinds of technologies we seek to build—and indeed to merge with. But deconstructing or seeing through the metaphysics of religion need not vitiate the redemptive aspirations of advanced technologies. We wish to live, and live more abundantly; it would be agreeable if we did so with maximum health and unlimited, unaging longevity, and in the company of a whole world equally blessed. We would like to go outward to the stars, perhaps, and inward to the depths of our complex, modular minds—and we will do so.

But success is only possible if we retain a cautious respect for the bugs in our evolved legacy code, all those messy adaptations piled one on top of the other that natural selection has conserved just because they did not work so badly that they killed their bearers. Humans are wonderful, but we have been built by a blind idiot. Perhaps posthumans, when they come, will prove a little more successful. At least they shall have been nurtured by conscious creators: by us, their forebears.

In fifteen or twenty-five years' time, we might well see computers that are as complex as human brains. Will they be people? We do not yet know. Will they be conscious? We do not know. It seems to me very likely that at least some of those machine minds will be conscious, will be *persons*. But the world is already filled with persons; the key point, the astonishing novelty, is this: once machines emerge that are as clever as people, they will start to rewrite themselves, rebuild their own architecture. We cannot do that to our own bodies or minds, except in very limited degree. A computer as smart as a human should be able to optimize itself, so a week after its emergence you might see one that is twice as smart. A week, or ten minutes, after that, it will be four times as smart, and then there is no stopping it.

So the world is bound to become very strange. There is no limit to what novelties will emerge.

It has been suggested, for example, that every household will have a solar-powered machine no larger than a microwave oven containing a soup of tiny gadgets the size of bacteria able to be reprogrammed as molecular assemblers.[55] They will take in raw material—carbon, oxygen,

---

[55] This might not be the most efficient way to implement nanofacturing, but it is not absurd. A much simpler model system has been analyzed by Chris Phoenix of the Center for Responsible Nanotechnology, in 'Design of a Primitive Nanofactory' (2003) , at http://www.jetpress.org/volume13/Nanofactory.htm

other elements readily available in the environment, stuff you can suck out of the air, out of the dirt in the backyard—and the nano machines will tear it down into the simplest possible atomic or molecular form, and then re-compile it according to stored templates, algorithms, recipes, building you useful things, or at least parts of useful things.

What kind? A Sunday roast if you are lucky, although that may take some time given that now it takes several years, starting from a baby cow, to build a Sunday roast. True, once you have the exact description of a roast, it should be possible to put it together inside a compiler—but that might be easier said than done. What is much easier is to make a perfect copy of a book, build a car or make a new computer. *Abundance* is what we can hope for. Once we gain the capacity to manufacture factories themselves, little gadgets able to copy themselves, it becomes trivially easy to spread their benefits around the world. They will not cost much to make, after all. The moment it becomes possible to download assembler templates or recipes off the Internet, anybody in the world will be able to manufacture any physical consumable for which somebody has made a nice description and posted it on the net, rather in the way that people pull MP3 music off the net now. It sounds in many respects like the traditional definitions of Utopia.

How long we expect to live—that most basic of facts—has nearly doubled this century. That is extraordinary. In 1900, Australia led the world, males at birth expecting to make 53 and females 57. Those figures are a bit misleading, of course, factoring in an intolerable child mortality rate, prior to the development of antibiotics. Still, at the start of last century even adults safely past vulnerable childhood could expect to die young by today's standards.

By 1950, life expectancy had shot up an extra 18 years for men and 20 for women. Those were not empty years, either, ruined by pain and senility. We got healthier and stayed active longer. Near the start of this new century, men in the First World expect to live to nearly 80, women older still. Fluoride halted the scourge of tooth decay. Now, though, the down-side of medical triumph is kicking in. Diseases that rarely show up in youth and middle-age can make extreme old age a drawn-out misery.

That might be temporary. Luckily, increasing mastery of the aging process will likely solve these hazards as well, as I detailed in *The Last Mortal Generation* (1999).

By 2050, medical science might have put an end to routine aging. Our cells, tissues and organs will be taught to repair and maintain themselves. Using techniques drawn from an unprecedented insight into the roots of mortality, we might gain an effectively unlimited lifespan. What we do with it—whether it hangs upon our shoulders like a curse or opens wonderful new pathways before us—is up to us.

Undying Love

> I am bullish on the prospects for indefinite lifespan.... In my opinion, there will be only a short interval between the time when we first have genuine life extension treatments and the time when we're improving those treatments faster than we're aging. My personal research goal is to achieve an indefinite lifespan for human beings, and I think we have a fair chance of doing it in about 25 years with the right funding. Given the present research and political environment, the actual timeline for achieving the first real healthy life extension breakthroughs could be anything from 15 to 100 years. Of course, we should all work hard to keep to the lower end of that range! By 'real' I mean treatments that at least double the remaining life expectancy of averagely healthy 70-year-olds. Treatments that do more will very probably follow rapidly—more rapidly than aging is occurring. For practical purposes we will by then have reached the cusp where individuals with the physiology of present-day 70-year-olds or younger will have an indefinite lifespan.
>
> Aubrey de Grey,
> 'Closing in on the Cure for Death' (2003)[56]

i

If we can change ourselves, there is no reason why humans have to remain the way that we happen to have evolved. If, by altering our genes, we can stop being as bloody-minded and as cruel, that is something that I would not mind doing to myself. Now it might be that, say, the desire to raise children runs very deep; after all, it underlies the whole genetic principle of evolution. So it might not be all that easy to snip out—or indeed very smart to do so, either—but it might be possible to suppress it. After all, I do not have any children myself; now that I have no opportunity to father any, I can reflect rather wistfully and nostalgically that it would have been nice to have had a couple of kids. But the lack of children of my own has not driven me mad or bitterly twisted with grief.

What happens when we rid ourselves of the ancient blight of mortality, if we do? I do not know, and as I approached my 60th birthday it seemed to me unlikely that medical immortality will arrive in time to

---

[56] http://www.longevitymeme.org/articles/viewarticle.cfm?article_id=15&page=1

save me. (Call it emortality, or amortality, if the quasi-religious term 'immortality' seems impious or daft—I just mean the end of the *necessity* of death by cellular degradation and disease.) Some argue that indefinite life spans would sap our will to push forward. If we expect to live a thousand years, does that imply that we will not want to get up in the morning, never get anything done? I do not think so, but I don't really know, and I don't care. So what if that turns out to be the case? Imagine a Lotus Eaters Future: for a thousand years people have happy, droning lives, refraining from murder or brutality, not polluting the planet, sparing the other species who share the world with us—that is okay, surely. That is how flowers and trees live now. In fact it is the way most of the living creatures on the planet exist; they simply... *exist*. True, we cannot really empathize with such a condition, it is almost beyond our grasp. So trying to imagine ourselves in such a world is pointless. Nothing is more pointless, however, and more cruel, than routine, unstoppable death itself.

I cannot imagine what is in anyone's head who disagrees with that assertion. Suppose you learn that over a period of weeks you are going to have your arms and your legs amputated as the result of a madman's lottery. Do you have any objections to this fate, one you cannot escape? Some features of the world *as it is right now* are precisely and obviously that atrocious.

We do not like getting sick, we do not like getting painfully old (although we might welcome the soothing pace of those more tranquil years, if our health remained fair), and it is not very joyous to see loved ones die. Some argue that death enriches life. It is true that the way we respond to *any* experience, no matter how vile and unconscionable, can enrich our lives. Fortitude and courage flourish under adversity, but so too do pettiness, evasion, fear, betrayal. Suppose you really did live in a demented regime where the authorities sent around a man once a year to cut off one of your fingers until they were all gone, and then started on your toes. (Impossibly silly? Think of cliterodectomy, imposed in some luckless communities by older women upon younger women in the name of tradition, decency, divine will.) If this happened to everybody, and always had done so back through the generations, I have no doubt people would adjust, would develop rich and meaningful spiritual experiences as a result. This is what we do, we humans, we deal with the real world. But that is hardly the optimal world to imagine living in.

A world in which we are doomed to sicken and die, and then rot, is even worse.

That is *this* world. Perhaps it need not be, and perhaps soon it no longer will be—unless those who enforce despicable horrors like genital mutilation prevent the change.

I am now entering the experience of getting old. Even in my 20s I could see that old age was not a very enviable prospect. I insisted to anyone who would listen that it would be a good idea if we could stop aging and death as soon as possible. Now that I am drawing closer to old age and death, I know directly and irritably how bad it is not to be able to see nearly as well as formerly, nor hear as acutely. Even sleeping; what a disaster. I used to have wonderful sleep, I'd hop cozily into bed, drop off instantly, wake up refreshed recalling rich dreams. That no longer happens so often nowadays. The aging body aches even in rest.

We have to put a stop to this pointless decay. Once, the best and the only relief people could anticipate was the surcease of death. Now we have a finer hope, one made possible in the brilliant exercise of intelligence and directed, experimental imagination: the end of aging, perhaps the medical recovery and maintenance of healthy youthfulness and, not impossibly, the death of routine death itself.

ii

Death is intensely personal. We are more moved by death than by any other passage—except, perhaps, birth. I myself have never seen a baby born, never fathered a child of my own, and indeed have taken steps to ensure that I never do. But I watched with great emotion as my father's elder sister quietly died in hospital, her face and body reduced to bones and rags by her final illness. A few years earlier my mother had died of cancer at just 66. Once that would have made her very old. Nowadays, it is no more than late middle-age. Such an incredible waste—she was still working through a degree she had started a few years before, after a lifetime of looking after the kids and her husband.

We take such tales for granted. After all, everyone gets old and eventually dies. But why should that be? Surprisingly, there is growing evidence that aging and its fatal consequence results from coding mistakes that accumulate in our cells and their genes. Some scientists now argue that these errors might be remediable, and that technologies to make those repairs can be expected during the next century, perhaps as early as the next couple of decades. Indeed, some of the key steps have already been achieved in the laboratory.

For example, healthy human skin slowly replaces itself following damage, but cells normally lose this self-repair capacity after some 65 or 80 divisions, and finally perish. Now such cells have been literally *immortalized*, in the lab, using a breakthrough discovery made by cell-biologist Elizabeth Blackburn, for which she received the prestigious Australia Prize in 1998 (prior to her ill-fated tenure with the Kass bioethics committee). In January 2000, it was announced that experimental human cell cultures had exceeded 500 divisions—some seven times as many as usual—and since then appear to have become permanent. Fix all the dividing cells in this way, and we would be halfway to an indefinite lifespan.[57]

iii

Death in aggregate tends to move us less fiercely than the passing of a loved one, or even of a pet. In the face of death as the reaper of millions we do not know, our kindest emotions sag beneath 'compassion fatigue'. And for the young, death and its mimicry can also provide the wildest of thrills. Healthy young gangs of men travel great distances to maim each other in soccer game riots, just for the pleasure of it. Vivid computer simulations allow youths to obliterate imaginary foes in gory detail— even to flash whole cities into nuclear fire. We embrace what terrifies us most. Or we ignore and suppress it. But death will not go away—unless we *make* it go away.

For the first time since single-cell life coalesced on this planet, we are perhaps within reach of doing just that.

Cautious skeptics regard the claim that death might be defeated within 30 or even 100 years as evidence of emotional arrest at the stage of denial. Death is so terrible, they say, so final, so unappeasable, that naive science groupies flee from its implacability into a fantasy of technical redemption or reprieve. Indeed, the environmentalist writer Bill McKibben has addressed my case for the abolition of inevitable aging and death in just these terms. In his eloquent but profoundly confused tract *Enough* (2003), McKibben states without feeling any need for supporting argument that Robert Ettinger and Hans Moravec and Gregory Stock and Robert Freitas and I advocate healthy life extension without our understanding how 'weird or gross or boring' living forever would be (156). Indeed, he assumes we are *afraid* of dying, rather than outraged by death's waste. He calls us 'true believers' (85) and 'unhinged by death' (147) when we point out that sometime in the medium-term future mortality will become optional—and yet McKibben does not dispute that this will become technically possible. The wish not to senesce and then die (at 80 or so, presumably, rather than humankind's traditional 25 or 35 or 55) is ipso facto 'unhinged'. It offends against 'gut feelings'.

Granted, as yet no method recommended by science—or by magic, affirmation or prayer, for that matter—has managed to extend human life beyond the naturally evolved limit of about 120 years. But what *has* changed lately is that geneticists have extended the lifespan of at least some living creatures, such as

---

[57] See, for example, http://www.senescence.info/clock.htm and http://www.swmed.edu/home_pages/cellbio/shay-wright/ publications/classic.experiment.pdf

nematode worms, allowing them to live as much as seven times longer than their unmodified kin. This is not yet the abolition of death—but it looks very much like the first step toward that goal. Cynthia Kenyon, who made these discoveries, comments:

> People have shown that the system first found in worms controls longevity in fruit flies and mice. That means it had to evolve early in a common precursor of mice, flies and worms. In genetics everything else that has been found to be true in mice, flies and worms has also been found in humans—with variation, of course, but the basic system is the same. We don't know for sure yet, but on rational scientific grounds the chances are very high.[58]

Suppose this remarkable claim is correct. The very possibility forces us to ask a quite profound question:

Must thinking about death in the somewhat remote and clinical mode of science distract us from the fundamental agony of loss whose truest answering voice is music and the hard-edged melodies of poetry? I am the last to dismiss the power of the arts; I have been publishing fiction for more than forty years, and hope to go on doing so for centuries yet—if I'm lucky, if we beat mortality to a standstill in the next 20 or 30 years, and learn how to repair the ravages of aging (a trick performed by every new baby, created from old cells in its parents' bodies).

I believe we are justified in confronting death with knowledge and determination, rather than trying to appease it by mythic verse and surrender. But solving death, and life, is not just a technical project. It embraces everything that makes us human. The first immortal generation will not be the children of science alone, but of law, art, music, writing—all the humane arts.

iv

When health and youthfulness are prolonged into the hundreds of years, will ordinary life, as we know it, persist? Almost certainly not. After all, an extremely hightech future is needed to support such medical triumphs, and that will create other unexpected discontinuities. I have tried to sketch how the work-force will alter in *The Spike*. Swiftly accelerating change in supercomputers, genomics and nanotechnology will ensure that by 2050 very few jobs will be unchanged. Most of today's work will

---

[58] http://www.newscientist.com/opinion/opinterview.jsp?id=ns24171

be either gone or on the verge of vanishing, done by smart machines using molecular manufacturing techniques still on the drawing board today.

So we will need to reorganize the economic bases of society, and nobody should expect that to be easy or painless—but the ageless will not face today's problems writ large. They will have problems of their own, no doubt, but new ones. Constructing utopia (and preventing horrific local warfare between restless new tribes and gangs) will give them something to do with all their free time...

Bill McKibben (like Leo Kass, and most others on the President's Committee) is appalled by the prospect. 'But you *can't* "enjoy the gift of life" forever. Maybe with these new tools you can *live* forever, but the joy of it—the meaning of it—will melt away like ice cream on an August afternoon. It is true that nothing short of these new technologies will make us immortal, but immortality is a fool's goal. Living must be enough for us, not living forever' (2003: 161).

My notion of joy is a little less saccharine than ice cream on an August afternoon, which is admittedly pleasant but not to die for, and I find McKibben's confident insight into the spiritual misery and existential emptiness of people 1000 years old entirely amazing. How can he *know* these things with such certainty? And how can he *know* that there will be no cure for the ailment (the achingly empty misery) that he just *knows* must afflict the optionally undying? I am not saying confidently that he is wrong—I don't know either. But his hubris in demanding that the gate be barred in our faces is breathtaking... literally.

The world of emortals surely will be increasingly strange. Many people will bend, eventually, under the shock of relentless change. Some of those will simply choose, either in despair or with dignity, to remove themselves from the project of endless life. That must be their privilege. But they will be missing out on some very interesting and rewarding times.

McKibben's certainty might derive from a traditional source. He lives with his wife and daughter in the Adirondack Mountains, where he is a Sunday school superintendent of the local Methodist church.[59] Might the ambition to attain indefinite life be seen, in and of itself, as an affront to God, a new impious Tower of Babel? I do not see why. The longer we have to savor the rich joys and tests of earthly life, the more opportunities we gain to mature, to love, help, build, to take and share responsibility. Life is as replete and meaningful as we make it, and if we can share in the glories of the world for a thousand years instead of a mere seventy or eighty, I cannot imagine that a loving deity would resent our tenure here, or punish us for living well and long.

---

[59] http://www.annonline.com/interviews/981217/biography.html

Within that passionate quest for understanding, we will surely also seek to nourish the quiet, serene arts of living well, and—if death is, after all, finally unavoidable, however long postponed—of dying well.

And in the meantime? How tragic to stand under the shadow of the executioner's sword even as the pardon is being rushed to us! If its sharp blade falls, we are as dead and gone as any peasant or priest or king in the suffering, long history and prehistory of the world. Plainly, the only prudent move is to do everything possible to forestall accidental or infective death during the next decade or three, and to adopt as many healthy practices as we can manage without altogether giving up on the vivid texture of life.

That much is under the individual's control. Social and political factors play a larger role. Mortality rates vary shockingly between nations and even states or regions within nations. If we mean to ensure the best feasible health for everyone, we need to start with the basics: Enough food and supplements for mothers and infants. Sufficient for the rest of the community as well. Clean water and air. Modern sanitation. Immunization programs. Decent medical and dental care.

The most frightening apartheid one could imagine is a future world in which extended life is allowed only to a few—the very wealthy, the political elite and their chosen followers, Mafia, military, scientists, sports heroes, movie stars. It is up to all of us to ensure that this future never happens. We will not best prevent it by denouncing technical advances and trying to blockade them, but in thinking hard, feeling deeply and wisely, debating the issues together, and acting as free men and women.

If we choose to enhance the human condition, to mitigate as best we can the horrors and blunders blind evolution has imposed, that will be a step toward diversity in unity, one taken in the confidence that old tyrannies were marked exactly by ferocious control and interdiction of knowledge. A deathless society without a free flow of information, and opportunities to choose, would indeed be dismal. We must ensure that the form of the future is not foreclosed by panic or mistrust. For doubters like McKibben, the pursuit of indefinite healthy longevity would be the slippery slope to the final erosion of meaning from our (formerly) mortal lives. That meaning, allegedly, derives from our transience and continuity with the rest of the natural world. This does not mean, somehow, that we have to give up reading or wearing clothes, even though sparrows and worms and bacteria cannot do that. How so? The argument falls away into a shrugging posture: if you don't see (or *feel*) why, evidently, it obviously shows how spiritually bankrupt you must already be...

For those of us who are now alive, the astonishing difference from the past is that we really *do* have a chance, finally. The twentieth century witnessed cruel oppression and phoenix recovery again and again, most poignantly perhaps in the survivors of the Holocaust. Millions died, but some prevailed even in those hellish conditions. Perhaps it will be that way for us, too, faced by the cruelty of evolution's strategies of death. We must live as vividly as we may, while life is ours—hoping that we will triumph, in the end, even over that final enemy. And not just passively hoping, but acting to make it so.

v

I was not there at the exact moment of my mother's passing away. But I had wept beside her sick-bed as we forgave each other for being fallible human beings, and spoke of our love, too late, too late. Now, well over a decade later, my father sits each day in a nursing home, held to his chair or bed by a strap lest he fall and break some part of his fragile old man's flesh. His mind is already broken, except for rare flickers of canny but usually madly irrelevant commentary.

You have to wonder if it is really necessary, all this pain, all this decay, all this pointless death.

If we or our children are to be the first *immortal* generation—the first for whom death is not an automatic imposition of our genes—then we must be prepared to fund the necessary research, demand that every effort be spent on that last and most extraordinary quest. Above all, we need to grasp this almost-unbelievable fact: that perhaps we have it within our reach to make the overthrow of routine human death our epoch's responsibility and wonderful privilege.[60]

---

[60] A start can be made by everyone who wishes to donate small or large amounts to Dr. Aubrey de Grey's Methuselah Mouse Prize, aimed at encouraging major longevity-enhancing research in mammals: http://www.methuselahmouse.org/

Virtual Realities

Once, at an Australian National University two-day conference devoted surprisingly enough to science fiction, I fell into conversation with one of the audience, a striking, vividly intelligent prostitute. Woody Allen has a routine about the Whore of Mensa; it took on fresh meaning. After the first day's academic sessions, we lolled about merrily discussing the Gnostic distinction between *pleroma* and *creatura*, you know the sort of thing. She doted on sf, she said, for the genre's intellectual cut and thrust, its fun and lack of bigotry. Her working partner turned up, quite exhausted by certain visiting diplomats. Where my new friend was charming and feisty, this woman was pure essence of hard-faced, nasal Australian pragmatism. 'Ravin' on again, is she? Bloody sci fi. Can't stand the stuff meself. Nothing *real* in it, is there?'

The Melbourne *Age* broadsheet newspaper, for which I wrote a regular sf review column throughout the 1980s, hired a new Book Pages editor. He was working on his own literary novel and told me he had never been able to read sf himself. He allowed, however, rather as one throws a mangy dog a bone, that his two boys loved the stuff. I regarded his youthful, unlined brow, and decided that this was not an encouraging line of thought for a grown-up sf writer. Just the thing for bored kids on a wet afternoon, eh?

He was right and he was wrong. I suspect he was thinking of the comic-strip sf of, say, *Star Trek*. Matters have moved along since then, and not just with the awesome sight of Arnold Schwarzenegger, before he took up the Governor's burden, ripping humans apart on the big screen, saying 'Fock you' in a muffled Austrian accent while the acne-faced kids in the audience guffaw, jolted by their new gushers of testosterone. Science fiction merged with postmodernism in the brief silicon flowering of cyberpunk, stories set in the mirrored interface between sense, thought and computer-generated virtual realities.[61] Did this new condition redeem sf for the grandees of literary taste? Not quite. For a time, the *Age* newspaper had the good fortune to run sf reviews by Peter Nicholls, founding editor of the massively authoritative (and entertaining) *Encyclopedia of Science Fiction*. Despite the presence of this icon of sf sense and sensibility, curious opinions were not absent from the newspaper's Book Pages, evidence that literary segregation remained as potent as ever. Witness a regular columnist's wonderful reinvention of the sf wheel.

'Remembering forwards is difficult for most of us,' the late Dr. Helen Daniel remarked, reminding us of the White Queen's preference

---

[61] See my *Reading by Starlight: Postmodern Science Fiction*, London: Routledge, 1994.

(in Lewis Carroll's *Alice*) for recalling 'things that happen the week after next'. These were the words of a critic of immense and variegated learning and an admirer of transgressive postmodern game-playing. All the more startling, surely, that she now proposed a *new kind of fiction!*—the 'futuristic novel', including the 'uchronia'. Sf readers have known this form for generations: tales of 'alternate worlds', in which some key event took a knight's turn into an alternative history—such as the outlaw bushranger Ned Kelly having become President of an Australian Republic.

As examples of such astonishing new forms, Daniel listed a dystopia by Ignacio de Loyola Brandao, Dame P. D. James's novel about universal human sexual sterility, and books with eco/environmental themes by Australians George Turner, Gabrielle Lord, Joan Dugdale and Blanche d'Alpuget. 'It's not easy remembering forward and thinking in the future tense,' she concluded. But a bit of remembering backwards and sideways might have done her argument—and the status of sf enthusiasts—rather a lot of good.

I am neither cringing nor complaining about this selective blindness. My point is that traditional literary critics and readers are short-changing *themselves* in failing to notice that whole ecospheres of 'futurist' novels and stories already exist in profusion, fictions that long ago populated those alien shores which daring traditionalists imagine have been visited only lately by a few brave explorers. This self-inflicted ignorance impoverishes readers afraid to cross genre barriers.

Of Daniel's six exemplary 'futurists', only Turner was an acknowledged sf novelist. Yet sf is the very habitation and name of her supposed breakthrough in shaping the forms of things unknown. It was not really sublimely inventive of P. D. James to posit a sterilized, childless world, since 30 years earlier the very good writer Brian W. Aldiss not only got there first, in *Greybeard,* but did so with Thomas Hardy-like poignancy. In *The White Plague*, Frank Herbert used the same device in a complex meditation on terrorism and the human condition. While plenty of sf is undeniably consumer pap—fairytales with starships—its evolution as a distinctive variety of popular fiction has mapped precisely that vast territory which postmodern literary theorists quaintly believe to be their new-found *terra nullius.*

As a quick exercise, I jotted down an alphabetical list of authors and titles—books that might not altogether unhinge the fragile non-sf reader, although some will seem difficult to enter. Consider these as essays in proleptic literature, in remembering the future or inventing the Other:

Brian Aldiss, *Greybeard*; Greg Bear, *Queen of Angels*; Damien Broderick, *The Judas Mandala*; Arthur C. Clarke, *The Fountains of Paradise*; Thomas M. Disch, *334*; Philip K. Dick, *Ubik*; Greg Egan, *Permutation City*; Karen Joy Fowler, *Sarah Canary*; William Gibson, *Virtual Light*; Frank Herbert, *The White Plague*; Dean Ing, *Soft Targets*;

Gwyneth Jones, *White Queen*; Daniel Keyes, *Flowers for Algernon*; Ursula Le Guin, *Always Coming Home*; Walter M. Miller, *A Canticle for Leibowitz*; Linda Nagata, *The Bohr Maker*; Rebecca Ore, *The Illegal Rebirth of Billy the Kid*; Frederik Pohl, *The Year of the City*; Daniel Quinn, *Ishmael*; Kim Stanley Robinson, *Pacific Edge* or his immense, Tolstoyan trilogy *Red, Green* and *Blue Mars*; Lucius Shepard, *Life During Wartime*; George Turner, *Brainchild*; John Updike, *Toward the End of Time*; Vernor Vinge, *Marooned in Realtime*; Connie Willis, *Passage*; Chelsea Quinn Yarbro, *Time of the Fourth Horseman*; Roger Zelazny, *The Dream Master*.

These are not necessarily science fiction's finest works, for sf's imaginative power is diminished by the timid request that its tales should begin in the near or recognizable future (a restriction I have relaxed slightly in any case). Some are hardly to my own taste, and not a few carry the taint of the genre's genesis in primary-color, headlong adventure. Yet each bears us confidently to an alien shore, over the horizon of the safely remembered.

ii

Back in the twentieth century, as I noted at the start of chapter 20, the two canonical emblems of comic book futurity were the year 2000, and humans on the Moon. When both came and went, each event was, inevitably, reduced on the instant to banality.

Twenty-five years before the Apollo Moon landing was 1944, the height of the war against Hitler, the year I was born, and everyone (so I'm told) brayed like jackasses when people like Isaac Asimov and Arthur Clarke told them humans would shortly be flying into space. I got the same reaction from an elderly teacher when I was in fifth grade in Jesuit primary school, and that was a mere two years before Sputnik and six before Yuri Gagarin rocketed into orbit.

Twenty-five years before the *faux*-millennial year 2000 was 1975. The personal computer revolution had not yet booted up. In 1975 the mirthful equivalent of *landing on the Moon* would have been, let us guess, *cyberspace* and *virtual reality*, although nobody had yet heard of them under those names. It was the year I mailed off to the United States a novel called *The Judas Mandala*, eventually published in 1982. Here is a fragment from that book, set in the remote world of 6039, when most of the world's remaining humans drift in dreams written for them by advanced cybernetic organisms or cyborgs. My 20th century lesbian narrator, who has been bushwhacked into the future, is trapped in just such a simulation:

> For the first time [she says], I understood the overwhelming lure of addiction, the honeys of

transcendental art. I understood how it could be that the Dreamvats of the cyborgs contained the majority of the world's living human beings, their brains afire on a junkie's junket of total fantasies.

For being on line to Dream circuits was the ultimate art. There was nothing paltry or imposed about cyborg fantasy. Verisimilitude was unsurpassed. Each character I encountered in the endless cast of my sleeping universe was rich with density, beyond the resource of a Murasaki, a Shakespeare, a Dostoievski. It was solipsism tuned bracingly to my supine needs.

I understood its addiction and its horror: The hunt is done and bellies are full. In the flickering firelight the tribe lean forward to hear and tell their boasts. The old ones sing, at last, the sagas of their once and future heroes. In the Dreamtanks, at the apotheosis of art, the old ones live and sing forever... (1982: 154-5)

I dubbed these machine-human hybrids 'cyborgs', drawing on the 1960 NASA analysis by the polymath Dr. Manfred Clynes and Nathan Kline[62]. Since then, the word has become so overused and debased, especially in the *Terminator* movies, that all its freshness was lost. What is more, since I wrote that novel my own attitude to living in cyberspace as an uploaded consciousness has mellowed. Uploading might well be the path of choice for advanced conscious beings, evading the deplorable tendency of flesh and blood to deteriorate and then perish in death. Uploads might die too, of course, but they have the option of backing themselves up or, less controversially, scattering redundant portions of their machine-implemented being through space, keeping them connected by radio or laser. That is not entirely weird and creepy, upon reflection; already we are a composite of left and right cerebral hemispheres, each of which emerges as a slightly different person if the neural cable linking them, the corpus callosum, is cut. Yet both normally work together to create our juggling-act sense of unified identity. Living inside cyberspace, rather than using it as an external communications medium, will utterly blur the boundaries between real and virtually real.

iii

The magisterial *Encyclopedia of Science Fiction* credits me with coining the term 'virtual reality' in that novel, written more than a quarter of a century ago. (It appeared on page 119 of my slim paperback.) The term is more generally attributed to Jaron Lanier, who in the real world did key work in

---

[62] http://www.superconductor.com/clynes/mcbiog.htm

developing simulation programs and hardware such as data gloves. Asked by Barbara Lamar if he had borrowed the term from me, he said:

> 'virtual world' was the term used by ivan sutherland, who made the first head-mounted display—'virtual reality' was meant by me to mean a kind of virtual world which was social—more than one person—so that people would see each other and have bodies, instead of just looking at the non-human environment—that was the purpose for the term 'vr'—(i made the first networked virtual world)—the term 'virtual world' was made up, so far as i know, by susanne langer, a philosopher of esthetics, in the 1950s.

As for the term VR itself:

> So far as I know I made it up, but who knows? The first use of the phrase was by Antonin Artaud back in the 1920s, though I didn't know about that at the time, which was about 1981.

Artaud's coinage did not denote, of course, what we have in mind today: William Gibson's cyberspace in *Neuromancer*, *The Matrix*, all that. Still, in *The Theater and Its Double* (1938), the deranged French playwright claimed that the alchemy of theatre yielded a 'la realite virtuell', intended to provoke a transformation of matter into mind, an image beckoning to us, he claimed, from 'the incandescent edges of the future'.[63]

Lanier added: 'The first programming language for vr was called Mandala, and was from about that time, so it is a double coincidence, I guess.'

I just thought I would mention that. Coincidences are such fun.

iv

How will it be like, living in such a profoundly modified and modifiable world? What kind of art will we create?

Consider Alasdair Foster's 2001 *New Australiana* photographic exhibition:[64] Stevie Everton-Smith's cheerfully vulgar *Skimpy Girls and Pissed Turkeys*, Gia Mitchell's surprise transsexual *Mutton Dressed as Lamb: The Journey of the Pineapple Princess*, Tracey Moffatt's voyeuristic *Heaven*. From the perspective of my pinched 1950s'

---

[63] Cited at http://www.dromo.com/fusionanomaly/antoninartaud.html from Erik Davis, *Techgnosis: Myth, Magic & Mysticism In The Age Of Information*.

[64] http://www.pica.org.au/artist01/australiana.html

childhood memories, Australia's pre-millennial decade was a literally unbuttoned and shocking utopia of the remote future. Still, when people someday start taking off their bodies instead of their clothes and their genitalia, and recreating them with new lurid prolificity, uploaded into cyberspace where it is larger inside than outside (computing new magical physics, so you can experience yourself—richly, physically—flying or teleporting, and morphing your body image in an instant to a horse, a cat, a cloud, a song), those photographs too will recall an innocent and cramped generation.

Famously, Karl Marx wrote in his youthful *Theses on Feuerbach*: 'The philosophers have only *interpreted* the world in various ways; the point, however, is to *change* it' (1959: 245). Looking at the hideous botch his avowed followers helped make of the twentieth century, it might seem that philosophers would do well to interpret the world *correctly* before troubling themselves to change it, especially with violence. But what happens when the world, however we interpret it, is changing whether we like it or not? And not just changing at the sluggish old rate that replaced caves and tents with high-rises (and, a little faster, horses with cars), but accelerating pell-mell into a future of unimaginable strangeness?

That convergence of advanced technologies seems likely to carry us beyond the horizon of the human future, into a realm where all bets are off and nothing can be predicted with certainty. If the Spike is truly on the agenda, driven by new science and technology, it will not wait around for the year 3000. And if the Spike is our future, will we any longer in that altered world be able to take a photo or paint a picture and display it, beyond the horizon of strangeness? Will there be anyone there with simple eyes to look at it?

Artists have never simply interpreted or represented the world; we have always been as much *makers* as *correspondents* who fetch back the news from the reality front, perhaps with a bit of expedient embellishment. The texts of makers need not correspond to anything given, not in a direct way. Roll the film, capture light in pixels, the process looks like representation—but of course the moment we select the frame, cut the sequence or crop the image, and then present the work to an audience, it is a made thing, a contrivance. Postmodernism taught us that much at least, even if it fell too far into the silly new age wistfulness that supposes we 'create our own reality'. Just as your right to throw your fist stops at the end of my nose, your ability to create your own reality stops there too, or maybe at your own mouth: imagine a delicious dinner as forcefully as you like, it will not nourish you for long. (Painting or photographing a meal might, of course, earn you enough to buy yourself one. It need not be enticing or beautiful. A dinner plate covered in gruesome mold or vomit fetches a steeper price from chic art lovers.) But in the next couple of decades, new technologies *will* close the gap between the solid and the imagined. We might end up eating our dreams, quite literally. Even before that curious economy of the electronic body/mind crystallizes in cyberspace, we shall surely inhabit a world made as much from mental images as any artist's reveries.

I mean that literally. In the almost immediate future, we can expect an explosion of new imaging and presentational media that will continue today's increasingly effortless transition from world to image to reception/re-creation. Hologram movies have been a long time coming and maybe they are still off in the middle distance, but right now the Xerox Research Center of Canada has developed a prototype polymer, polythiophene, that will allow organic transistors to be built—or grown—on a flexible plastic substrate. So we can forget Palms and other hard, lumpy storage and display gadgets. We can anticipate cheap drivers and liquid crystal displays on a surface you can fold, spindle and mutilate, or stuff into your pocket, or drape over the cat like something out of Dali.

Meanwhile, the *Journal of Chemical Physics* reports that a black and white image 32 pixels on a side has been stored and retrieved in... a *single molecule*. University of Oklahoma researchers into a coming 'molecular photography' used 19 hydrogen atoms in a liquid crystal molecule to store more than a thousand bits of data inside the whirling magnetic moments of the protons.[65]

These two experimental technologies already make a new digital camcorder seem a tad like a box Brownie. But why use physical media to represent and create images? Why not enhance or bypass the eyes entirely? As noted in chapter 18, neuroscience is starting to unlock the fantastically complex wiring and processing of the brain's visual system. Exponential increases in computer power at cheaper prices make it likely that communities will deploy dispersed systems of nodes or localizers bringing us overlays via dedicated miniaturized contact lenses or induced feeds to the occipital regions of the brain. Vinge's imaginative novella 'Fast Times at Fairmont High' (2001), winner of a Hugo Award, explored such a moderately near-term future. His schoolboy Juan notes that the wind is blowing through his hair in a way impossible to emulate without 'gaming stripes'. But the visual illusions are complete:

> With all enhancements turned off, the houses were low and stony-looking, set well back from the street. Some of the yards were beautifully kept, succulents and dwarf pines... Others were workaday neat...

---

[65] 1024 bits stored in a molecule:
http://science.slashdot.org/article.pl?sid=02/12/02/005232&mode=thread&tid=134
polythiophene organic semiconductor:
http://www.nytimes.com/2002/12/03/technology/03XERO.html?todaysheadlines

Juan turned on consensus imagery. No surprise, the street was heavily prepped. The augmented landscape was pretty, in an understated way: the afternoon sunlight sparkled off fountains and lush green lawns. Now the low stony houses were all windows and airy patios.. But there were no public sensors. There was no advertising and graffiti. The neighborhood was so perfectly consistent, a single huge work of art. (419, 424)

Such a world might be plagued with spam ads on every surface, as in Spielberg's *Minority Report* (2002). In my novel, *The White Abacus* (1997), most people see the world as a composite of concrete reality and elaborate, optional decoration. That can cause confusion to anyone luckless enough (like the boy in the following scene) to be excluded from the internal display system:

Despite the day's brightness and evident heat, [the man] was lavishly clad, from his broad heavy shoes to his bulky sleeveless gown, furred in ermine... Under the gown he wore waistcoat, jerkin, doublet opened at the bulging codpiece. His massive arms, swinging, moved easily in sleeves slashed and puffed. It was a formidable display. Fashion glosses flickered: **Hans Holbein the Younger, Henry VIII,** items of garb orbiting an historic attractor in couture dataspace...

'Citizen! The red singlet!'

For an instant I, too, was confused... I understood, then, with something of a shock, that the boy was somehow operating without Gestell access.

Tsin said at the same moment, 'You'll notice, Sen, that the young man is in vanilla mode. No aks.'

I plunged into the tuple field, fetched out [the man's] unaugmented appearance. He was indeed wearing a shabby red singlet stained under the armpits in sweat, sloppy shorts of an execrable tartan, and a pair of heavy walking boots. I let the eidolon cover him again decently. (8-9)

This needs quite a bit of unpacking, since the narrator's terminology reflects lived experience in that future. Readers slowly grow to understand that most of the humans (hu) and artificial intelligences (ai) are linked by a super-Internet called the Gestell, which they access (aks) at will. 'Gestell' comes from German philosopher Martin Heidegger's fiercely negative analysis of the global technological system we are already embedded in. Much of the terminology (tuples, etc) comes from David Gelernter's fluent analysis, *Mirror Worlds*; tragically, Dr. Gelernter was a victim of the notorious and cowardly Unabomber, whose explosive device ruined the computer scientist's hands. The approach to the Singularity will be a race between headlong technology and such Luddite foes.

Like Vinge and earlier sf writers such as Samuel R. Delany, I propose that a kind of augmented or enhanced reality will be commonplace in the future. The world's drab surfaces might be cloaked by eidolons or trompes (from *trompe l'oeil*, the old art of fooling the eye into seeing depth in a flat painting). In Vinge's tale, the tricky images arrive via smart contact lenses that collect data beamed from localizer nodes scattered around the landscape. My Gestell works directly through the tweaked genomes of my future communitarian anarchists; they have modified organs able to create and detect the world-building imagery mediated by the Gestell.

That vista, though, is surely too far off into the exponential future, one short step from a world where we humans replace ourselves with posthumans. (Not *necessarily* replace, however: they might be our children, or even ourselves, drastically enhanced, rejuvenated, rewritten, transcended.) A more plausible tomorrow, though, might somewhat resemble the augmented reality that Vinge and I and others have imagined in science fiction. Let me return to the opening of *The White Abacus*, where my young ai enters the rococo Melbourne Opera House, a blend of old and new:

> A Gestell gloss flickered: the nanosurfaces of this public room were tromping the Amalienburg pavilion in Munich's Nymphenburg Palace... Gloss pop-ups cascaded an Archive hyperspace as I glanced admiringly at the wonderful snaking curves of the room's mirror panes: my riffling background attention snared for a moment on **Nymphenburg porcelain** (c. 1755) and *Anton Bustelli*'s theatrical, delicate rococo figurines: luscious masquers from the commedia dell'arte, richly draped patricians, cavaliers' elegant ladies... The building's ambient audio filler—crystalline fractals rotating in a serial space—segued to ocean hushing on a shore, accompanied by a single clarinet scat... Korngold's sunny invention seemed to fill the room, impeding the conversation of the five hu at the room's far end, until I realized that I was taking a node-feed from a private transponder. (5-6)

Even compared with the buoyantly tolerant permissiveness of today's Australia, this is a media-engulfed and googled world. The reality will be a future beyond media, but only because it is so thoroughly entangled in the technologies of inventive figuration.

Next to that ambiguous quote from Marx, we might place one from free market economist Ludwig von Mises, in his book *Theory and History*: 'The outstanding fact about history is that it is a succession of events that nobody anticipated.' If so, is it foolish to predict so radical a dislocation as the Spike promises to be? Perhaps not. It is precisely its unknowability, the curtain it draws across tomorrow, that makes the Spike's shadow so disturbing. 'The fallacy inherent in predicting the course of history,' von Mises went on, 'is that the prophets assume no ideas will ever possess the minds of men but those they themselves already know' (1957: 378-9). Nothing could be farther from the perspective of the technological singularity, where all certainties dissolve except the assurance of drastic change.

Wonderment and Science

> Fools have said
> That knowledge drives out wonder from the
> world;
> They'll say it still, though all the dust's ablaze
> With miracles at their feet; while Newton's laws
> Foretell that knowledge one day shall be song,
> And those whom Truth has taken to her heart
> Find that it beats in music.
> Even this age
> Has glimmerings of it. Newton never saw
> His own full victory; but at least he knew
> That all the world was linked in one again;
> And, if men found new worlds in years to come,
> These too must join the universal song.
> Alfred Noyes ('Sir John Herschel Remembers')[66]

i

Science is under bitter assault for the way its motivating *interests*—set by policy and ideology alike—have often deformed its growth, and damaged its victims. So pervasive are these factors that they are mostly hidden in plain view. It took a lot of spade-work by the women's movement before we could even detect the patriarchal cast of the reductionism of traditional scientific practice. Until then, the domination of research and teaching by senior men, with their specific (some would say ruthless) cast of mind, seemed ordinary as the sun's rising.

Still, even if we grant that the activity of science has mixed motives, might not we prefer to support molecular genetics over, say, the ignorance of common-sense or the absurdities of astrology? Despite scandals and demystification, isn't the scientist still our epoch's pre-eminent creative seeker after truth?

Alas, it is not that simple. David Foster, Australian novelist and former cancer researcher, once caustically asserted that the scientist is the operational definition of a hack. Despite those soaring quests among the stars for the Mind of God, in reality the highest ambition of the scientist is a set of procedures, or algorithms, so banal and repeatable that anyone possessing the appropriate trained skills can obtain reliable results by joining the dotted lines.

Happily for fans of science, there *is* that other way of regarding the scientist seethed in her own juices. Countering Foster's scorn (mimicked

---

[66]. ftp://ibiblio.org/pub/docs/books/gutenberg/etext04/wtcsk10.txt

in its way by pragmatic philistines) is a surprising image from the late Lewis Thomas, former director of the Sloan-Kettering Cancer Center and extraordinary rhapsodic, polymathic essayist: 'Scientists at work are rather like young animals engaged in savage play. When they are near an answer their hair stands on end, they sweat, they are awash in their own adrenalin' (Thomas, 1974:118).

Thomas was an experimentalist as well as an administrator; his description finds a striking echo from Richard Feynman, whose Nobel Prize was for theoretical work in quantum electrodynamics, that ultimate abstraction:

> Sometimes I feel like an ape, trying to figure out how nature's going to behave, fooling around with all those symbols.... You get so excited you can't calculate, you can't think any more. It isn't just that nature's wonderful, because if someone tells me the answer to a problem I'm working on, it's nowhere near as exciting as if I work it out myself. (cited Calder, 1970:215; cf. Feynman, 1986; Gleick, 1993.)

On philosopher Thomas Kuhn's now-famous account (1962), science is by turns classical and romantic, austere and explosive, conservative and revolutionary. Beyond those binary oppositions (nowhere in reality found so neatly), there exist shades of tone and mood. Science is also, in a psychological sense, *magical*. (In the academy, this was recognized by French philosopher of science Michel Serres, who stands with his alchemic patron Hermes Trismegistus at the boundaries of myth and science.) For while science may usually be hackwork, it can clearly stir the hairs on the neck. Describing a Wood's Hole beach where marine biologists eat their lunch, Lewis Thomas captured something lyrical which transcends the myth of the cold laboratory elitist:

> You can hear the sound from the beach at a distance ... that most extraordinary noise, half-shout, half-song, made by confluent, simultaneously raised human voices, explaining things to each other as fast as their minds will work. (Thomas, 1974:73)

For a non-scientist, the sole access to that joyous babble is a voyeuristic eavesdropping, recalling an ancient tension between painter and audience. What we as witnesses create (re-create) in the canvas has only a tendentious intersection with the sweating impulse that laid down its shaped edges, its fields of color. Art-as-consumable-object is a piece of social technology, twin to the physical technology that is at once the motivating spur and the merest by-product of Feynman's terrible excitement.

ii

During recent decades, even as the art market boomed and interviews with artists and writers were everywhere published, there was a strenuous and principled repudiation of the consumer aesthetic. The artist might not be dead in fact but there are sound reasons for acting *as if* death separates us from his or her authoritative hand. Strikingly, this is the tack we *automatically* take with science and its works. Today, it is the air we all breathe (or choke on).

Technological cultures are simply too diverse to sustain any wistful return to the often-mooted Aboriginal or Balinese equation of Social-Life-as-Art. The major obstacle in the way of any non-alienated dream is precisely this: that much of the creative thrust of a high-energy, high-information culture is expressed in scientific research, usually founded in daunting mathematics, of a thousand different and baffling varieties. What we lack is a conveyable poetics of science by which the non-specialist, the non-scientist, might grasp that fierce excitement of which Thomas and Feynman sang. Adapting a celebrated line from Susan Sontag: perhaps we need an erotics of science.

A grimmer, more pragmatic response than Lewis Thomas's has become fashionable among non-scientific intellectuals, blending clear-eyed cynicism toward the actual practice of science in centralized technocracies, with (all too often) considerable ignorance of the results and procedures of science.

It is instructive to see how many feminist women have responded to new reproductive technologies. Overcoming their aversion to the cold Frankenstein patriarchal horror of it all, they swot up their recombinant genetics and molecular biology, the better to arm for combat. The sentiment is often backed by gruesome example. Yet frequently it proceeds from a fundamental mistrust and (as it seems to me) misunderstanding of what impels scientists, male and female, in their efforts. Anxious and revolted spectators will never apprehend the joyful, ferocious delirium Feynman expresses, because most of the time we non-scientists, would-be polymaths or not, simply have no idea what a given research issue actually is. We must wrestle second-hand with a variety of tentative answers offered by working scientists. Here in awful earnest, half a century on, is Lord Snow's 'two cultures'.

Still, it is possible to begin by seeking out that peculiar kind of elevated pleasure gained in simply listening to those confluent human voices *explaining* things. Is this a regressive and dangerous pleasure? Perhaps; but it is also an aspect of maturity to rejoice in the activity of complex discourse. I cannot disguise the romantic cast of this view of science, and yet it is a romance not at odds with the spirit of the Enlightenment. Finally, it seems to me, a skeptical spectator's appreciation of current scientific knowledge, conjectures and practice might be less fruitfully grounded in suspicious rancor than in recognition of the joyous intoxication which makes hairs lift off one's neck.

'This passion of our kind

'For the process of finding out,' declared W. H. Auden,

'Is a fact one can hardly doubt

'But I would rejoice in it more

'If I knew more clearly what

'we wanted the knowledge for.'

Richard Feynman was furious. Here was one of the premier poets of the age of science 'directly confessing not understanding the emotional value of knowledge of nature.' James Gleick, in *Genius*, cites the great vulgarian scientist's necessary and sufficient retort: 'We want it,' Feynman wrote, 'so we can love Nature more' (1992:444).

iii

The future, Sir Arthur Clarke liked to say, is not what it used to be. That is a comment capturing our despondency at the way the latest millennium has not yet turned out to be the marvelous fantasy land we so long anticipated. But Clarke was a great technological optimist, and never pinned his hopes to a definite tomorrow. On the contrary: the first two chapters in his strange, sublime book *Profiles of the Future* were candidly and exuberantly, about 'the hazards of prophecy'.

Most know Clarke via the glacial majesty of Stanley Kubrick's great film *2001: A Space Odyssey*. Yet long before that movie astonished audiences in 1968, he was hailed as inventor of the communications satellite. Today the world is skeined with computerized comsats in low-earth orbit worth many billions of dollars, linking the planet into a global culture of many mansions. Clarke's triumph of prophecy is matched in hindsight by its comic pratfalls: his 1945 invention conceived three mighty space platforms high in geostationary orbit, crewed by technicians handling switchboards.

Seventeen years later, not long after the earliest primitive sputnik beeped from space, Clarke published his book of linked visionary essays that announced three whimsical laws. The first: when a distinguished but elderly scientist states that something is possible, he is almost always right. When he states that something is impossible, he is very probably wrong. The third law, more famous, states baldly: any sufficiently advanced technology is indistinguishable from magic. Utterly mind-bending if you were a teenager in 1964 when it came out in paperback, it still is, refurbished in a fourth edition for the jump to this new millennium.

Aptly, the future's revised portrait, like the future itself, is not what it used to be. In the early 1960s, Clarke's methodical originality pushed then-current physics to the boundaries of possible knowledge. Today the fascination of those early dreams is mixed with amused chagrin at the occasional blooper. Four decades ago, it seemed plausible that hovercraft might replace other forms of transportation, erasing the shoreline's natural boundary. In fact, the brutes are rowdy fuel-guzzlers. Clarke ruefully describes his own four-seater, which almost immediately broke down on a Sri Lankan beach and got handed off as an exhibit at the University of Moratuwa's engineering department (47-8).

In other predictions, Clarke suffered the very hazard he denounces, failure of nerve. Nowhere in the universe, he guessed in 1962, would gravity exceed a few hundred thousand times the force we feel on Earth. Within a few years vastly massive neutron stars were located, swiftly followed by black holes where gravity bends light itself. He did wonder if anti-gravity might some day be attained, but had no inkling that by the end of the 20th century astronomers would blame the very expansion of the universe on a cosmic burst of reverse gravitation (not tapped so far, however, for domestic appliances).

Still, there is also a kind of exultation in finding how far, and fast, real history has carried us toward the limits of the possible. Can we shrink people to the size of bugs? No, but maybe we will link our senses to theirs, sharing the world of ant and bee. That is, indeed, a form of virtual reality, glimpsed decades ahead of its real reality. Will we travel cheaply into orbit? Yes, if those space elevators can be built, hanging down like gigantic inverted beanstalks. Clarke popularized that prospect in 1979, and the strong carbon structures called buckytubes, as we saw in chapter 19, now make skyhooks a genuine engineering possibility.

Do we face resource exhaustion? Not soon, Clarke points out, because science repeatedly does more with less. Assuming we use it wisely, that is. 'In this inconceivably enormous universe, we can never run out of energy or matter. But we can all too easily run out of brains' (144). No fan of environmental despoliation, Clarke hopes that 'one day our age of roaring factories and bulging warehouses will pass away... [and our offspring] will remember what many of us have forgotten—that the only things in the world that really matter are such imponderables as beauty and wisdom, laughter and love' (150).

And if another of his futuristic prospects is won—indefinitely extended longevity—some of us might also still be here to share that lesson. The sequential editions of *Profiles of the Future* comprise a rich and illuminating patchwork of time, reminding us repeatedly how much has already changed. Initially, Clarke dated his roster of wonders as feasible within the next 500 years; now he slashes that to a mere century (and I think he is being rather conservative). A computer equal to a human brain, Clarke estimated in 1962, would require 'a single floor of the Empire State building'. Today it is 'a matchbox' (198). This will be surpassed in turn by the coming impact of molecular nanotechnology, programmable matter and genomics/proteomics.

Clarke does not deal with these newest expectations in detail, directing readers to my own futurist book *The Spike* 'as a more imaginative sequel' to *Profiles* (148). That dreaming youth in 1964 could hardly have dared predict such a delightful future surprise. Back then, reviewing the first Pan paperback edition, I vowed that we must offer to those disciplined prophets who blend science and poetry 'the tribute of leaping ahead of their visions and bringing them the future in their old age'. By the end of that millennium, in his mid-eighties, Clarke was dwelling in a future as remarkable as any he predicted. In the end, literally, his vision is elegiac and spine-prickling, an essence of wonderment. Our universe, he says, 'is in the brief springtime of its life'. While, in the deep eons ahead, our descendants 'will have time enough … to attempt all things, and to gather all knowledge … for all that, they may envy us, basking in the bright afterglow of Creation; for we knew the universe when it was young' (210).

X-Files Reality

> I have always thought it a wonderful irony that
> America's Budd Hopkins, the ufologist who is arguably
> the chief patron of the art-form known as the UFO
> abduction story, is by training and profession an artist.
> Would that he could apply his artist's insight to the
> tales of his abductees, which as a ufologist he takes to
> be literally true. As an artist, he once recounted a gentle
> parable about the human impulse to confuse the
> products of the mind with exogenous experience and
> revelation: 'A kindergarten teacher asked the children in
> her class to paint whatever they wished. Later, she
> enquired of each child what subject he or she was
> painting. A picture of Mommy or my cat were typical
> answers. One child, however, said "I'm painting a
> picture of God." How can you paint God? the teacher
> asked. "No one knows what God looks like." "Wait till
> I finish my painting," the child replied.'
>
> Jim Schnabel, 'Genuine Art' (1994)[67]

i

Is the Truth, as Agent Mulder hoped before he vanished from our TV
screens, really Out There? What lay behind the *X-Files* assertion,
surprisingly popular and given a surprising degree of credence, that
thousands of hapless humans are being routinely abducted by UFO aliens
and subjected to tasteless sexual experiments? Hybrid human-alien
babies, humiliating anal probes, reptoids walking among us, that sort of
thing. George Adamski (*Flying Saucers Have Landed,* with Desmond
Leslie) started it all fifty years ago with faked photos of a flying saucer
that took him, and his readers, for a ride. Whitley Strieber cashed in
decades later (1988, 1989) with scary 'true' tales about small gray aliens
with huge dark eyes and dubious reproductive plans for the human race.

Three quotations, and a fumarole:

> Binnungar was known to the tribes as 'Big Ears', the
> frill-necked lizard. He would convey messages in the
> sand with his feet and tail because he lived on the
> ground... One day Binnungar was given a very
> important message to deliver to the elders of the tribes.
> It was a message from the Sky Spirits. However,
> Binnungar was too busy having fun with his friends.

---

[67] Cited http://www.pause.demon.co.uk/windows2.0/rodtext.html

> When the message didn't arrive, the Sky Spirits got very
> angry and called a great wind, called a willy-willy, to
> take Binnungar far up into the sky.

I heard this charming story about the southern skies told in his soft, burred voice by the late Gaparingu Naputa, who died at a tragically early age after a life spent largely behind bars. His sky myths, devotedly gathered from tribal groups throughout Australia, have been collated in word and image, and mapped on a circular celestial chart by amateur white astronomer Gordon Patston.

Here is a second sky story of origins:

> Could our universe exist on the inside of a single
> magnetic monopole produced by cosmic inflation?...
> Such a monopole would look like a magnetically
> charged black hole, connecting our Universe through a
> wormhole in spacetime to another region of inflating
> spacetime... The result is a never-ending fractal
> structure, with inflating universes embedded inside each
> other' (Gribbin, 1996: 277).

That is a creation tale invented by Moscow-born Stanford University cosmologist Andrei Linde.

Here is a third sky tale, even more modern, just as ancient:

> The woman tells me about the afternoon her husband
> saw a bright light emanating from within their garage.
> 'That was the first experience,' she says. 'He was by
> himself. It wasn't until a couple of weeks later that
> someone else saw that very, very bright light with him.
> There was a doorway cut out of the air—there was no
> door frame, just a doorway shape—and behind it,
> through it, he could see that there was a room... on a
> ship—which is just a science and technology above what
> we commonly know.' She tells me their four children,
> ranging in age from three to fifteen, have 'open
> relationships' with the aliens' (Bryan, 1995: 29-30).

That is testimony gathered at the 1992 Abduction Study Conference, held at the Massachusetts Institute of Technology under the auspices of psychiatrist John E. Mack, a distinguished Harvard professor and Pulizer Prize-winning biographer of T. E. Lawrence, now an abduction believer hounded by his peers, and M.I.T. physicist David E. Pritchard, told to Courtlandt Dixon Barnes Bryan, an upscale journalist and historian published by the *New Yorker*, *The New Republic* and *Rolling Stone*.

Here is a fumarole (which is a crack in the side of a volcano, emitting spumes of hot gas):

The UFO abduction/cattle mutilation mythos is clearly nonsense from top to bottom. Anyone with even the most elementary scientific training who takes it literally is a gullible goose. This, very briefly, is why I say that so bluntly: Suppose we stand on the verge of as yet un-known physics, or of known physics applied in some startling new way. It follows that in the future humans might well harness this physics into machines able to transport people or information through spacetime. It also follows that other intelligent species elsewhere in the cosmos will eventually develop these capabilities, or have already done so. What militates against this perspective as an explanation for UFO reports is that such craft or apertures might be expected already to have maximally exploited our resources (Darwinian competition pressure), or to hide themselves, whether they are space devices or time machines. (UFOlogist Jacques Vallée has suggested one elusive escape clause [1976]: perhaps those behind the UFOs are manipulating human culture in a mysterious control program. As a counsel of intellectual despair, this is inarguable, and untestable.)

Today's core UFO abduction narrative is obviously laughable: beings allegedly able to traverse vast space or time, pass through walls, change shape, etc, *who still need to use reproductive technologies already years out of date in our own medical science!* In general, it is obvious that the linear analyses of technology which underpin standard explanations of UFO-as-craft are as comical as, say, some 19th century extrapolation that might have seen them as mighty steam engines running between the stars or 'dimensions' on gleaming steel rails. The technological convergence we are already witnessing with the birth of molecular nanotechnology, genomics/proteomics and machine intelligence seem bound to change our own culture to an immeasurable degree within half a century. To imag-ine that alien civilizations fly around the galaxy in spinning tin saucers, or even hyperplasma antigravity black triangles, is not *way out there* and *wildly futuristic*, it's absurdly old-fashioned.

But then I do not think it is very likely, either, that Binnungar actually got himself turned into a group of stars, or that the Tasmanian Tiger got his stripes defending Polana, son of the Sky Spirit Moinee, from a ferocious attack by Tarner the kangaroo. I am nearly as suspicious of inflating monopole cosmology, but it has the saving grace that Linde is impelled by a thoroughly postmodern sense of fun and provisionality.

What gets me *really angry* is mush-headed theft of hard, rigorous, limited, testable ideas from science. Yes, of course we all agree that science is based on metaphor, like all discourse, but that fact should not license the warping of its hard-won findings by desperados who wish to shore up their angst with a miasma of quantobabble. C. D. B. Bryan reports, with controlled incredulity, that someone at the abduction conference asked hypnotherapist Yvonne Smith 'if, after alien examinations, there are any indications of healing. Smith replies, "I have an HIV-positive abductee who now tests negative"' (24). Then again, UFO cures are not rare. Eddie, a 20-year-old, had his right eye pulled out and replaced by the aliens, which hurt a lot but fixed his visual impairment. Well, not altogether. Medical records show that he has switched from a green to a blue-yellow lack, which admittedly is preferable to his original profound color blindness (33).

Aboriginal sky stories, too, have their practical side. In northern Australia, a certain bright star figure is the crocodile. 'When Ingalpir was seen in the early morning sky during the month of December, tribes around the northern coast knew that they would see Malay traders arrive to exchange knives and axes for the trepang or sea cucumber, which would then be traded to the Chinese.' Western astronomers also keep tabs on recurrences, such as the solar cycle with its waxing and waning sunspot count. At the time when the Greenhouse effect was first attracting substantial attention, the Sun had just been through an active phase when its diameter shrank by about 0.02 percent, which might have nudged up temperatures on Earth (Gribbin, 1996: 368).

I confess a partiality to the scientific myths lovingly and extensively detailed in popular science books. However, for hours of amazed hilarity, I recommend studies of those who study the aliens who study us, falling like Wahn the Crow in their ships of light to inform us yet again of cosmic bliss, or doom, by and by, high in the sky. Bryan's book is one; another is *Dark White* (1995) by Jim Schnabel, a sympathetic investigation of this strange epidemic. Schnabel, as funny as P. J. O'Rourke, but in a kinder, gentler way, escalates his tale in jumps of lunacy that have you laughing and groaning and staring wildly by turns. And his explanation for it all would appeal to experimental psychologists and neuroscientists such as Nancy Andreasen and Antonio Damasio, tracking these powerful delusions back to 'promiscuous neuronal intercourse'-intense dissociative states where the temporal lobe gets cross-wired.

iii

The UFO rumor, craze, myth or narrative fad, then, has taken on a fresh lease of life in recent decades. Perhaps its biggest boost came in 1988 with a vast-eyed neotonized Grey gazing out from hundreds of thousands of paperback covers of *Communion,* horror writer Whitley Strieber's purportedly true story of alien abduction. It had already entered mass culture with Spielberg's 1977 *Close Encounters of the Third Kind,* and is now firmly entrenched, via the *X-Files* and the *National Enquirer.* What is going on? Are aliens really abducting and anally probing or fetus-harvesting thousands of reluctant people, perhaps for their entire life-time and even beyond death into endless hybrid rebirths? That is a less interesting question, for Terry Matheson, English professor at the University of Saskatchewan, than the puzzle of this narrative's immense popularity in a culture ostensibly shaped by rational bureaucratic and scientific canons.

Matheson proposes that the UFO narrative gains its force from its adoption as a myth, an organizing structure that (borrowing from Northrop Frye, Roland Barthes and other mythologists) blends dream and ritual to 'reflect a culture's preoccupations and concerns as well as the things it fears', ordering and structuring (although hardly *explaining)* 'certain aspects of the world that would otherwise remain unintelligible or objects of dread' (1998: 285). Some of these elements are age-old—the nature of cosmic, social and interpersonal forces, often allegorized in astrological or sacred doctrines—while others are typical precisely of our technological and allegedly rational epoch.

Ancient Greeks figured powerful ambiguities of lust, war and political power in such mythologized tales as Leda's rape by Zeus and her subsequent triple impregnation with twins Castor and Pollux and the Helen fated to ruin two cultures in protracted battle. Today, Matheson argues, we find in the bleak, emotionless and literally faceless UFO aliens a strikingly vivid figuration of postindustrial life at its worst—but also at its darkly numinous, with technology's ceaseless parade of wonders, medical promises, its ambiguous offer that we might soon transcend human limitations.

Matheson's approach is historical (technically, diachronic), tracing the slow waxing and waning of subordinate elements in this developing mythos (a narrative form often regarded as timeless or synchronic). While he claims to bracket off the question of whether UFO abductions are real or not, attending solely to the narrative or semiotic codes and forces in play, this is disingenuous; the book is published by Prometheus Press, notable for its sturdy inquisitorial list of texts by people friendly to the skeptical Committee for the Scientific Investigation of Claims of the Paranormal (CSICOP) and other ardent skeptical organizations. His method is known in literary studies as *close reading:* in a forensic way, he examines the claims and descriptions in several notable books by and about abductees, testing them for consistency, plausibility, sequential influence, as well as for their rhetorical design and devices.

Narratologists and morphologists have shown that written testimony is not a clear windowpane through which we can see the truth of reported events (see Broderick, 1994, chap. 8). Authors help form and reshape the tale they tell. Even in legal narrative, the courtroom 'construction of truth' is 'primarily a matter of the *overall* narrative plausibility' (Matheson, 37), the case as a whole, rather than the details. Still, he notes, realistic details help, and it is noteworthy how many get inserted later into abduction narratives as authors tidy up the blurts and scraps or summarize floods of verbal and pictorial testimony. Avowals of integrity and probity are frequently used to fill the void left by the inevitable absence of hard or compelling evidence, so such books usually begin with 'an introduction or preface written by a presumably objective third party who often possesses impressive academic credentials' (38). Such strategies are not invoked to deceive, but are part of the protocols and practice of writing and reading, which impose certain 'resemblances... from account to account [that] may say more about the nature of a realistic narrative's inner logic' (39) than speak to their truth content. All this is compelling, yet Matheson's skeptical presumptions can lead him astray. Citing a certain blatant inconsistency in John Fuller's *The Interrupted Journey*, he remarks: 'Because Fuller makes no attempt to resolve this, the Hills' credibility is bound to suffer' (53). Yet it did not do so among believers, on that basis at least, which is a surprising fact that Matheson's methods do not quite resolve.

His investigation proper launches from that key 1966 text, which dealt with the celebrated early 1960s case using hypnosis to uncover (or perhaps instill) the terrifying Ur-abduction reports of Betty and Barney Hill. In the four decades since, its core story has gathered fresh elements, dropped others, strengthened that early reliance on hypnosis while abandoning the stuffy requirement that trained psychological specialists should do the honors, and in general has followed a course convincingly seen as the elaboration of a living myth.

Matheson takes us through consecutive versions from Raymond Fowler (Betty Andreasson's abduction and space tour, replete with fundamentalist imagery and glossolalia appropriate to her Christian faith—and Fowler's own abduction, belatedly realized) to Travis Walton's self-authored testimony, Ann Druffel and D. Scott Rogo's treatment of several gay women who oddly enough were spared the usual phallic probing, the vatic arrival of Budd Hopkins with his menacing extraterrestrial aliens and Strieber with his even more terrifying occult shapeshifters, Ray Fowler again with four men in a boat whose drawings and stories do not especially resemble each other, despite the extensive interpretative zeal and leading questions of their interrogator, concluding with the arrival of the big guns from academia, historian Dr. David Jacobs and John Mack.

Matheson adopts an annoying tic in these analytic recountings: often, sentences tell us that 'many readers may be inclined to' (86), 'some readers may conclude that' (117), 'many readers will emerge from this section having concluded' (208), and on and on. This is exactly the kind of narrative bullying Matheson discerns so frequently in the abduction documents. I found myself wondering if the first draft had been a straightforward skeptical demolition of these often woolly, dreamlike, perverse and inconsistent narratives, lightly re-jigged with slightly old-fashioned narratological gadgetry in order to gain a publishing niche.

Still, Matheson's account is persuasive, as far as it goes. According to structuralist Claude Lévi-Strauss, myth is an ideational and affective ensemble of stories that articulates schemata of expected behaviors while specifying and defusing its culture's antinomies or internal contradictions. Its aim is the coercive institution of order, regularity, harmony—even if those ends are met, at times, through controlled ritual passages into frenzy, carnival and hysteria. This is the type of analysis adverted to by Matheson, although rarely attempted in any subtlety. Occasional references to Thomas Bullard's 1982 PhD thesis, the only work I know of other than Jacques Vallee's to look closely into the folkloric and mythological components of the emerging mythos, make one wish to see more detailed analytics: a far more exact semiotic unmasking of the codes at work, rather than vague if plausible generalizations about the impact of science fiction iconography on vulnerable people at the ends of their 20th century tethers.

Structuralism, of course, is now out of fashion, replaced in the humanities by variants of critical theory, Lacanian psychoanalysis, poststructuralism and discourse theory, approaches that emphasize a shimmering uncertainty where earlier models sought a reliable if abstract binary algebra. Even so, like Lévi-Strauss's myths and Jung's archaic dreams risen from a postulated collective unconscious, discourses are held by contemporary literary theory to possess an eerie autonomy, indeed a pre-eminence over any thought or intention that one might suppose lies behind the utterances they 'enable'. Like cosmic radiation, discourses *traverse* the fragmented subject. Meanwhile, as we saw earlier, cognitive and experimental neurosciences replace old folk images of a unified self with modular brains and multiple intelligences. Consciousness, individual and collective, is prey to memes, the inward ecology of mental viruses that might, indeed, in their totality *constitute* the parliament of the self. On this view, a myth might be a kind of commensal package of memes, a roaming mental genome that infests us even as we learn some local patois and hear or speak its latest modish utterances.

Can hermeneutic, narratological, semiotic or discursive analyses take us much farther than Matheson manages in his intriguing but frustrating book? He provides a telling critique of the major texts in the abduction industry, but does not go very deep, or venture far from the books under consideration. There is no discussion of the murky undergrowth that preceded and paralleled the invasion of the gray gynecologists: the delicious semi-occult contortions of John Keel (especially) and Brad Steiger, let alone the subterranean foliations and filiations of mind cults and more reputable marginal belief systems: the suicidal Heaven's Gate dupes, Scientology with its space opera theogony, Theosophy and its

Ascended Masters, all the charmingly crackpot scholarship that Desmond Leslie assembled in *Flying Saucers Have Landed*. The vimanas of ancient Atlantis and Mu might not seem direct ancestors of John Mack's aporias, half in this world and half beyond it, but I scent a narrative trail.

And there remain endless apertures for an inventive reader of these accounts. Andreasson's friendly ufonauts passed along *faux*-explanations Matheson finds 'unedifying', cast in 'pseudoscientific language' (198). This is so, but consider this amusing coincidence: the hybrid-engineering aliens must 'put their "protoplasma" in the "nucleus of the fetus and the paragenetic"', and Betty mentions 'balancing "the oscillating telemeter wheels" ' (ibid), although this latter task apparently relates to their propulsion or guidance systems. But Betty simply might have been confused. Recall that biologists have recently found they can significantly extend the lifespan of *in vitro* human fibroblasts by inserting into the nucleus a genetic package that codes for the enzyme telomerase. That prompts the chromosomes to repair their ever-shortening telomeres (key to their replicative capacity), which very recently were found to form a wheel or loop at the ends of DNA strands. Surely that is not what the aliens were telling Betty, but I would not be surprised if the evolving abduction mythos incorporates such a reading with a cry of recognition.

The abduction mythos *is,* of course, as Matheson argues, a culturally-created phenomenon, or perhaps a spontaneously emergent one, catching in its slowly shifting narratives the changing pressures, fears and hopes of turn-of-millennium technological societies. It speaks to a hunger inside many First Worlders whose lives have been stripped of ritual and metaphysical drama. The task of providing a satisfying alternative lies ahead for new Enlightenment polymaths.

Yesterday's Dreams

> Most Gaians believe that the 'something else' that is
> missing from reductionist descriptions of nature
> impinges on the physical world via living things, and is
> subjectively experienced by each living organism as its
> *self*... To use a spiritual term, it is very close to the core
> of what is meant by the term *sacred*.
>
> Richard Heinberg, 1999: 76

i

Are all purported mysteries dissolved so readily as the UFO mythos?
Perhaps not. Let us admit this much, in the interests of open-minded
inquiry.

Classic Vitalism, humankind's favored explanation for what sets life
apart from dead matter, has been known for more than half a century to
be mistaken. That scandalous fact was fixed at the heart of biology with
the discovery in 1953, by Watson and Crick, of the simple chemical code
that compiles unliving matter—molecules of carbon, hydrogen, nitrogen,
phosphorus, oxygen—into life (Eigen, 1992). If any doubt lingered, it
was quashed in July, 2002, when a polio virus was literally assembled
from brute components strung together in a laboratory according to its
documented genome.[68] While a virus is not strictly alive, since it needs a
host to make its copies, there can be little doubt that an entire bacterium
will soon be built from nothing more than a genomic recipe plus a
handful of lifeless chemicals.[69] But that, of course, is how life proliferates
anyway, parent to child, in a lineage stretching back to the first simple
chemical replicators on a barren world. In this sense, then, life requires
no spirit breathed into its nostrils before it awakens from dust. The right
kind of common elemental dust, guided by an evolved, conserved
molecular recipe and energized by the Sun's thermonuclear light, does
the job of being alive all by itself.

Many people, perhaps most, still tremble at this fact, preferring to
turn aside in denial. Surely such raw lessons from biology can tell us
nothing important about life, especially human life? Even a child knows
the difference between a rock and a kitten, the one inert and changeless,
the other squirming with joy and naughtiness, like the child herself. Yet
the deepest mystery for an adult, the mystery withheld from the child's
eyes as long as possible to protect her innocence, is that all warm flesh
some day will chill, stiffen into nothing better than stone. Those sweet
lips breathe no more, nor speak to us; those poor dead eyes stare without

---

[68] http://news.bbc.co.uk/1/hi/sci/tech/2122619.stm

[69] http://sciscoop.com/story/2004/3/30/64612/5378

seeing, stones indeed. The heart we loved, which loved us in turn, or hated us, is stilled; spirit has left its dwelling.

But has it gone anywhere—if it is indeed a *thing*, rather than a *process*? Has it found another home? Is it nestling, even as we mourn, into unformed embryonic tissue fated to unfold *in utero* into a new person? Or does it sport (or suffer for sins of the flesh) in some place untouchable by mortal hands, unreachable by living tread? Humankind has held tight to those assumptions, those terrified hopes, for a hundred thousand years.

Evidence has always seemed abundant, even aside from our desperate wish and consolatory belief that it be so. In dreams, our lost ones return to us, if we are lucky (or perhaps unlucky, should their message be vituperative). Analogy tells us that a flame blown out is gone, but only for a moment; a spark will rekindle its fire. A song dies on the lips, but is harbored in the heart, in the folds of the brain, until we call it forth effortlessly once again to move the air in patterned waves of beauty, melancholy, martial zeal. Must it not be like this with the human spirit? Is not death merely a temporary occlusion of the light, never truly lost if always somehow altered for a time, hidden from our sorrowing gaze, brought back in new birth, or perhaps in some empyrean continued, elevated above corruption, ruin, change, disappointment?

Such, at any rate, seems to be the almost universal instinctive belief of humans now and in the past. It seems a temptation written into our genes, this consoling or sometimes frightening belief, as is the very template of our capacity for language and personhood (Pinker, 1994). If so, that need not vouch for its truth, alas. Vitalism once seemed as true, as self-evident, as anything in the world or our experience of the world. It seemed as lasting and undeniable as—well, as the flatness of the earth, stretched to its four Scriptural corners, circled by its tiny Sun. Then we learned, with astonishment and resentment, that this flat cosmos is a small portion of a vast globe, that the small brilliant luminous ball crossing the sky is a sustained hydrogen bomb explosion over a million kilometers broad, and that life is patterned matter. Vital force, *élan vital*, fell out of the scientific lexicon, along with the forces of the ancient astrologers who in their conceit took the vastly distant blazing stars for maps to local destiny.[70] Can spirit-like powers have more durability than these lost guesses?

---

[70] On the other hand, an interesting connection between paranormal effectivity and a certain locus in the sky is argued by James P. Spottiswoode, Cognitive Sciences Laboratory, Palo Alto, CA, in 'Apparent association between Effect Size in Free Response Anomalous Cognition Experiments and Local Sidereal Time', claiming remarkably that 'the effect size increased 340% for trials within 1 hour of 13.5 h LST ($p = 0.001$)'. See this and other papers at http://www.jsasoc.com/library.html

An unfashionable minority opinion among the well-informed today (but a persistent majority opinion among the poorly educated) is that apparently paranormal phenomena provide just the evidence we need to sustain spirit in the heart of matter, at least of human, conscious, loving, willing matter. Matter itself, after all, is now not the hard, definitive stuff it was deemed to be a century ago. Matter, and energy, the impulsive force that gives it motion and sustains its structure, have grown wispy and immaterial, a haze of quarks and stringy membranes, a dance of mathematical symmetries on an eleven-dimensional manifold no human eye is keen enough to witness nor human hand fine enough to shape (Greene, 1999). In an epoch of such drastic reinterpretation of spacetime and energy-matter, might we find an explanation, indeed a privileged place, for those rogue and damnable phenomena claimed anciently by witchcraft, formerly by spiritualism, today by statistics-trained specialist researchers into canonically anomalous events and patterns?

The point need not be labored: if a wonder-worker could, for example, without pressure bend metal at a whim, read intentions and mental images from a distance, foresee with uncanny accuracy some unexpected future event, draw a convincingly detailed picture of some remote object hidden from sight—let alone float unaided in the air, heal the incurable or raise the dead, transform one thing into another, cause an object to vanish from here and appear there, instantly—would this not be evidence of spirit, or at least of a breakdown in recognized scientific verities? Better yet, what if these feats could be elicited also among the rest of us, just plain folks who turn our interested and somewhat skeptical attention to uncanny activities usually scorned as delusion or conjurers' trickery? Perhaps not all of us would attain such gifts, even with expert guidance; after all, only a few can aspire to run a four minute mile or calculate partial differential equations in our heads. Those are astonishing performances, yet hardly controversial, let alone paranormal. But suppose that sufficient candidates came forward for investigation by unprejudiced scientists, genuine psychics able to perform such feats repeatably, perhaps astonishing even themselves. Would this suffice to remake our scientific models and certainties?

More profoundly, would it require those who respect evidence to readopt, whether grudgingly or gladly, a dualistic stance to the cosmos, to rediscover merits in a worldview that has been eroding for more than a century? Indeed, would it cause the traditionally religious to rethink their own views, confronting them with a miraculous order of reality that so many prelates have explained away as parables and allegories of a less educated time?

Perhaps it seems obvious that people would hasten to embrace such support for long-held human yearnings. After all, some do so already, at the mere hint of miraculous manifestations, cures, tears falling from the plaster or marble eyes of holy statues. The rest of us shake our sensible heads sadly. That kind of gullibility, however, is not the postulated case under consideration. Suppose remarkable, inexplicable powers of mind *were* demonstrated, repeatedly and almost upon demand, as nowadays we take it for granted that the flick of a wall switch fills a dark room with fluorescent light brighter than any fire, the turn of a key activates the quiet but immense power of an automobile engine stronger than any hero or beast of burden. Science and technology provided those benefits, the fruit of long, careful investigation of how things work, and of theories marked by increasing depth and extent, mapping the secret workings and patterns of the world. Would a purported spiritual appearance in the midst of our workaday world cause us to reshape our lives? Is a paranormal epiphany, even one we can turn on at will, the kind of experience we might expect to bring peace to the feuding, love to the loveless or hate-poisoned, food and comfort to the wretched, wisdom to the ignorant or puffed-up and, most poignantly, authentic meaning to the well-off whose hearts and lives are empty?

It might seem so, for our legends, myths and sacred teachings insist that teachers gifted with power and insight beyond the usual in a greedy, carnal world will prove their credentials by signs and wonders.[71] Paradoxically, however, those same sources teach that miracles are unimportant, trivial, distracting compared with heartfelt faith: an inward knowledge embraced precisely in the absence of empirical evidence or the scrutiny of logical reasoning. As Karl Popper (1983) and other philosophers teach, we must assess this claim with the greatest wariness for, while it is found on the lips of the authentically holy, its shield also protects charlatans, the deluded, the honestly mistaken wedded to their errors.

iii

More confrontingly still, we must acknowledge that the Western world's history is precisely unique in its characteristic methods of empirical science and materialistic technology, which summoned into routine reality a host of benefits (and some disasters) that a thousand years ago certainly would have been considered paranormal miracles.

---

[71] In an unfortunately influential passage, Paul wrote to the Romans that 'We know that the law is spiritual, but I am carnal... For I know that nothing good dwells within me, that is, in my flesh' (Rom. 7:14, 18). Yet even materialist monists may still embrace the word *spiritual* to signify profound realities, our heightened response to rapture, insight and love, knowing this need not imply a ghostly 'soul' independent of the flesh.

Why levitate when you can catch a plane? Saints, mystics and sorcerers were said to relieve pain and heal the ill, or curse the healthy into infirmity. Today professionals in medicine and surgery do just that (within limits) and far more reliably than those who lay on hands or pray for results. Extreme claims have been made for healing by miracle: even that the dead have been revived. Yet in some measure, that is attained already with heart transplants; in coming decades, it is plausible that cryonics patients now frozen or vitrified after death will be recovered, fatal illnesses repaired, youth rejuvenated, by an emergent nanotechnology working on damaged tissues at the molecular level (Perry, 2000).[72] If so, it literally will be true that these were not dead, only sleeping.

Meanwhile, most in the Western world daily live more richly than kings of the ancient Orient. We might not be showered in gold and perfumes, but our deodorants are superior, our meals more various, our knowledge far more extensive. At the touch of a switch we see the far places of the world, and our small machine deputies fling back to us images of other worlds from the edges of the solar system. This much is commonplace: we gaze upon atoms, or at the ancient universe nearly back to the Big Bang of Creation. No other people has been as fortunate, as rich, as distracted by wonders. Perhaps distraction's lure is the key to what we are considering.

It cannot be astonishing wonders alone, whether technical or paranormal, that will renew the world. Arguably the world already grows closer knit than ever before. If we are often distracted, alienated from loam, flower, beast, from collective passionate fellowship (corroboree, liturgy, even tribal warfare), the instruments of diversion serve also to show us the faces of those beyond our borders, the damage done by violence and natural disaster to our foes as well as to many people and creatures our ancestors never even knew existed. A night club is torn by a suicide bomber, and we see it; a village is bombed from the air, killing women and children, a town is lost to fire or flood, and despite the fatigue of compassion we do know some measure of empathy, it grows a little harder for us to treat other people as irrelevant. Would access to genuine paranormal abilities augment the better face of information's Janus-blend: care for others, versus hunger for base amusement?

Perhaps it would. It is true that First Worlders can dial friends anywhere in the world on a mobile phone, our words shot nearly instantly via a satellite hung like a star in space, like whispering in a messenger angel's ear. Conceivably, true telepathy might do what such technologies can never achieve: place us womb-deep within the

---

[72] U.S. National Science Foundation Report on Converging
Technologies, 2002: http://itri.loyola.edu/ConvergingTechnologies/.

consciousness of another (Wolman, ed., 1977; Jahn and Dunne, 1987; Radin, 1997). If it is true, as some parapsychologists hope to establish, that random systems resonate to those agonies and triumphs shared by masses of humans[73]—when we are brought to simultaneous focus, ironically, by those very instruments of technological communication— then perhaps we might finally cultivate a deeper fraternity. Yet we might still ask if these putative wonders of the mind must necessarily open an aperture into some superior, redemptive realm.

Some scientists use anthropic reasoning to deduce that the cosmos is too cozy for life and mind to be accidental, that its fundamental parameters seem too neatly tuned to life's requirements. Lee Smolin (1997) and his colleagues show how the quantum vacuum itself might bud off sub-universes through black holes. But we never experience *nothing*, only the absence of certain *things* as they are transformed into different *things*. It is more than eighty years since Karl Barth announced the 'wholly otherness of God'.[74] Even as some scientists seek to marshal anthropic arguments and paranormal phenomena in a renewed argument for spirit, for a Being Who can bind the sweet influences of the Pleiades, or loose the bands of Orion, deconstructive theorists blend Heidegger, Derrida and the pseudo-Dionysus in dazzling feats of negative theology (Hart, 1989). Faith, by definition, must evade and even challenge rational grasp. Barth and his theological followers would have argued that any naturalistic quest for spirit risks ending in the bathos that closed John Updike's 1986 novel *Roger's Version* (a fictional computer search for the face of God, like the Shroud of Turin, painted in pixels on the monitor), or the mathematically impossible epiphany in which Carl Sagan's astronomer heroine, in *Contact* (1986), located a perfect circle inscribed millions of digits into the expansion of pi.

If telepathy, remote viewing, precognition, levitation, psychokinesis become repeatably demonstrable (Schnabel, 1997), they will enter the realm of regular science, gifts granted us by rational inquiry, evidence, hard and imaginative thinking. Will they—*can* they—in addition yield metaphysical insights, keys to happiness, intensity, existential meaning, a sea-change in social direction? Only as much, perhaps, as a Cezanne rendering of a peach caught in light (which once brought me, motionless and timeless in front of a museum exhibit, to astonished tears), or a Bose-Einstein condensate of sodium gas poised a hair above Absolute Zero, or a Hubble portrait of the cosmic dawn of galaxies burning in illimitable night.

An acquaintance who combines wizardly skill in artificial intelligence design with a mystical bent sought counsel from a Zen

---

[73] The Global Consciousness Project data and analyses are at
http://noosphere.princeton.edu/

[74] Karl Barth, *Der Romerbrief*, 1919, cited: http://www.faithnet.freeserve.co.uk/barth.htm

Buddhist abbot with a PhD in physics.[75] He was told this: 'The mystic's view is that truth—Reality—is only ascertained once we have transcended the mental framework of experience—or, in Buddhist lingo, cause and effect. We (our brains) talk about reality in terms of sensory input, but the mystic subtracts all the sensory input from the equation and says that what's left is all that is real, and true. Intellectually, this is appalling... to suppose that we can't think our way to the truth.' If it is so, perhaps paranormal phenomena will prove to be a gateway to some spiritual truth surpassing scientific knowledge. The long and often disappointed history of psychical research suggests otherwise, however.[76]

If it is not, their authenticity—once proved—will stand at the least as compelling, invigorating evidence that the world contains more than we have yet uncovered and explained. But this knowledge is already the true heart of science, which replaces dogma, bit by bit, century by century, with subtle understanding. Perhaps this will prove to be so in the case of those strange, intimate, persistent experiences we are currently obliged to name negatively, in our continuing partial ignorance, as *paranormal*.

---

[75] Cited with permission from Dr. Ben Goertzel, Novamente AI Engine Project: http://www.realai.net/

[76] For an excellent account of the early years by an open-minded but level-headed historian, see Brian Inglis (1977 and 1984).

Zeitgeist Engineering

> To make the case against ageless bodies...to say no thanks to the prolongation of one's life—one has to make an argument for human mortality.... Shakespeare tells us that the human story is one of inexorable ripening and rotting. But what if biotechnology allowed us to alter the effects of time, to suspend aging or to disentangle the desired effects of aging from the undesired? What if we could ripen without rotting? What if we could arrest not the maturation of our minds and spirits, but the senescence of our bodies? How would the human tale change, and would it change for the better?... [M]ortality is, if not precisely a good thing, then at least the necessary foundation of other very good things... there is something misguided about the attempt to overcome mortality.
>
> Professor Diana Schaub, Loyola College of Maryland (speaking December 9, 2003 at AEI panel discussion of the President's Council on Bioethics' report, *Beyond Therapy*)

i

One of the more tedious clichés of the day is the admonition to *Think Outside the Box*. Meant to convey daring disruption of the status quo, it can strike the mind with the same heavy thud as those campus posters that advised dutifully daring students to *Subvert the Dominant Paradigm*. Outside the Box is where we should all go to 'think different', Apple and Ikea and The Gap assure us (while, absurdly, offering standardized garments and goods).[77] Inside the box is where the round pegs are, slithering in through the holes the square pegs couldn't manage. Inside the box is the comfortable bourgeois illusion of well-being and security. Thinking inside the box just won't do, we're told by marketeers with designs on our purse. What nobody seems to think to ask is whether the box can be changed. Maybe we can add a picture window, or an extension. Indoor plumbing would be a convenience. Get the box connected to the Internet. *Fix* the damned box.[78]

---

[77] http://dir.salon.com/tech/feature/2000/11/22/old_navy/index.html

[78] I know, the cliché doesn't really refer to a box but to a square made of nine dots that must be joined using only three straight lines without lifting the pencil: http://www.ihi.org/resources/qi/qitips/ci0202tipp1.asp, an exercise in lateral thinking devised by Carl Drucker and popularized in Paul E. Plsek's book *Creativity, Innovation, and Quality* (1997). The lines have to extend beyond the outer perimeter of the 'box'.

Perhaps it takes a polymath to re-jig a constricted box, because polymaths are accustomed to swapping their attention span across a number of compartments. Alas, it looks as if polymathy is not in itself the cure for what ails us. Diversity of understanding needs to be powered—to be *illuminated*—by that very respect for practical wisdom and theoretical reasoning (*phronesis* and *theoria*, in Aristotle's terms) which marked the first Enlightenment. There is little doubt that conservative ethicists such as Dr. Leon Kass can be polymathic in their grasp of multiple fields of human knowledge. Yet their capacity to extend an imaginative embrace to our new possibilities seems crippled by some desperate yearning for the box as it is, as they fondly suppose it has always been. Or indeed as it used to be before people acted in the disgusting ways they do nowadays—by, for bizarre example, eating ice cream in the street (ironically, Bill McKibben's idea of heaven). Here is Dr. Kass a decade before his elevation as US bioethics czar, exercised by a shocking sight, denouncing

> those more uncivilized forms of eating, like licking an ice cream cone—a catlike activity that has been made acceptable in informal America but that still offends those who know eating in public is offensive.
>
> I fear that I may by this remark lose the sympathy of many readers, people who will condescendingly regard as quaint or even priggish the... view that eating in the street is for dogs... This doglike feeding, if one must engage in it, ought to be kept from public view, where, even if *we* feel no shame, others are compelled to witness our shameful behavior. (1994: 148-49)

Yes, the box has been altering its dimensions year by year, decade by decade, even as we struggle, with ruffled uncertainty, within its shifting frame. There are more serious indices than gustatory manners. A century ago, those living inside the First World segment of the box had a life expectancy of 47.3 years. Today, the US population, minorities included, has a life expectancy of 77.4 years but even that rise only takes us to two-thirds of the age of the oldest human reliably recorded. (Nor have mean increases stopped; life expectancy for Japanese females reached 85.23 years in 2002.) Most of us, presumably even conservative bioethicists, would be outraged if a government ordained that the earlier 'natural' abbreviated figure should be respected, perhaps by denying babies or the elderly the benefits of clean drinking water and routine medical care. The box representing our received worldview has expanded, in other words, even as the world's population has swollen suffocatingly inside its previously narrowed expectations.

According to advocates of the status-quo, those of us who wish to see increased healthy longevity, augmented emotional and intellectual depth, and the capacity to do very much more with much less, are greedy, grasping and immature... and that's that, no argument. Bill McKibben, for example, is sure that the way people happen to be *just now*, in the planet's dominant culture, is about right, as long as we don't get too uppity:

> Most of us mature only partway: we learn—it's to be hoped that we learn—to place our family or our community or our deity nearer the center of our lives, but only in rare cases do we fully vanquish that compulsive striving, that grasping for more. And in recent centuries we've come to embrace our selfishness—our hyperindividuality—with an almost religious fervor... The choice between Enough and More has always been a choice we could put off a little longer, both in our own lives and in the life of our civilization.

With a burst of religious fervor of his own, he warns: 'But now the hour draws near' (210).

He closes his book by describing an autumnal run he had just completed, which echoes a hard-won marathon run recounted in the opening pages, and then points out that we need no alarming technofutures; no, we can just get by with Enough. When I was McKibben's age I could run, too, it was lovely. Now I have some trouble getting up the stairs (knee joints damaged, ironically, by a decade of running, worsening my inherited arthritis) or even just walking the dog fast. Enough, indeed! This is nothing but priggish and distressingly self-satisfied sanctimony.

Do we have a moral responsibility to deny ourselves the novelties provided by keener scientific insight and ingenious technical application? In some cases, I suspect we do, for the same reason that we need to struggle against our inherited urges to gobble up as much sugar and fat as we can lay our hands on. That made sense in the frugal Pleistocene to which our physical constitution is optimally adapted, but in an era of plenty (for some) it is a recipe for self-inflicted injury and woe.[79] It might be that access to simulated realities of vile cruelty and insensate imaginary death-dealing, the offspring of computer games, should be relinquished if it is demonstrable that they do corrupt the vulnerable (which might be most of us). Other

---

[79] '[O]besity now rivals smoking as the largest cause of premature death [in the USA]. The Centers for Disease Control reckons that obesity contributes to about 400,000 deaths annually, just behind tobacco (435,000) and ahead of alcohol (85,000), car accidents (43,000) and guns (29,000). Obesity and its complications—more diabetes and heart disease, for instance—now account for an estimated 9 percent of U.S. health spending.' Robert J. Samuelson, 'The Afflictions of Affluence', *Newsweek*, March 22, 2004.

opportunities will soon arise, the pharmacological, genomic or nanotechnologic equivalents of eye-glasses for the sight-impaired: tailored neurotransmitters that enhance our mental focus, will power, sensory scope, intelligence, even sanity. Should these also be rejected without any further consideration, on some blanket 'precautionary principle' shaped by dread of the unknown? Is all this novelty no better than *reason run mad*, rationality unhinged from a decent respect to the opinions of current humankind? The philosopher Daniel Dennett is crisp:

> We happily lean on the prostheses that *we* find valuable—that's the beauty of civilized life—but tend to begrudge those that others need. Once we understand that this is an arms race, we can fend off the absolutism that sees only two possibilities: Either we are perfectly rational, or we are not rational at all. That absolutism fosters the paranoid fear that science might be on the verge of showing us that our rationality is an illusion, however benign from some perspectives. That fear, in turn, lends a spurious attractiveness to any doctrine that promises to keep science at bay, our minds sacrosanct and mysterious. (2003: 271)

Still, it must be granted that the ferocity and sometimes appalling attraction of rational polymathy might have dubious roots. That is something everyone who aspires to a renewed Enlightenment polymathy must guard against. Richard Webster is scathing about those intellectuals (he is thinking of poststructural psychoanalyst Jacques Lacan especially, ironically enough)

> who have become completely unhinged from their own emotional life and from ordinary human relationships. The tragic predicament of such thinkers is that, driven by terrifying feelings of insecurity and emptiness, they mistakenly conclude that intellectual truths can be an adequate substitute for emotional warmth. Craving distinction and imagining that abstract intellectual formulations can alone fill the void they feel within them, they develop a voracious appetite for such formulations, anorexically judging their goodness by the degree of difficulty or abstraction they possess. Believing that what they have devoured is intrinsically nourishing they are impelled to share their 'truths' with others. Like a starving man who compels others to eat the diet of stones he believes has saved him, they give abundantly of their

poverty out of a genuine conviction that they are
enriching others. (1997)

Significantly, this diagnosis resembles Peter Gay's account of the clerisy
of the eighteenth century: 'The great majority of pastors wasted their
time by parading abstruse learning, interpreting obscure biblical
passages, and spinning out etymological quibbles' (1977: 350). More
than one postmodern professor might wince in recognition. That sort of
polymathy is not what the Enlightenment stood for, even if parading
esoteric knowledge is perhaps always a hazard among know-alls. It is,
though, exactly the kind of brow-beating, 'Tyrant of the Breakfast
Table', neo-colonialist, dead white male oppressiveness which the term
'Enlightenment' tends to bring instantly to mind nowadays. It doesn't
help that the eighteenth century *philosphes* were nearly all men, and that
women's conditions generally *deteriorated* during that period.

> In many ways, the position of women was seriously
> degraded during the Enlightenment. Economically, the rise
> of capitalism produced laws that severely restricted
> women's rights to own property and run businesses. While
> Enlightenment thinkers were proposing economic freedom
> and enlightened monarchs were tearing down barriers to
> production and trade, women were being forced out of a
> variety of businesses throughout Europe. In 1600, more
> than two-thirds of the businesses in London were owned
> and administered by women; by 1800, that number had
> shrunk to less than ten percent. While the Enlightenment
> greatly changed the face of education, the education of
> women simultaneously expanded in opportunity but
> seriously degraded in quality.[80]

But enlightenment polymathy is not inevitably a Y-chromosome trait,
except where punitive and exclusionary cultural forces make it so (and
indeed the Enlightenment was largely fueled by the support of wealthy
women, who began to speak in their own voices with Mary
Wollstonecraft's *Vindication of the Rights of Women* at the close of the
eighteenth century). Let me tell you about one of today's polymaths: my
American wife, Barbara Lamar.

For some years, Barbara ran, by herself, her own 160-acre permaculture
farm in the parched sandhills of Caldwell County, Texas, raising her daughter in a residence she had designed (using skills acquired during studies in
architecture) and built herself (using skills acquired as she went along)

---

[80] Richard Hooker, 'Women during the European Enlightenment',
http://www.wsu.edu/~dee/ENLIGHT/WOMEN.HTM

powered by solar cells and connected to the rest of the world by satellite uplink. Formerly a system designer for a major accounting firm, she read widely in many fields, played the piano, trained her own horse, and was a competition cyclist (before blowing her knees out, a hazard of the sport), and a pilot of small aircraft. Barbara was one of the founders of a women's shelter in Caldwell County, has written a novel, raised and butchered animals for their meat, faced down feral crack dealers with a shotgun in her hand, and grown beautiful gardens in sand. I was not surprised to find that she speaks Spanish as well as English, has a degree in mathematics, a higher degree in business management, and a Juris Doctorate from the University of Texas Law School. Starting with a pittance saved from tips she earned as a waitress, she built up a million dollar business buying old houses and apartment buildings and repairing them for a tidy profit, until the ruinous oil shock recession in the Texas economy of the late 1980s took it all away (along with a number of banks). She is possessed of a forthright, generous, insightful and occasionally ferocious mind. Recently, she has returned to her tax law practice, interrupted during those self-sufficiency experiments on the farm, with clients around the world, and in her spare time is completing her PhD in decision theory. This is exemplary polymathy, a new enlightenment polymathy without the stain of sexism. The planet needs more of it.

ii

Still, ours seems not to be a time that welcomes new knowledge, turning instead again and again for guidance to old errors (astrology, *feng shui*, Dark Age theology) and ornate bogus waffle (mystic quantobabble, post-empirical embrace of 'knowledges'). Even as our robot deputies sent back word from Mars that they were roaming ancient sea beds, perhaps the home of martian life, the US President's ethicist was releasing a sturdy anthology pretending, among other things, that Jonathan Swift's surreally satirical *Gulliver's Travels* provided all the evidence we need for the assertion that an indefinite lifespan must inevitably be atrocious—as if Dean Swift spoke with the authority of a 21st century gerontologist rather than as an early eighteenth century moralist and wit:

> *When Gulliver first learns about the[deathless] struld-brugs from mortal Luggnaggians, he is 'struck with in-expressible delight.' Prompted by them to describe how he would have lived, had he been one, he imagines per-petual study, ever-growing wisdom, service to humanity, and the comfortable fellowship of his own kind. His in-terlocutors laugh and set him straight. Though they are immortal, the struldbruggs enjoy neither perpetual*

youth nor perpetual prosperity and health. They live anything but enviable lives.[81]

Frederick Crews, now Professor Emeritus of English and former Chair of the English Department at the University of California at Berkeley, situated the problem with his habitual uninflated eloquence in an archival interview with Harry Kreisler. I will quote his observation at length, since it reflects just the kind of polymathic, tolerant openness which opponents of the new Enlightenment ridicule as toxically scientistic, reductionist, blind to the mysteries of art and heart. It is a standpoint consilient with what I, a paid-up postmodernist, once called 'the insistence of the empirical', as well as the always-already-social context within which such a responsible and reasonable attitude *has any meaning*:[82]

> Virtually all philosophers of science today would deny that there is such a thing as the scientific method in the sense of an algorithm that leads us to correct results in our propositions about the world. That was the dream of logical positivism, and it's been exploded.... What interests me is general rationality, of which science is a part. General rationality requires us to observe the world carefully, to consider alternative hypotheses to our own hypotheses, to gather evidence in a responsible way, to answer objections. These are habits of mind that science shares with good history, good sociology, good political science, good economics.... the 'empirical attitude.' It's a combination of feeling responsible to the evidence that is available... including the evidence that is contrary to one's presumptions, and responsibility to be logical with one's self and others. (Kreisler and Crews, 1999)

Empiricism in this sense does not imply that nothing exists except what we can see, prod and record with instruments. It is primarily a demand for publicly assessable evidence, which includes shared experiences of a certain robustness and generality. We establish the reality, the objectivity, of these experiences by telling each other about them, by mutual recognition and skeptical trust, by our fellowship in the human estate (which need not exclude non-human intelligence and consciousness when and if that arises, or is confirmed in creatures such as great apes and

---

[81] http://www.bioethics.gov/bookshelf/reader/chapter7.html#introduction

[82] Broderick, 1994: x. I added that this insistence of the empirical 'would compensate for that drastic dispersion of subjectivity into volatile discursivity which is the specific hazard of postmodern theory.'

certain marine mammals that rival our own brain-to-body index). So the requirement is not *viciously or repressively* reductive. Nor does it commit the alleged intellectual crime of the earlier ambitious Enlightenment polymaths, an assumption of sovereign reason ruling all other aspects of an individual's life. For every individual is human only in the context of many others, most of them somewhat or even considerably different from him or her self, all of them (all of us) passionate and at least partially opaque to ourselves. This, then, as Crews argues,

> is an ideal that is not so much individual as social. The rational attitude doesn't really work when simply applied to one's self. It is something that we owe to each other. We submit our ideas to each other in a way that enables them to be clear enough, non-contradictory enough, to be accessible to refutation. And that's as true of propositions about literature as it is of propositions about quarks and protons.... What's happened in the humanities is a general assault on the idea of the empirical, the very idea of the rational, which is now associated with such social evils as racism, patriarchy, and so forth. And in the vacuum that is created by this denigration of the empirical, nothing is left but cliquishness, nothing is left but power.

iii

In a resolute essay affirming the radical core of the Enlightenment project, and its continued centrality to our culture, my friend Greg Burch acknowledges that the future 'has not been finally won for the value of humane progress' while asserting that 'we must continue the process of vigorously promoting the idea that things can and will get better. And that there is a clear path forward—even in the face of strong opposition' (Burch, 2001). A litigator specializing in maritime, international and commercial law, with a degree in Chinese language and culture, Burch is a composer, space exploration advocate and scuba diver whose Houston household contains, extraordinarily, a happy lemur and a two-toed sloth; a polymath, that is to say—a human possessed by hungry curiosity.

> The rush of insight and philosophical optimism that marked the early radical Enlightenment was based primarily on a very few theoretical and empirical scientific breakthroughs, primarily those of Newtonian physics, observational astronomy empowered by the invention of the telescope, and a first view of the world of microbiology made possible by the development of the microscope.

These dislocations and expansions of our shared world were very much a leap of faith, beyond any existing world-view, driven by disquieting evidence and a sense that ancient models of the cosmos must be inadequate to this freshet of new knowledge.

> Wholly lacking at the time was the kind of theoretical framework that would make possible a real science of life, both at the biological and behavioral levels, much less the depth of empirical observation necessary to validate such theories. Also missing was what we would call a theory of information, much less the deep unity of the life sciences and information theory that we perceive today.

That lack of a deep and appropriately theorized consilient narrative of the world left the emerging Enlightenment at a disadvantage, allowing its best impulses to be stifled on the one hand, and on the other perverted into the bloody excess of the French Revolution.

> Thus, the opponents of progress took root and flourished in the blank spaces on the cognitive map created by those who developed the modern conception of the world. In a very important sense, the Enlightenment world-view was significantly premature: In the first flush of excitement engendered by the power of the Cartesian method and Newtonian physics, the leading edge of the modern world-view rushed ahead of what could be established with the methods and with the values upon which it was based. This created the environment in which romantic Naturism, technocratic Guardianism and reactionary spiritualism could thrive.

Those remain three major threats to Enlightenment values, as diagnosed by Burch. The cult of Nature and a wholly imaginary 'noble savage', popularized by Rousseau, reappears in our time as extreme Green or Gaian activism, some of it terroristic; only 'Man' is vile, while the natural order is purportedly timeless and immutable except for human meddling. Platonic hopes for an order of powerful monitors to oversee an easily-corrupted citizenry were apotheosized, notoriously, in the Soviet gulag state and the Nazi death camps, and can be witnessed today in violent technological incursions around the planet and in a menacing blizzard of spy cameras, Internet traffic snoops and other Orwellian encroachments against free speech and assembly (after all, we are assured, 'Only criminals have anything to fear'). The revival of faith-based activism takes many forms: bans on life-enhancing stem cell research driven by muddy theological reasoning, assaults on abortion availability and even on the lives of health workers and, in the most terrifying form, terrorist barbarities like the destruction of the World Trade Center in September 2001 and the murderous attacks in Bali, Madrid and elsewhere. 'It should not surprise us,' Burch notes, 'that the most common reaction to the notion that humans can progress beyond their current nature by their own initiative is to condemn such ideas as blasphemous.' The faithful are conveniently blind to their complicity in this compulsive irrationality, due to those evolved cognitive and emotional motives we considered in chapter six. When the Taliban denied schooling for girls over eight years old and destroyed millennium-old statues of the Buddha in a taunting public act of holy vandalism, when women in Africa and other places continued to suffer clitoridectomy under the auspices of Muslim tradition, the West was shocked and affronted. Yet when many in the West insist on retaining references to the deity of their choice in the official utterances of a nation where Church is avowedly and deliberately separate from State, when they interfere with school curricula to bowdlerize evolutionary findings, or reject equal treatment under the law for homosexual citizens, few notice the muted likeness to those other faith-driven power plays against culture and individuals.

Is it possible to modify, even engineer, such currents in the Zeitgeist? Burch's policy recommendations for the defense of a new Enlightenment culture are threefold, and increasingly drastic: Contesting the Middle Grounds, Fortification of the Core, and Strategic Displacement. Conventional political success is often attributed to seizure of the middle ground of debate. At a time when reasoned argument and appraisal of robust evidence are under renewed attack, contesting the neutral overlap between right and left, credulous and skeptical, nationalist and global, and the rest of the standard binary contrasts might not remain possible for long, or effective. So Enlightenment polymaths might first find themselves obliged to shore up 'key cultural, institutional and legal factors that protect our right to continue to pursue progress and work to strengthen them' against the onslaught of foes of progress.

If appeals to liberty and freedom of thought and research fail in turn, Burch proposes a genuinely radical step: retreat from confrontation, withdrawal to clandestine '"free science" enclaves', perhaps located in the Third World. To me, this suggestion smacks a little too much of Ayn Randian heroism, a self-declared Atlas of knowledge, inventiveness and power shrugging off the burden and taking a knight's move into a secured redoubt, there to carry forward researches of a Promethean kind despite the vehement and perhaps violent opposition of those who demand that enough is Enough, that we must Relinquish studies and activities too dangerous to our material flesh and too corrosive of our spirits. Yet I am forced to admit that such an apparently melodramatic agenda might indeed exert attraction upon those who see, for example, crucial breakthrough work on stem cells conducted in South Korea[83] because the United States Congress refuses funding to any lab performing such blasphemous research, meddling with the sacred stuff of life: upsetting, in short, the prejudices of those who confuse their provincial and visceral gut revulsion for divine inspiration.[84] (Recall the gloomy prophecies of ruin and spiritual harm by none other than then-Georgetown University bioethics professor Leon Kass when the first *in vitro* pregnancies were announced a quarter century ago; today the procedures are almost routine, if still expensive and only successful a quarter of the time—but more than half a million fully human lives have started in a Petri dish.)

Let us consider the startling fact that as few as 20 percent of human fertilized eggs survive the rigorous process of implantation, pregnancy and birth. Four out of five blastocysts, embryos and fetuses perish due to natural processes and attrition, quite independent of any human intervention, let alone deliberate abortion. But many people, especially those of the religious right who gained President Bush a second term in 2004, must believe that these represent lost souls, since (they claim) with each fertilization their deity implants a fresh soul into the tiny ball of growing cells. But how many people *really* believe this, believe it all the way down? I occasionally offer the sardonic but doctrinally consistent suggestion that virginal nuns, impelled by all that's decent and moral and Christian, should surely host-mother those poor shivering orphan embryos trapped in ice. It is not as if there would be any unlawful sex involved. Recently, I was astounded to read that the US government, busy lobbying for a UN vote against all stem cell research, is ready with just such a helping hand for the pre-voters.

In the US, the federal Department of Health has given nearly $US1 million to organizations such as the Snowflake Foundation as part of its embryo adoption campaign. The goal is to find a home for an estimated 400,000 embryos held in frozen storage across the country.[85]

I also note that none of the 'pro-life' religious folks seem eager to locate, baptize and consign to the soil in tiny caskets, with full burial rites, the 80 percent of spontaneously aborted pre-painters, pre-mechanics, pre-politicians, pre-parents and pre-clerics, which look to the eye like bloody clots. Why ever not? Are these not alleged to be complete human persons with souls? How vile to let them just slide away with the sewage. But handling cognitive dissonance of this order is an old, old game: eyes wide shut, that's the ticket.

---

[83] Hwang WS, Ryu YJ, Park JH, et al., 'Evidence of a Pluripotent Human Embryonic Stem-Cell Line Derived from a Cloned Blastocyst,' *Science*, Vol. 303, No. 5664, 1669-74, March 12, 2004.

[84] Decisions condemned by Elizabeth G. Phimister, Ph.D. and Jeffrey M. Drazen, M.D., 'Editorial: Two Fillips for Human Embryonic Stem Cells,' *New England Journal of Medicine*, Vol. 350, No. 13, 1351-2 March 25, 2004.

[85] http://www.theaustralian.news.com.au/printpage/0,5942,11395316,00.html

A different and less embattled attitude is advanced by another poly-mathic friend, the frighteningly articulate Berkeley University rhetorician Dale Carrico, a postmodern theorist of 'queer'. His persuasive approach insists that opposition to science-driven radical change is *not* always irra-tional and, even when it is, the best way to persuade people of the virtues of progress is neither to display one's ferocious mentality in a menacing, brow-beating fashion, nor to abscond to a super-scientific Fortress of Solitude (even assuming that this is possible outside a *Superman* movie or Greg Egan novel). Carrico notes that 'when radical implications are proposed and swift timelines projected, a properly scientific attitude would demand that these claims be highly caveated in a way that often they are not.' Is this nothing better than advocacy of 'philosophical stealth', as has been suggested by a critic? Not at all. It is practical, effective communication, but it is principled as well. Carrico comments (as an atheist):

> I am satisfied that perfectly reasonable people can make their own accommodations between science, democracy, technological power, worldly pleasure, and whatever spiritual or aesthetic private projects constitute their own flavor of self-creation. Many mainstream human-ists are religious or at any rate tolerant of religion... So long as we are forceful in our insistence on separations of Church and State, and our support of scientific and critical thinking education, we should leave religious and spiritual people alone to make their contributions to the future as they see fit.[86]

The question is, will people outside the small catchment zone of the poly-mathic and neophilic new Enlightenment *philosophes* extend the same courtesy? Gloomy images of Bruno at the flaming stake and Galileo forced to recant the Sun-centered solar system might rise irresistibly to mind, but their rise should be resisted anyway. Politics is an art of conversation as well as the imposition of raw or cooked power. Our human and perhaps post-human futures will grow out of astonishing, unpredictable work being conducted right now in a thousand labs, but also from the conversations—clichéd, impassioned, ignorant, learned—between millions of people, thou-sands of millions, in this pivotal century.

---

[86] Both comments are from recent posts to an Internet email list, cited here with the author's permission. Is this a conservative position for an avowedly Enlightenment mind? Ferocious enough on occasion in his intellectual attack, Dale Carrico positions himself far from the Greg Burch's strategic ground: 'I have always valued the reasonable over the original. I am far too earnest to be cool, far too lazy to be hip, and far too middling to be truly original. And I am in any case quite happy to stick with what appears to be working' (17 Feb 2004).

Some of them will be the ferocious minds we have looked at briefly and promiscuously in this book, and many other like them.
One of those conversing people will be me.

Another will be you.

Sources cited

Andreasen, Nancy C. *Brave New Brain: Conquering Mental Illness in the Era of the Genome*, Oxford; Oxford University Press, 2000.

Appleyard, Bryan *Brave New Worlds: Genetics and the Human Experience,* London: HarperCollins, 1999.

Asimov, Isaac 'The Sound of Panting', *Astounding Science Fiction,* LV, 4, June 1955.

—— *In Memory Yet Green,* New York: Doubleday, 1979.

—— *Asimov's New Guide to Science,* London: Viking, 1985.

—— (ed. Janet Jeppson Asimov) *It's Been a Good Life,* New York: Prometheus Books, 2002.

Aunger, Robert (ed.) *Darwinizing Culture*, Oxford: Oxford University Press, 2001.

Baker, Simon, and Jake Chapman, 'Jake Chapman on Georges Bataille: an Interview with Simon Baker, *Papers of Surrealism*, 1, Winter 2003. http://www.surrealismcentre.ac.uk/publications/papers/text_only/issue_1/issue1_contents.htm

Barbour, Julian *The End of Time: The Next Revolution in Our Understanding of the Universe*, London: Weidenfeld & Nicolson, 1999.

Barnett, S. Anthony *Science, Myth or Magic*, Sydney: Allen & Unwin, 2000.

Barth, Karl *Der Romerbrief* , 1919, cited: http://www.faithnet.freeserve.co.uk/barth.htm

Batchelor, John Calvin *The Further Adventures of Halley's Comet,* [1980] London: Granada, 1984.

Behe, Michael *Darwin's Black Box: The Biochemical Challenge to Evolution,* New York: Simon & Schuster, 1998.

Berlin, Sir Isaiah *The Age of Enlightenment*, New York: Mentor, 1960.

Blackmore, Susan *The Meme Machine*, Oxford: Oxford University Press, 1999.

Bolton, Melvin *The Road to Now: Taking Stock of Evolution and our Place in the World,* Sydney: Allen & Unwin, 2001.

Broderick, Damien *The Judas Mandala,* New York: Pocket Books, 1982. Revised: http://fictionwise.com/eBooks/DamienBroderickeBooks.htm

—— *The Lotto Effect: Towards a Technology of the Paranormal,* Melbourne: Hudson, 1992.

—— *Theory and Its Discontents,* Melbourne: Deakin University Press, 1997.

—— *The Architecture of Babel: Discourses of Literature and Science,* Melbourne: Melbourne University Press, 1994.

—— *The White Abacus,* New York: Avon Books, 1997.

—— *The Last Mortal Generation: How Science Will Alter our Lives in the 21st Century,* Sydney: New Holland, 1999.

—— *The Spike: How Our Lives are being Transformed by Rapidly Advancing Technologies,* New York: Tor, 2001.

Bronowski, Jacob *Science and Human Values,* Harmondsworth: Penguin, 1964.

—— *The Identity of Man,* Harmondsworth: Pelican, 1967.

Bronson, Po 'A Prayer before Dying,' *Wired,* December, 2002: http://www.wired.com/wired/archive/10.12/prayer.html?pg=1&topic=&topic_set=

Bryan, C. D. B. *Close Encounters of the Fourth Kind: Alien Abduction and UFOS: Witness and Scientists Report,* London: Orion, 1996.

Burch, Greg 'Progress, Counter-Progress and Counter-Counter-Progress', 2001: http://www.gregburch.net/progress.html

Calder, Nigel *The Mind of Man: An investigation into current research on the brain and human nature,* London: BBC, 1970.

Campbell, Frank, review of James Oliver, *Weekend Australian,* 15-16 March: R12, 2003.

Chalmers, David J. *The Conscious Mind: In Search of a Fundamental Theory*, Oxford: Oxford University Press, 1996.

Cioffi, Frank 'Freud and the Idea of a Pseudo-Science,' in Robert Borger and Frank Cioffi, eds., *Explanation in the Behavioural Sciences*, Cambridge: Cambridge University Press, 1970: 471-99.

Clarke, Arthur C. *Profiles of the Future: An Inquiry into the Limits of the Possible*, [1962] London: Gollancz, 1999.

Colapinto, John *As Nature Made Him: The Boy who was Raised as a Girl*, London: HarperCollins, 2000.

Copleston, Frederick, S. J.. *A History of Philosophy*, Vol. 2 *Mediaeval Philosophy*, Part II, New York: Doubleday Image, 1962.

Crews, Frederick *Skeptical Engagements*, New York: Oxford University Press, 1986.

Crick, Francis *Life Itself: Its Origin and Nature*, London: Macdonald, 1981.

Curthoys, Jean *Feminist Amnesia: The Wake of Women's Liberation*, London: Routledge, 1997.

Damasio, Antonio R. *Descartes' Error: Emotion, Reason and the Human Brain*, Picador, 1994.

—— *The Feeling of What Happens: Body and Emotion in the Making of Consciousness*, New York: Harcourt Brace, 1999.

Davies, Paul *The Mind of God: The Scientific Basis for a Rational World*, New York: Simon & Schuster, 1992.

—— *Superforce: The Search for a Grand Unified Theory of Nature*, Harmondsworth: Penguin, 1995a [revised ed.]

—— *About Time: Einstein's Unfinished Business*, London: Viking, 1995b.

Davis, Erik *Techgnosis: Myth, Magic & Mysticism In The Age Of Information*, New York: Harmony Books, 1998.

Dawkins, Richard *Climbing Mount Improbable*, London: Viking, 1996.

—— *Unweaving the Rainbow: Science, Delusion and the Appetite for Wonder*, London: Allen Lane, 1998.

Dennett, Daniel C. *Consciousness Explained*, London: Allen Lane, 1991.

—— *Darwin's Dangerous Idea: Evolution and the Meanings of Life*, London: Allen Lane, 1995.

—— 'In Darwin's Wake, Where am I?', APA Presidential Address, December 29, 2000. Archived at http://ase.tufts.edu/cogstud

—— *Freedom Evolves*, New York: Viking, 2003.

Desmond, Adrian *Huxley: The Devil's Disciple*, London: Michael Joseph, 1994.

—— *Huxley: Evolution's High Priest*, London: Michael Joseph, 1997.

Dover, Gabriel *Dear Mr. Darwin: Letters on the Evolution of Life and Human Nature,* London: Weidenfeld & Nicolson, 2000.

Drucker, Peter F. *Managing in Turbulent Times,* New York: Harper & Row, 1980.

Edwards, Bradley C. and Eric A. Westling *The Space Elevator: A Revolutionary Earth-to-Space Transportation System,* self-published, 2003.

Eigen, Manfred *Steps Towards Life: A Perspective on Evolution*, Oxford: Oxford University Press, 1992.

Ekman, Paul *Emotions Revealed: Understanding Faces and Feelings*, London: Weidenfeld & Nicolson, 2003.

Farrell, B. A. *The Standing of Psychoanalysis,* Oxford: Oxford University Press, 1981.

Ferguson, Kitty *Stephen Hawking: Quest for a Theory of Everything*, London: Bantam, 1992.

Feynman, Richard P. *'Surely You're Joking, Mr. Feynman!' Adventures of a Curious Character*, [1985] New York: Bantam, 1986.

—— *The Meaning of It All*, London: Allen Lane, 1998.

Foster, Alasdair, 'New Australiana' (curator): http://www.pica.org.au/artist01/australiana.html

Foucault, Michel, 'What is Enlightenment' (1969) in *The Foucault Reader*, ed. Paul Rabinow, New York: Pantheon 1984, translation here modified.

Fukuyama, Francis, *Our Posthuman Future: Consequences of the Biotechnology Revolution*, London: Profile Books, 2002.

Gardner, Martin *Fads and Fallacies in the Name of Science*, New York: Dover, 1957.

Gay, Peter *The Enlightenment: An Interpretation. I: The Rise of Modern Paganism*, [1966] New York: W. W. Norton, 1977.

—— *The Enlightenment: An Interpretation. II: The Science of Freedom*, New York: Alfred Knopf, 1969.

Geison, Gerald L. *The Private Science of Louis Pasteur*, Princeton, N. J.: Princeton University Press, 1995.

Gleick, James *Genius: Richard Feynman and Modern Physics*, London: Little, Brown, 1992.

Gould, Stephen Jay *Rocks of Ages: Science and Religion in the Fullness of Life*, New York: Ballantine, 1999.

—— *The Hedgehog, the Fox, and the Magister's Pox: Mending the Gap between Science and the Humanities*, London: Jonathan Cape, 2003.

Greene, Brian *The Elegant Universe*, London: Jonathan Cape, 1999.

Gribbin, John *Schrödinger's Kittens and the Search for Reality*, London: Weidenfeld & Nicolson, 1995.

—— *Companion to the Cosmos*, London: Weidenfeld & Nicolson, 1996.

Grünbaum, Adolf 'Does Psychoanalysis Deserve a Second Century of Influence?' 2003, www.unics.uni-hannover.de/zeww/lecture_3.pdf

Hart, Kevin *The Trespass of the Sign: Deconstruction, Theology and Philosophy*, Cambridge: Cambridge University Press, 1989.

Heinberg, Richard (foreword by Dorion Sagan and Lynn Margulis) *Cloning the Buddha: The Moral Impact of Biotechnology,* Wheaton, Illinois: Quest Books, 1999.

Inglis, Brian *Natural and Supernatural: A History of the Paranormal from Earliest Times to 1914,* London: Hodder & Stoughton, 1977.

——— *Science and Parascience: A History of the Paranormal, 1914-1939,* London: Hodder & Stoughton, 1984.

Jahn, Robert G. and Brenda J. Dunne *Margins of Reality: The Role of Consciousness in the Physical World,* NEW YORK: Harcourt Brace Jovanovich, 1987.

Jones, Steve *Almost Like a Whale: The Origin of Species Updated,* London: Doubleday, 1999.

Kaku, Michio *Hyperspace: A Scientific Odyssey through Parallel Universes, Time Warps, and the Tenth Dimension,* New York: Oxford University Press, 1994.

Kanigel, Robert *The Man who Knew Infinity: A Life of the Genius Ramanujan,* New York: Scribners, 1991.

Kass, Leon *The Hungry Soul: Eating and the Perfecting of Our Nature,* Chicago: University of Chicago Press, 1994.

——— Chairman, *Human Cloning and Human Dignity: An Ethical Enquiry.* The President's Council on Bioethics, Washington, D. C., July, 2002. http://bioethics.gov/reports/cloningreport/fullreport.html

——— Foreword, *Beyond Therapy: Biotechnology and the Pursuit of Happiness.* A Report of the President's Council on Bioethics, New York: Dana Press, 2003.

Kolata, Gina *Clone: The Road to Dolly and the Path Ahead,* London: Allen Lane, 1997.

Konner, Melvin Book Review: *Evolutionary Psychology and Violence* edited by Richard W. Bloom and Nancy Dess, *Evolutionary Psychology,* 2: 28-31, 2004.

Kreisler, Harry, and Frederick Crews, 'Criticism and the Empirical Attitude', August, 1999: http://globetrotter.berkeley.edu/people/Crews/crews-con0.html

Kurzweil, Ray *The Age of Spiritual Machines: When Computers Exceed Human Intelligence,* London: Allen & Unwin, 1999.

Laing, R. D. *Wisdom, Madness, and Folly: The Making of a Psychiatrist, 1927-57,* New York: McGraw-Hill, 1985.

Lavers, Chris *Why Elephants Have Big Ears: Nature's Engines and the Order of Life,* London: Gollancz, 2000.

Lewontin, Richard *It Ain't Necessarily So: The Dream of the Human Genome and Other Illusions,* London: Granta Books, 2000.

McCarthy, Wil *Hacking Matter: Levitating Chairs, Quantum Mirages and the Infinite Weirdness of Programmable Atoms,* New York: Basic Books, 2003.

McIntosh, C. B. G., J. M. Foyster, and A. W. C. Lun 'The classification of the Ricci and Plebanski tensors in general relativity using Newman–Penrose formalism,' *Journal of Mathematical Physics,* Vol. 22(11) 2620-2623. November, 1981.

McKibben, Bill *Enough: Staying Human in an Engineered Age,* New York: Times Books/Henry Holt, 2003.

Malik, Kenan *Man, Beast and Zombie: What Science Can and Cannot Tell Us About Human Nature,* London: Weidenfeld & Nicolson, 2000.

Margulis, Lynn *The Symbiotic Planet: A New Look at Evolution,* London: Weidenfeld & Nicolson, 1998.

Marx, Karl, *Theses on Feuerbach:* in Marx and Engels, *Basic Writings on Politics and Philosophy,* New York: Anchor Books, 1959.

Matheson, Terry *Alien Abductions: Creating a Modern Phenomenon,* Amherst, New York: Prometheus Books, 1998.

Miller, Geoffrey *The Mating Mind: How Sexual Selection Shaped the Evolution of Human Nature,* London: Heinemann, 2000.

Millett, Kate *Sexual Politics,* New York: Equinox/Avon, 1971.

Mises, Ludwig von, *Theory and History: An Interpretation of Social and Economic Evolution,* Yale University Press, 1957.

Moravec, Hans *Mind Children: The Future of Robot and Human Intelligence*, Cambridge, Mass: Harvard University Press, 1988.

—— *Robot: Mere Machine to Transcendent Mind,* New York: Oxford University Press, 1999.

Naputa, Gaparingu and Gordon Patston, *Aboriginal Sky Figures: Your Guide to Finding the Sky Figures in the Stars,* Sydney: ABC Books and Audio, 1996.

Nettle, Daniel *Strong Imagination: Madness, Creativity and Human Nature*, Oxford: Oxford University Press, 2001.

Olson, Steve *Mapping Human History: Discovering the Past through our Genes,* London: Bloomsbury, 2002.

Pais, Abraham *Niels Bohr's Times, In Physics, Philosophy, and Polity*, Oxford: Oxford University Press, 1991.

Park, Robert L. *Voodoo Science: The Road from Foolishness to Fraud,* Oxford: Oxford University Press, 2000.

Parker, Andrew *In the Blink of an Eye: The Cause of the Most Dramatic Event in the History of Life,* London: The Free Press, 2003.

Perry, R. Michael *Forever for All: Moral Philosophy, Cryonics, and the Scientific Prospects for Immortality,* Universal Publishers, USA: 2000.

Pinker, Steven *The Language Instinct: The New Science of Language and the Mind,* London: Allen Lane, 1994.

—— *How the Mind Works,* London: Allen Lane, 1997.

—— *The Blank Slate: The Modern Denial of Human Nature,* London: Allen Lane, 2002.

Popper, Karl R. *Realism and the Aim of Science,* London: Routledge, 1983.

Radin, Dean *The Conscious Universe: The Scientific Truth of Psychic Phenomena*, New York: HarperCollins, 1997.

Robinson, Paul *Freud and His Critics*, Berkeley: University of California Press, 1993.

Sagan, Carl *Contact*, New York: Random House, 1986.

—— *Pale Blue Dot: A Vision of the Human Future in Space*, New York: Random House, 1994.

Schnabel, Jim *Dark White: Aliens, Abductions, and the UFO Obsession*, Harmondsworth: Penguin, 1995.

—— *Remote Viewers: The Secret History of America's Psychic Spies*, New York: Dell, 1997.

Shermer, Michael *The Borderlands of Science: Where Sense Meets Nonsense*, Oxford: Oxford University Press, 2001.

Sicher, F., Targ, E., *et al.*, 'A randomized double-blind study of the effect of distant healing in a population with advanced AIDS: report of a small scale study,' *Western Journal of Medicine,* 168(6): 356-63, 1998.

Smolin, Lee *The Life of the Cosmos*, London: Weidenfeld & Nicolson, 1997.

Spottiswoode, James P. 'Apparent association between Effect Size in Free Response Anomalous Cognition Experiments and Local Sidereal Time', at http://www.jsasoc.com/library.html

Steele, Edward J., Robyn A. Lindley, Robert V. Blanden, *Lamarck's Signature: How Retrogenes are Changing Darwin's Natural Selection Paradigm,* Sydney: Allen & Unwin, 1998.

Stock, Gregory *Redesigning Humans: Choosing our Children's Genes,* London: Profile Books, 2002.

Strieber, Whitely *Communion: Encounters with the Unknown,* London: Arrow Books, 1988.

—— *Transformation: The Breakthrough,* London: Arrow Books, 1989.

Sulloway, Frank *Freud, Biologist of the Mind: Beyond the Psychoanalytic Legend,* New York: Basic Books, 1979.

Sulston, John and Georgina Ferry *The Common Thread: A Story of Science, Politics, Ethics and the Human Genome*, Bantam/Random House Australia, 2002.

Sykes, Bryan *Adam's Curse: A Future without Men,* London: Bantam Press, 2003.

The Skeptic, Autumn 2002, Vol. 22, No. 1: 9-10.

Thomas, Lewis *The Lives of a Cell: Notes of a Biology Watcher,* [1974] New York: Bantam, 1984.

Thornton, Elizabeth *Freud and Cocaine: the Freudian Fallacy,* London: Blond & Briggs, 1983; slightly revised as *The Freudian Fallacy: Freud and Cocaine,* London: Paladin, 1986.

Toulmin, Stephen *Return to Reason,* Cambridge: Harvard University Press, 2001.

Turner, George *In the Heart or in the Head: An Essay in Time Travel,* Melbourne: Norstrilia, 1984.

U.S. National Science Foundation Report on Converging Technologies, 2002: http://itri.loyola.edu/ConvergingTechnologies/.

Updike, John *Roger's Version,* New York: Knopf, 1986.

Vallée, Jacques *The Invisible College: What a Group of Scientists Has Discovered About UFO Influences on the Human Race,* New York: Dutton, 1976.

Vinge, Vernor *Marooned in Realtime,* London: Pan, 1987.

—— Talk given at VISION-21 Symposium sponsored by NASA Lewis Research Center and the Ohio Aerospace Institute, March 30-31, 1993.

—— *The Collected Stories of Vernor Vinge,* New York: Tor, 2001.

Webster, Richard, 'Lacan goes to the opera', *New Statesman,* July 1997. Archived: http://www.richardwebster.net/lacangoestotheopera.html

Weir, Allison *Sacrificial Logics: Feminist Theory and the Critique of Identity.* New York and London: Routledge, 1996.

Wheeler, John Archibald (with Kenneth Ford) *Geons, Black Holes & Quantum Foam: A Life in Physics,* New York: Norton, 1998.

White, Michael and John Gribbin *Stephen Hawking A Life in Science,* London: Viking, 1992.

Wilmut, Ian, Keith Campbell and Colin Tudge *The Second Creation: The Age of Biological Control by the Scientists who Cloned Dolly*, London: Headline, 2000.

Wilson, Edward O. *Consilience: the Unity of Knowledge*, London: Little, Brown, 1998.

—— *Naturalist*, Washington: Island Press/Shearwater Books, 1994.

Wolman, Benjamin B. ed. *Handbook of Parapsychology*, New York: Van Nostrand Reinhold, 1977

Wright, Elizabeth *Psychoanalytic Criticism: Theory in Practice*, London: Methuen, 1984.

INDEX

www.ingramcontent.com/pod-product-compliance
Lightning Source LLC
Chambersburg PA
CBHW022017090426
42739CB00006BA/174